'*Beryl* is quite simply a tour de force – and a worthy winner of the William Hill Sports Book of the Year Award. It charts the most incredible of sporting endeavours and gradually reveals Burton to be both admirable and troubling. She would have stormed the Olympics had it allowed female cyclists, and her story demanded the attention to detail that Wilson affords it' Alyson Rudd, chair of the William Hill Sports Book of the Year Award

'I had never realised the longevity and scale of achievement. I'm in awe' Dame Katherine Grainger

'The subtitle – *In Search of Britain's Greatest Athlete* – is not hyperbolic. A phenomenon' Robert Crampton, *The Times* Best Books of 2022

'The complex and enigmatic Beryl Burton is given the literary treatment she so richly deserves in Wilson's rigorously researched biography. Britain's greatest cyclist' Waterstones Best Books of 2022

'Hands up if, like me, you had never heard of Beryl Burton. Shame on us. Jeremy Wilson brings alive this extraordinary woman's achievements (and problems, too) in this fabulous biography' Roger Alton, *Daily Mail*

'I simply cannot exaggerate how bloody great this book is and how inspiring Beryl's story is' Emma Cole, *Cyclist* magazine

'Jeremy Wilson finds the human heart of a story that gets more extraordinary as a unique athlete recedes into history. Very highly recommended' Richard Williams, *Guardian*

'Beryl was a woman ahead of her time – an incredible athlete with an inspirational mindset and we are only left to imagine what she would have achieved given the same opportunities as the women's peloton now. Generations will be eternally grateful for the path she paved' Lizzie Deignan, world champion cyclist

'My 97-year-old mother-in-law has no interest in cycling but picked it up from our kitchen table, took it home, and loved it. A story that cuts beyond sport' Alastair Campbell

'A fabulous book which brings the person and her phenomenal, groundbreaking achievements out of the shadows. Inspirational. I couldn't put it down' Chrissie Wellington, four-time Ironman Triathlon World Champion

'A beautiful book that tells us not just what she did, but who she truly was' Michael Hutchinson, author of *Faster*

'One of the best sporting stories – men's or women's – told superbly. A funny, endearing and truly extraordinary read' Fiona Tomas, *Daily Telegraph*

'The most comprehensive chronicle of its kind' *Yorkshire Post*

'Beryl Burton was, and is, a beacon … a guiding light, a warning signal, a fire in a high place. Her flame burns all the brighter thanks to Jeremy Wilson's fine book' Carlton Kirby, Eurosport cycling commentator

'So wonderfully researched, so many things I didn't know. Beryl's story is mind-blowing, and this really puts her on the roster of legends. A marvellous book' Maxine Peake

'A remarkable biography of a remarkable cyclist' *New European*

'Absolutely extraordinary. I feel like we ought to have a statue to her' Mishal Husain, BBC Radio 4 presenter

'What a story Wilson has uncovered. No one in the history of sport can have worked with quite the self-sacrificing single-mindedness ... a woman of thermonuclear levels of competitiveness' Jim White, *Oldie*

'This is not a hagiography, and all the better for it. Wilson brings her personality to life, faults and all. Meticulously researched. Compelling' Isabel Best, author of *Queens of Pain*

'There's been many plaudits for Jeremy Wilson's amazing book, but a common thread is how thoroughly researched it is. Fascinating and brilliant' *Cyclist Magazine Podcast*

'The subtitle may not even be hyperbolic. Jeremy Wilson retrieves an astonishing life' Simon Kuper, *Financial Times* Best Books of 2022

'Loved it, as everyone else has, and recommend people get it, read it cover to cover, and be amazed by the life of Beryl Burton' *Spokesmen Cycling Podcast*

'Subtle, full of insight, extensively researched and a joy to read' Paul Jones, author of *End to End*

'A masterpiece in many different ways. Spellbinding' Michael Caulfield, Premier League sports psychologist

'Jeremy Wilson set out to learn more about Beryl Burton and, after a long investigative odyssey into a miraculous life, ended up convinced she was this country's finest athlete. Who are we to argue?' *Cycling Weekly*

ABOUT THE AUTHOR

Jeremy Wilson is the Chief Sports Reporter for the *Daily Telegraph*. He was voted investigative sports reporter and national journalist of the year for his work on football and dementia. His sports writing was again highly commended in 2021 at both the British Press Awards and the British Journalism Awards. A lifelong club cyclist, he worked previously as a sports journalist for the *Guardian*.

BERYL

BERYL

In Search of Britain's Greatest Athlete

JEREMY WILSON

PURSUIT

This paperback edition first published in 2023

First published in Great Britain in 2022 by
Pursuit Books
An imprint of Profile Books Ltd
29 Cloth Fair
London
ECIA 7JQ
www.profilebooks.com

1 3 5 7 9 10 8 6 4 2

Typeset in Sabon by MacGuru Ltd
Printed and bound in Great Britain by
CPI Group (UK) Ltd, Croydon CR0 4YY

A CIP catalogue record for this book is available from the British Library.

ISBN 978 178816 293 7
eISBN 978 1 78283 574 5

MIX
Paper | Supporting
responsible forestry
FSC
www.fsc.org
FSC® C171272

Contents

A Note on Names

The decision to largely refer to Beryl Burton by her first name rather than the more conventional biographical surname gave pause for thought. The central importance to the story of two other Burtons – Charlie and Denise – was one reason, as was their preference for 'Beryl'. It also *felt* right. It was how she was simply known by just about everyone in her sport.

Similarly, the majority of my interviewees thought that it made most sense to refer to them by the surname they were best known by in cycling, whether that was their maiden name or their married name.

The magazine now called *Cycling Weekly* has chronicled British cycling, especially time trialling, since its inception in 1891. It has gone by various names, but has mostly been known just as *Cycling* and is referred to as such throughout.

Various competitions and organisations were central to Beryl's career and are known by the following acronyms:

British Best All-Rounder (BAR): Annual time trial competition for the woman with the fastest average speed for their best rides over 25, 50 and 100 miles. For men, the average speed is calculated over 50 and 100 miles as well as 12 hours.

British Cycling Federation (BCF): The governing body for track racing and mass-start road racing. Now known as British Cycling (BC).

Cyclists' Touring Club (CTC): Founded in 1878 to support recreational cycling on British roads. Now known as Cycling UK.

Road Records Association (RRA): British organisation founded in 1888 to adjudicate various place-to-place time and distance records.

Road Time Trials Council (RTTC): The governing body since 1922 for time trialling in Britain. Now known as Cycling Time Trials (CTT).

Sports Journalists' Association (SJA): Formed in Fleet Street in 1948 and organisers of the oldest annual British sports awards for the outstanding sportspeople of the year.

Union Cycliste Internationale (UCI): The world governing body of cycling.

Women's Cycle Racing Association (WCRA): Founded in 1949 to further women's cycling by organising races and campaigning for inclusion in events like the world championships and Olympic Games. Disbanded in 2007, having achieved its aims.

Prologue
Why Didn't I Know Her?

It is a unique and yet instantly recognisable sound. The whirring of a bicycle wheel freely rotating until it slowly stops, not because a brake has been applied but because the momentum from the last push of a pedal has gradually ceased. It was the fading sound that accompanied the last breath of Beryl Burton after she collapsed on the side of the road in May 1996 while out riding her bicycle on the outskirts of Harrogate. It was also the sound that cut poignantly through the silence during an afternoon play on BBC Radio 4 some sixteen years later, when the actor Maxine Peake recreated her sudden death. The play, written by Peake herself, was adapted for the theatre in 2014, and a capacity audience for the opening night at Leeds Playhouse included Beryl's daughter, Denise, and her then eighty-five-year-old husband, Charlie.

Denise gazed across a theatre filled with more than 1,000 people who had known little of her mother's extraordinary life only two hours earlier. 'People were sobbing,' she said. 'It was surreal. Just incredible.' And then, as a projector replayed rare footage of Beryl powering along on two wheels, the statistics from a career that was quite plausibly the finest in all cycling history were narrated by Peake:

Time trialling: British Best All-Rounder, champion 25 successive years. The first woman to beat a time of 1 hour for 25 miles. The first woman to beat a time of 2 hours for 50 miles. The first woman to beat a time of 4 hours for 100 miles.

Track racing: 3,000 metres pursuit, world champion five times, national champion thirteen times. The first woman to beat a time of 4 minutes. Road racing: world champion twice, national champion twelve times. In 1967 she became the only woman to beat a men's competition record, riding 277.25 miles in 12 hours. Awarded the MBE in 1964 and the OBE in 1968. Beryl Burton.

As the curtain came down, the tears that had just been shed slowly turned into a climax of cheers. People rose to their feet and loudly acknowledged the accomplishments of a local champion who had literally pedalled herself to death just a few miles up the road.

The sudden end to Beryl Burton's life following heart failure while out delivering invites for her fifty-ninth birthday sent a jolt shuddering through British cycling. The years when she dominated the sport had long passed, but she remained a familiar face on the domestic scene and, although it was a time when such news travelled more slowly, the outpouring of correspondence that appeared in *Cycling* magazine just four days later was overwhelming.

It underlined not just the shock at her unexpected passing but also an enduring and undiluted awe at her achievements. Graham Webb was the 1967 men's world amateur road race champion and had competed against Eddy Merckx when cycling's 'cannibal' was in his prime. Webb wrote in to assert that 'Beryl was the greatest racing cyclist who ever lived'. Eileen Sheridan, another pioneer for women's cycling, described her as quite simply 'the greatest sportswoman of all time'. Peter McGrath, the chairman of the Road Time Trials Council, said that Beryl was 'not just one of the greatest cyclists ever, but one of the greatest athletes'. Beryl's club-mate and friend Malcolm Cowgill contended that 'undoubtedly the greatest cyclist of all time' was also unfortunate. 'If she had achieved comparable feats in a different era or in a more popular sport, often beating the best male competition, she would have been a household name all over the world,' he wrote. The *Yorkshire Evening Post's* John Morgan agreed that Beryl would have 'earned a million or more on the continent' and 'walked as tall as the Eiffel Tower'.

*

I saw Beryl Burton in person just once, in the summer of 1984. I was eight and, although that may seem like an impossibly young age, it was sufficient to leave a lasting impression. Sebastian Coe and Daley Thompson at the Los Angeles Olympics and Everton's FA Cup triumph against Watford at Wembley are literally my only other memories of that entire year. Beryl was riding in the national women's 25-mile time trial championship, which was being staged in Ringwood, about 35 miles from our home in Andover. My father was a keen club cyclist, very much of the touring rather than racing variety, but sufficiently curious to join a considerable roadside throng. It was a time when cycling had a rather different place in the fabric of British sport and, although Beryl could have walked down the nearby Bournemouth promenade unnoticed, this was a vibrant little pocket of European culture in which she was revered.

Three things still clearly stand out through the mist of what was a delayed 6 a.m. start. The first was after the event, noticing how other cyclists – fully grown men – sought out Beryl's autograph. An autograph! Such behaviour bordered on the outlandish amid a cosy post-race scene dominated by Thermos flasks, homemade cake, peaked caps, ruddy cheeks and the clunking sound of metal cleats. And yet all this had become perfectly normal for the icon dressed in tracksuit bottoms, knitted jumper and moccasin slippers, who, between catching up on the gossip with friends she had known for thirty years, carefully signed the words 'Best wishes, Beryl Burton OBE' for each admirer. 'That's *her*,' whispered my father, discreetly pointing, and it was soon apparent that the eyes of just about every other nearby stranger were being drawn in the same direction. Chris Boardman later told me that one of his first cycling memories involved approaching Beryl before a race in Harrogate to secure her autograph. Boardman would famously later triumph at the 1992 Barcelona Olympic Games, and it is easily forgotten that the marketable distinction of becoming the first British cyclist since 1920 to win a gold medal was largely achieved only because women – and thus Beryl – were excluded from Olympic cycling events until 1984.

Beryl was forty-seven by then, the very same year as our distant encounter, but still exuded an unmistakable presence and authority. This was reinforced once she got on a bike. Not because she was guaranteed still to be the fastest among competitors largely from her daughter's generation but because of her style. With her flat back, rock-solid body and supple pedalling stroke, few people in any sport have married grace and power more efficiently. Like Roger Federer with a tennis racket or Allyson Felix on a running track, she performed with an aesthetic quality that somehow elevated her beyond even the finest contemporaries. Alf Engers, another celebrated British cyclist of the era, simply told me that Beryl was 'perfection' on a bike.

The final memory of that June morning in 1984 was rather less romantic, but would have been what mattered to Beryl: the result and the time. First place in 56 min. 47 sec. to average a speed still of 26.41 mph in her solo ride against the clock. Beryl was no longer annihilating the opposition as she had on a routine basis throughout the 1960s and 1970s, but she was still fastest by 4 seconds in a full field of more than a hundred of the best women cyclists in Great Britain. It was her twenty-fifth victory in the blue riband national '25' time trial championships and it would also prove to be the last in an unbroken streak of twenty-seven years – yes, twenty-seven consecutive years – in which she won at least one national senior title.

*

Maxine Peake would discover Beryl Burton rather later in life, but was then quicker to act. Her partner, Pawlo Wintoniuk, is an art director who enjoys building bikes; while browsing for spare parts on the internet, he stumbled across an old copy of Beryl's autobiography on eBay. He decided that it would make a good present for Peake's thirty-seventh birthday. 'He put a note on the cover which said, "Get yourself a curly perm and there's a film part in this",' says Peake. She duly read the book, which was published in 1986, and, despite knowing little about cycling, instantly wanted to know more than just the times, dates and records. She was captivated by the people, the sacrifices, the family relationships, the social context and what it told us about northern communities in the decades immediately after the war. She adored the myriad of homespun anecdotes and the way the Burton family, with little more than their bikes, a small tent and a camping stove, went out and conquered the world. And the more she researched Beryl's life, the more she became baffled by her relative anonymity, especially at a moment when cycling was booming and Olympic, World and Tour de France champions like Sir Bradley Wiggins, Sir Chris Hoy, Laura Trott, Victoria Pendleton, Mark Cavendish and Chris Froome were household names.

'I was transfixed, just fascinated that this woman in the late 1950s and 1960s had been so successful,' says Peake. 'A house wife and mother, who worked full-time, and yet this incredible specimen of an athlete. Maybe the best we have ever seen. But how often do we see women captured in that light? I hate the word "ordinary". But she was ordinary extraordinary. Her story is mind-blowing. Why didn't I know her? Why hadn't Beryl filtered through to the mainstream? I thought it was criminal.'

Timing provides one part of the answer. Lesser British cyclists who have followed in Beryl's path received disproportionately more acclaim from the general public, if never comparable affection among the sport's aficionados. The overarching explanation, however, is simple. This was an era in cycling when the institutional sexism that runs through many sports was shockingly evident. As well as being more than fifty years behind swimming and athletics in gaining inclusion for women at the Olympics, the first year of any female equivalent of the Tour de France was also 1984. It was then only staged intermittently, and over varying distances, before the relaunch in 2022 of an event to finally compare with the men's race. This all left Beryl with only two realistic world championship options throughout her career: the 3,000 m pursuit around an outdoor velodrome, which, as a timed and essentially individual race, partially suited her phenomenal endurance; or the road race, which, as a much more tactical mass-start event over a distance of around 35 miles for the women, compared with 90 miles now, was also skewed towards more explosive riders. Beryl still excelled. To this day, no man or woman has won more world championship pursuit medals, and she remains Britain's only double world road race champion, but her most outstanding discipline, the individual time trial, would not be staged in the women's world championship or Olympics until 1994. Beryl was fifty-seven by then.

It leaves her decades of jaw-dropping performances in domestic time trialling, the so-called 'Race of Truth', where riders set off at 1-minute intervals and race alone over the same course, as the clearest guide to just how far she was ahead of her contemporaries. To continually win the prestigious British Best All-Rounder (BAR) competition – for the time triallist with the fastest average speed for their annual personal best over 25, 50 and 100 miles – for a quarter of a century represents the longest individual winning streak in any serious sporting competition. A second incomparable achievement was her world best in 1967 for the distance cycled in 12 hours when she not only set a new women's landmark but decimated an entire field of ninety-nine men and beat their record. A four-word headline in *Cycling* following a rare defeat that year neatly captured her unique dominance. 'Hey! Men Beat Beryl', it simply said. It would take two years for a man to regain 'their' record. Despite all the vast advances in bicycle technology, her women's 12-hour record stood for half a century. Thanks to extensive modelling of her various records by sports scientists and experts in aerodynamics, which were carried out in a wind tunnel at the Silverstone motor-racing circuit exclusively for this book, we can now say with certainty that the best athletes even of today could not have matched the standards she set.

It is part of what makes these 'lists' of the greatest cyclists or sportspeople so maddeningly flawed. Beryl's achievements have never been ignored, but the acknowledgement is generally cursory and lacking any substantive appreciation of their scale and circumstance. My own newspaper, the *Telegraph*, was among the culprits, placing her eighty-fifth in a list of the greatest British sportspeople in 2016, just behind Gavin Hastings and Sandy Lyle. Such injustice was further brought home during a conversation with Simon Richardson, the editor of *Cycling* magazine. He recalled how Beryl had been fifth in a poll of Britain's greatest riders at the turn of the twenty-first century. It was before anyone had seriously contemplated a British Tour de France winner or cyclists with knighthoods, and yet there she still was behind a clutch of men: Boardman, Tom Simpson, Robert Millar and Reg Harris. Fifteen years on from the poll, the same question was asked. But here's the twist. Beryl was unmoved. Fifth again, except that the identity of all those ahead of her – Wiggins, Cavendish, Froome and Nicole Cooke – was different. Richardson tried to rationalise the anomaly. 'The top four from 2000 have all since had their achievements surpassed in some way,' he said. 'But Beryl's have never been matched. They stand the test of time.' That was true, but an additional explanation is that the list was wrong in 2000 and remains so to this day. For what sets Beryl apart is not just that she was the first to some particular landmark but that we can suspect with some certainty that she will also be the last.

By effectively judging her career through the prism of events that she was not allowed to compete in, we simply repeat and reinforce the sexism.

Does all this really matter? Yes, because it means that the inspiration and lessons that could be derived from Beryl Burton have gone largely unnoticed, and, as Peake says, 'We need role models, especially female role models, more than ever.' With girls statistically still less likely to take up sport and reap the lifelong benefits of being active, that is especially true of trailblazing sportswomen. It is something that Billie Jean King and Dame Mary Peters, two champions during the 1960s and 1970s in women's sports that had far more exposure than cycling, both highlighted. King says that sports literature 'needs more stories of women who dare', while Peters, who got to know Beryl and was a huge admirer, became so frustrated by the under-representation of women's sport in her local Belfast bookshop that she promptly wrote her own book on the subject.

Recognition or money never remotely motivated Beryl, and so what remains is a largely unknown story of breathtaking achievement and copious charm. At its root is the humble simplicity and bloody-mindedness of a woman who was as pure and unquestioning in loving her chosen sport as anyone who ever lived. A woman who thought nothing of cycling 170 miles home to Leeds from London after completing a morning 50-mile time trial. Or who could be seen vomiting by the side of the A1 in Yorkshire from the sheer effort of her training and then later sat in the corner of the Lighthouse Café near Doncaster, complete with a mug of tea and the knitting that she always carried in her saddlebag. 'I can still picture her – a pair of plus fours, no socks, plain black leather cycling shoes and a lime green woolly cardigan,' says Chris Sidwells, a cycling historian whose uncle was Tom Simpson, the 1965 world road race champion. Beryl was always utterly approachable and, having never stopped working herself – mostly in a rhubarb farm – would sound off to Sidwells about the new breed of 'lazy blighters' who thought it beneficial to combine training with

1. At the edge of the Yorkshire Moors in 1961.

part-time work. Beryl firmly believed that having the flexibility to cycle only when the weather was set fair, or when you felt sufficiently 'rested', was a one-way street to a weakened soul.

Not only did Beryl compete obsessively and ferociously until the day she died, but the bike was also her primary mode of transport and the focal point for every social activity or holiday. It became nothing less than an expression of self. In a speech to the Sports Journalists' Association in 1970, which has been preserved among hundreds of previously unseen documents, letters and photographs, including handwritten talks and notes in the months leading up to her death, she began by outlining that overriding feeling. 'Cycling, for me, isn't just a sport – it's a way of life,' she said. This basic sentiment provides the immovable trunk of her story, but it also should not conceal a fascinating mass of branches that stretch far beyond the domestic cycling scene. A journalist at *Le Monde* once said that, had Beryl been French, Joan of Arc would have taken second place. Her global dominance during the 1960s was of sufficient fascination for the Soviet Union to dispatch two of their coaches to visit the Yorkshire rhubarb farm on which she laboured to get a better understanding of how she kept beating their best riders. Her international celebrity was such that she was invited to race as far afield as Australia, Africa and America, and she was years ahead of her time in opting to spend an early spring month off work abroad, generally in Benidorm or Mallorca, for warm weather training. As her numerous letters to friends back home confirm, she would cycle from the airport with all her belongings in a saddlebag and live an entirely self-sufficient month alone, or with her husband, Charlie, eating the local produce and amassing thousands of training miles.

Beryl also competed frequently in East Germany at the height of the Cold War, and the infamous state security service, the Stasi, would monitor her movements during any visit. She was among numerous potential victims of the doping that would so disfigure women's international sport, even if it was still the entrenched sexism that most limited her career. The heroic Eileen Gray, always her great ally in the otherwise all-male committee rooms of world cycling, would later describe the sport's officials as 'saboteurs'. 'We had British men out to stop British women racing,' said Gray. 'Isn't that shocking? But it's absolutely true.' It was also repeatedly noticeable, while researching this book, how often people still look differently at sportswomen who are willing to sacrifice everything for their dream. While anecdotes of male sporting selfishness are invariably the stuff of legend (like the day Boardman missed the birth of his daughter Harriet to recce a hill he would race up the following week), a simmering disapproval can endure about how Beryl brought up her own daughter Denise without ever compromising her cycling. It was also striking that the most cutting observations come not from Denise, who mixes vast pride with blunt Yorkshire honesty in describing her mother's

personality, but from now elderly rivals who had themselves con-
formed to society's expectations.

Beryl Burton's story is not some unblemished fairy tale. She
was seriously ill during what was a traumatic childhood, and there
were later difficulties in her relationship with Denise, who would
grow from an infant permanently parked on an accompanying
bicycle seat to one of the main threats to her mother's cycling dominance. Some of the stories about how Beryl would treat Denise
– given her absolute tunnel vision about meeting her own cycling
needs – do not make for easy reading or listening. Nor does her
refusal to stop competing seriously or the remorseless demands
she made of her body through a career that began when Winston
Churchill and Clement Attlee were respectively Conservative and
Labour leaders and ended when Tony Blair and John Major were
vying for Downing Street. And yet it is these flaws, frailties and
struggles that now most resonate with those who work in the bur-
geoning study of great sporting champions. When I met Chelsea
Warr, UK Sport's former performance director and co-author of
The Talent Lab, a book that details how Warr helped turn Great
Britain into an Olympic superpower, her eyes visibly widened
when I began telling her about Beryl. Warr then sent me an email
later that evening. 'That was indeed fascinating!' she wrote. 'What
a project! Beryl Burton ... I would like to have met her!'

*

My conversation with Maxine Peake had extended into its second
hour when the subject finally turned to Beryl's death, and how
she simply kept cycling until her heart stopped. What was she still
chasing? Or should we instead have been thinking about what she
was running from? As our voices faltered almost simultaneously,
we were both then left wondering how this amateur cyclist, who
never earned a penny from her sport and whom we had never
actually met, could continue to stir such emotion some twenty-five

2. Beryl Burton at her happiest – racing solo against the clock.

years after her death. 'I actually found getting to the essence of Beryl quite difficult,' said Peake. 'When I was writing the play, I got to a point where I kept on saying out loud, "C'mon, who are you, Beryl?" She's a tough nut to crack. The women were often very much in charge back then. Getting things done. The matri-archs. Personalities of no nonsense. Strong women. Hard women. Never give up. Contained and disciplined. Private. No fuss. I'm not saying that's healthy, but that's how it was. You battled your own demons, alone, whatever they may be.

'Cycling is also quite an insular sport. It's you and the bike. Your focus. Your concentration. Your physical power. What did that infuse in her that made her unable to step away? There is something poetic about Beryl on a bike and there is something about that which really moves me. I believe there was something deeper going on. I feel protective of her. I don't know what it is, but I do get a bit tearful when people mention her now or I see pictures. I love her ... and I didn't even know her.'

Part One

TRAILBLAZING

1

The Greatest Ride

Beryl Burton woke shortly before 4.30 a.m. on the morning of Sunday, 17 September 1967. She liked to be up for a few hours before racing and, after a simple breakfast and last check of her kit – bike, cycling shoes, spare wheels and tyres, water bottles, flasks of tea and the small parcels of food that would be passed to her by husband, Charlie, every 15 miles – the family, including eleven-year-old daughter Denise, were ready. They squeezed into their Cortina car and set off on the short journey towards the Yorkshire market town of Wetherby, where, at 7.11 a.m., Beryl would begin an attempt at the record for the longest distance cycled in 12 hours. It had already been one of the finest years of her career. She had regained the women's world road race championship in the Netherlands the previous month, breaking away from the Soviet Union's Anna Konkina and Lyubov Zadorozhnaya to win by more than 2 minutes. She had also again swept the board domestically in the various British national championships and, at the age of thirty, was so superior to her opponents that she was effectively engaged in a personal battle to see just how far she could take her talent.

Beryl had spent the previous day baking and preparing her food: rice pudding, pears, dates, fruit and honey cake, malt loaf, tomatoes, banana sandwiches, grapes and pieces of sausage and steak that husband Charlie would cook by the roadside on a Primus stove and pass up during the race. Her Morley clubmate and employer Norman ('Nim') Carline had dropped around to the family home in Woodlesford the previous night to discuss what lay ahead and was startled to see how much food was being prepared. 'Oh, yes. I'm going to enjoy myself,' Beryl told him.

It was a gloomy, drizzly morning but relatively warm for the time of year and, most importantly, there was barely any trace of wind. Beryl completed a 3-mile warm-up before discarding her tracksuit top to reveal the same blue and red Great Britain team jersey that she had worn while winning her seventh world championship three weeks earlier. She let the jersey hang over her short black woollen shorts and then gently pedalled up behind a small queue of the last men's riders. The cyclists departed at 1-minute intervals and, as they patiently waited their turn like a seasoned rank of cab drivers, an air of tension – perhaps even dread – was conveyed in the absence of conversation. Beryl preferred not to stand for too long before any time trial in order to conserve energy in her legs, and so briefly sat down next to the grass verge. It was a ritual she had undertaken thousands of times before, but she still felt nervous and harboured private doubts over whether she would complete the race. As Ian Walsh, a pusher-off from the Otley Cycle Club, took hold of her gleaming blue 'Jacques Anquetil' bike – one hand at the back where the seat tube meets the seat post and one hand at the front on the head tube – Beryl firmly tightened the straps around her black leather cycling shoes and then slapped the flesh on her thighs before clasping the dropped handlebars.* 'Thirty seconds,' said the timekeeper, Joe Kipling, who was holding a stopwatch on top of his clipboard. Beryl nodded. And then the words that will forever send a surge of adrenalin through the body of any time triallist: '5, 4, 3, 2, 1, Go!' Beryl muttered a 'thank-you', stood up on the pedals and pressed down to propel herself forward. 'Do your best, lass – make it crack' were Charlie's last words as his wife disappeared into the distance for

---

*Cyclists are held up by a 'pusher-off' before starting a road time trial or a track pursuit, although automatic start gates are now used at an elite level.

3. The start of one of cycling's most epic days: 7.11 a.m., 17 September 1967.

a sporting achievement that would shatter all preconceptions of a woman's capabilities in endurance sport.

*

To appreciate the importance of this record, you need also to know something of British cycling's history. Track and road racing may be the major contemporary focus for elite riders, but in the decades before and immediately after the Second World War priorities were different. At the start of the century, the Road Time Trials Council (RTTC) had issued a snappily entitled statement, 'The Menace of Mass Start Racing on the Highway', which asserted that 'road races violate every one of the principles of clean amateurism, authenticity, and regard for public safety'. Group racing was outlawed and, with track facilities desperately scarce, time trialling was the way British people raced their bikes. This was initially done secretly, on routes that, to this day, retain their own unique code. The 'Otley 12', for example, took place on what was called the 'V181' course. It was all strictly amateur, but on any weekend across the country thousands of people would take part in these early morning events.

Time trialling is a discipline in which no rider can hide. Shielding oneself from the wind by following closely behind a competitor – a standard tactic in the massed peloton of any road race – is strictly prohibited. It is just a bike, the undulating road, a ticking clock and the limitations of both your mind and your body. This particularly appealed to Beryl and an outlook on life that could not easily compute shades of grey. 'It's a completely honest form of competition – the fastest and strongest rider wins,' she would say. Standard British time trial distances are 10, 25, 50 and 100 miles. For the more sadistic, there are also championships and records over a set time for the distances cycled in 12 and 24 hours. Time trials remain the bedrock of club cycling across Britain and have long been a pivotal part of major stage races like the Tour de France, as well as an individual event both in the Olympics and world championships.

The 1960s and 1970s, however, were what Sean Yates calls its 'golden age' and, even after a career that included riding the Tour de France eleven times before managing the likes of Lance Armstrong, Sir Bradley Wiggins, Alberto Contador and Chris Froome, the greats from this era remain his heroes. 'The world of time trialling was what inspired me,' says Yates. 'There was a mysteriousness about it. You would see the start and finish areas and there would be hundreds of people watching. There were barely any cars on the road then and you had all these characters and eccentrics. Alf Engers was a major draw with his sheepskin coat and Jaguar car. Eddie Adkins was known as the Emperor. You had Nim Carline who was this amazing mile-eater. They were like rock stars to me.' Beryl was unusually versatile and a world champion in road and track racing, but time trialling was the kingdom over which she ruled supreme like no one before or since. 'She was far and away the best – I was in awe,' says Yates.

*

Mike McNamara was another mainstay of the scene and a formidable athlete and character. After spending two years in North Africa completing his national service, he began combining his cycling passion with working on the furnaces at the Hadfield steel factory. Regardless of the time of year or weather, he would make the 30-mile round trip from his home in Swinton to the centre of Sheffield by bike. It was a routine that continued until the day he retired, aged sixty-five, in 2000. McNamara never went on holiday. Time off was simply spent accumulating as many miles as possible on his bike. His brother John was his main support by the side of the road during a 12-hour time trial and, once the pubs were opened at 11 a.m., he would be instructed to pass up a freshly pulled pint of bitter. 'I would pour it straight into a flask, run out of the pub and hand it over as he cycled past,' says John. The nutritional logic may baffle today's teetotal champions but long-distance cyclists have a surprisingly close relationship with alcohol, which was used in the Tour de France, largely for pain management, right up until the 1960s. McNamara also had his own targets that year. He would ultimately finish in the top twelve of the men's BAR competition eleven times between 1964 and 1977, but 1967 was also his physical peak and, with the racing season drawing to a close, he believed that eclipsing the existing men's 12-hour record was possible. 'It was something he always talked about,' says his brother.

McNamara was the top-seeded rider in the Otley 12 event, and so the last of the ninety-nine male competitors to start. The first rider had begun at 5.30 a.m. and, with the rest of the field departing every 60 seconds, McNamara began his effort at 7.09 a.m. There was then a 2-minute gap to Beryl and what was ostensibly a separate women's race of just four riders. McNamara had been given the number 129 to fix on to the angle of his frame. Beryl had 131. The fact that she was the first of the women to start became a point of minor controversy. Convention would have had Beryl setting off last and, although catching and passing the other women would have been a swift formality, such close proximity to the men meant that she was soon riding through their field and effectively part of their race. A rare copy of the official start sheet also confirms that Beryl was the only woman permitted to ride the men's 'full course' and the only one not to follow a modified route. 'It meant that Mike was always the hare for Beryl to chase,' says John McNamara. That was true but, with 21 miles' difference between the respective men's and women's records, and 12 continuous hours of cycling ahead, no one seriously expected this to have any bearing on the outcome.

After a fast stretch of road up the old A1 between Wetherby and Boroughbridge, the circuit moved into what were largely deserted country roads before zigzagging north as far as North-allerton via Tadcaster, York and Thirsk. McNamara recalled a course that was 'sporting', and, although the particularly hilly parts of Yorkshire were avoided, it was far from flat. The ride was bucolic, passing through rolling green countryside that formed a stunning backdrop to the industrial heartlands that powered the nation. The one really significant hill would be encountered when the riders later moved on to the finishing circuit, a 15.87-mile course that circled the roads south-east of Boroughbridge. The purpose of this shorter final loop is to provide a route that can be easily patrolled by marshals and timekeepers in order to calculate accurately where riders have finished once their 12 hours have elapsed.

It quickly became clear that both McNamara and Beryl could break the respective records. Beryl had obliterated the previous women's mark by more than 12 miles when she rode 250.4 miles in 1959. The men's all-time record of 271.8 miles had also stood for almost a decade. McNamara went through the first 100 miles in 4 hrs 14 min. 55 sec., powering along at an average speed of almost 24 mph and a pace that would put him beyond 280 miles. Beryl was only 58 seconds slower, but, as she would later explain, had been 'riding easily' at the start. 'Time passed pleasantly for the first few hours,' she said. 'I had no intention of going for anything fancy. I felt good, the wheels hummed, and so did I now and again. It was like super touring with food and drink passed up.' Beryl duly covered the next 100 miles in a remarkably even-paced 4 hrs 17 min. 44 sec. to move 18 seconds ahead of McNamara. The peculiarities of interval starts, however, meant that she was physically still behind on the road and unaware that she was now leading the race. It had passed 4 p.m. and, despite having both been riding continuously since just after 7 a.m., that initial 2-minute starting gap was almost exactly intact. An extraordinary personal duel would come down to an exhausting final 3 hours.

*

There is some wonderful footage of Beryl in time-trialling action in the documentary titled *Racing is Life*, including her undertaking an old Mk 1 Cortina on a roundabout and then passing two elderly male marshals who are sitting by the side of the road on foldaway chairs. Unaware of the camera, one turns to the other and loudly exclaims, 'Look at the gear!' Beryl's great strength meant that she could turn uncommonly high gears, and she would spend most of the Otley 12-hour churning a 107-inch gear, which equates to respective front and back chain rings of 57 teeth and 14.* Beryl had a similar 'get the miles in' training philosophy to McNamara, even if his friendship with the 1965 world road race champion Tom Simpson had just begun to inspire greater variation. Simpson had discovered the benefits of interval

---

*Gear inches are a relative measure of bicycle gearing. Road bike values typically range from 30 (very low) via 72 (medium) to 125 (very high). As in a car, low gearing is generally for ascending hills and high gearing is for fast speeds, when a single pedal revolution will propel you further forward.

training – alternating periods of ultra-high-intensity cycling with low-intensity 'recovery' periods – that was more common among continental road racers and is now a cornerstone of training for all endurance sports. Simpson had died only two months earlier on the slopes of Mont Ventoux during his tragic attempt to win the 1967 Tour de France, and at the funeral both Beryl and McNamara had stood among mourners from across the cycling world, including Eddy Merckx. Beryl cycled the 90-mile round trip to the village of Harworth on the Yorkshire–Nottinghamshire border, and photographs from the day show her standing next to Merckx in a large rain cycling cape. The epitaph that was inscribed on Simpson's gravestone was one every serious cyclist could relate to: 'His body ached, his legs grew tired, but still he would not give in.'

*

The need to absorb discomfort was being fully tested by the time Beryl reached the finishing circuit following 206 miles through Yorkshire. Club riders and spectators had begun gathering in unusually large numbers as word spread locally that something special was happening. Beryl was now ignoring Charlie's suggested pre-race schedule of 255 miles but was still puzzled by increasingly hearing the word 'Mac' being shouted at her. She had initially discounted the possibility that McNamara could be within range. After completing the first finishing circuit, Beryl had moved 42 seconds ahead of McNamara in terms of timing, and so physically only 78 seconds behind on the road. Charlie, who had positioned himself around the course at regular intervals to pass up food and drink, began shouting times at Beryl as she passed, increasingly excited by what might be. His wife still felt physically strong but had developed stomach cramps, which were ultimately relieved by a Rennie washed down with a mouthful of brandy.

A bigger difficulty then arose when Beryl heard a huge crack from the back of her bike. A spoke had snapped, leaving her afraid of changing gear for fear of further damaging the wheel. Beryl shouted and raised her right arm to signify that she needed a rear wheel replacement when she next passed Charlie, who, as ever, was only a few minutes up the road. He hurriedly drove half a mile in front and, with the help of his friend Eddie Whiteley, who had been firing up the Primus stove to cook Beryl steaks from the front of a moving car, they were able to grab hold of her bike as she slowed. 'She didn't get off,' says Charlie, describing how Whiteley held the now stationary bike upright (with Beryl still on board) as he went to work. 'I remember shouting at her, "for crying out loud, keep steady," while I was trying to fit the wheel into the forks.' Beryl shouted back in protest at how long she had been forced to ride with the handicap, but judging by the results, a Formula 1 team could hardly have dealt more efficiently with the situation. 'She set off again like a rocket,' says Charlie, proudly.

McNamara had a different problem. 'He was desperate for a toilet stop,' says his brother. 'He knew Beryl was coming but he did not want to let her pass and so he put it off for an hour and a half. It started to affect his riding, and Beryl was closing in.' One can only imagine the discomfort of riding at such speed with both a full bladder and just about every part of his body now screaming out in protest at having remained in a tucked racing position for more than 200 miles. At first, as McNamara came into view, Beryl was not certain who was in front of her. It was now early evening, and the light was just beginning to fade. They may have been the two leading riders on the course, but there were still other lapped competitors as well as casual cyclists on what were open public roads. As the silhouette of another rider drew gradually closer, it slowly dawned on Beryl that it was McNamara. She recognised the multicoloured stripes of his Rockingham Cycling Club jersey and, by the time and effort it was taking for her to reel him in, knew that it could only be another unusually fast cyclist.

They had been on the road for more than 10 hours and had

both caught every rider who started in front of them. They were each on course to set a new record. But Beryl was catching Mike. She finally approached his back wheel on a quiet stretch of road after 235 miles. They were completely alone. No other eyewitnesses were present for this unique moment in sporting history. Beryl later recounted her thoughts in a talk to the Cyclists' Touring Club and in her autobiography *Personal Best*:

> I drew inexorably closer, the wheels humming along the country lane, just two riders bent on great athletic endeavour. No cheering crowds at this point, no excited television reporters, just the occupants of the occasional car that passed unaware of the drama. I came to within a few yards of him and then I froze, the urge in my legs to go faster and faster vanished as though with the click of a switch. Goose pimples broke out all over me, and for some seconds I just stared at his heaving shoulders, the sweat-stained jersey. I could hardly accept after all those hours and miles I had finally caught up with one of the country's great riders who himself was pulling out a record ride. 'I'll have to pass him,' I thought. 'Poor Mac, it doesn't seem fair.' I drew alongside, both of us still striving, every yard of ground being greedily covered as the minutes ticked by to the end of the 12 hours. Then came the moment which has now passed into cycling legend.

Speak to almost anyone – male or female – who raced in British time trials during the 1960s or 1970s and they will invariably tell you about the experience of being caught by Beryl. She saw other cyclists the way a swallow might view a fly, gobbling up literally thousands in her career. Most just ignore the person they are passing, but it is considered good etiquette to offer a word or two of encouragement and, whatever the circumstance, Beryl *always* said something. But she would only deliver praise if she deemed it deserved and, in her blunt Yorkshire twang, was just as likely to say something cutting. Her brother Jeffrey would also regularly take part in club time trial events. 'I would usually start five or six minutes ahead but, not far up the road, she would come flying past and shout, "C'mon lad, you're not trying." I would be shattered, sweat dripping off me and shout back, "I am, I am!"' Beryl once caught the *Cycling* journalist Dennis Donovan, who had at the time put on some weight. Donovan was an influential figure in the sport, but there would be no tact or deference. 'Dennis, you are disgusting,' she shouted, before disappearing into the distance. There could be encouragement as well. Derek Orr, another club cyclist, recalls how she would shout an upbeat 'Stick in there, chuck' whenever she whizzed by. 'Being passed by a woman was just something you got used to when she was around – you had no choice,' says Brian Keighley, who was handing out drinks and sponges as a seventeen-year-old volunteer at the Otley 12. 'She usually looked to give you words of encouragement but must have studied past results because she always seemed to know how you were doing. If you were going well, she would look across and say, "Dig in here, lad. You are on a good one."'

So what would Beryl say to McNamara, the leading men's time triallist of the time, who was himself producing the best performance of his life? 'Mac raised his head slightly and we looked at each other side by side,' she said. 'Goodness knows what was going on in my mind but I thought a gesture was required. I was carrying a bag of liquorice allsorts in the pocket of my jersey and on impulse I groped into my sweetie bag and pulled one out. It was one of those Swiss-roll-shaped ones. White, with a black coating. "Liquorice allsort, Mac?" I shouted and held it towards him. He gave a wan smile. "Ta, love," he said, popping the sweet into his mouth. I put my head down and drew away. There I was, first on the road, ninety-nine men behind me, not knowing whether to feel elated or sorrowful. Mac was doing a sensational ride but his glory, richly deserved, was going to be overshadowed by a woman.'

The drama had still not quite ended. As soon as he had been caught, McNamara finally stopped for that comfort break. Seeing her clubmate and work colleague Sheila Broadbent by the side of the road, Beryl also sought relief behind a hedge. 'She handed me the bike and began laughing – she didn't seem tired at all,' says Broadbent. Beryl was soon 2 more minutes up the road but McNamara, invigorated, came back in the closing stages and the two remained within sight of each other throughout most of the final 45 minutes. Marshals were positioned around the finishing circuit and, with his 12 hours up at exactly 7.09 p.m., McNamara was signalled to stop. Beryl had another 2 minutes to go and, having pedalled a further three-quarters of a mile up the road, flopped down on a large patch of grass by the A59 with 45 seconds remaining, unable to face the circuit's hill again. Her final distance read 277.25 miles, amounting to an average speed of 23.1 mph through 720 continuous minutes of effort. She had ridden almost 40 miles further than the next best woman had ever managed and almost 6 miles more than the previous men's record, which had itself been broken 2 minutes earlier by McNamara. 'It was just out of this world – we were almost dancing up and down,' says Charlie. So did they celebrate? 'Oh yes. All the riders congregated at a field near Wetherby. We sat down and all had tea and sandwiches. It were quite a jolly do.' As first man, McNamara was given an envelope containing £4. And for Beryl? She had just delivered one of the greatest performances in sport but, despite setting a world record for either sex, was deemed only eligible for the top women's prize. This was £1.10 – the equivalent of about £16 today.

The Burton family were home shortly after 9 p.m. and, although Beryl was soon asleep, her alarm sounded at 1.30 a.m. She had promised to appear at The Cycle Show in Earls Court the following day and wanted to clear all the rubbish that had accumulated in the car before setting off, with Charlie at the wheel, at 3 a.m. Beryl was then on her feet all day, before being taken in the evening to Wembley Arena, where she was introduced to a

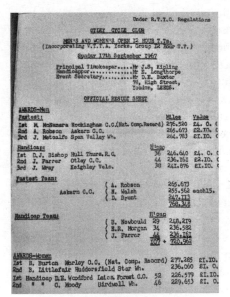

4. The 'official result sheet' confirms
two record-breaking rides – but a
stark discrepancy in prizes even for the
woman who had beaten all the men.

5. Mike McNamara: 'his
glory, richly deserved, was
going to be overshadowed
by a woman'.

packed crowd of cycling fans at the start of the Six Day London
track race. News of her 12-hour record was already reverberating
through cycling and, in the company of some of the world's best
male professionals, she was given a standing ovation before being
driven home by Charlie. They arrived back in Yorkshire shortly
before 4 a.m. Both had given up two days of holiday to be there
and, in keeping with her strictly amateur status, she was not paid
a penny for her appearance.

*

Beryl Burton's 12-hour women's record would stand for fifty years
before finally being broken by Alice Lethbridge, several decades

after cycling's aerodynamic revolution had transformed time-trialling speeds. To put that into some sort of athletic perspective, Bob Beamon's supposedly unbeatable long jump record, set at the 1968 Mexico City Olympics, stood for twenty-three fewer years. 'As far as I know, in all of sport, it has never happened that a woman has broken a men's record,' said the cycling commentator Phil Liggett. 'Not only that, it happened on the same day and in the same event. No one could say that Beryl did it on a better course or better conditions. It was a coveted record. It should have been front-page news but it almost slipped under the doormat. Only the cycling fraternity knew the enormity of what she had done.' Aware of her disappointment that women would not be allowed in the 1968 Mexico Olympics the following year, *Cycling* did obtain permission from the Bank of England to create a coin made of Mexican gold. On one side it simply said 'Cycling' and, on the other, 'Beryl Burton. First woman to break a men's athletic record. Otley CC 12. 17.9.67 (277.2 m)'. In their coverage of the race, the magazine also rightly predicted that 'the day long duel that these two fought will be forever remembered in years to come as the greatest of its kind'.

McNamara did also fulfil a lifetime's ambition later that year by winning the men's BAR title, even if the reaction to his own 12-hour record was inevitably distorted. 'Sad roadman', said the headline above his photograph in *Cycling*. 'Beryl's ride did overshadow what Mike achieved and I think deep down it grieved him a little bit,' says his brother John. 'It was all, "Have you seen what Beryl's done? She caught Mike!" He had still broken the men's record and it was an afterthought but we really don't want that to sound like sour grapes. We loved Beryl. She was an extraordinary athlete, a remarkable person and she never let success spoil her.' McNamara died in May 2021, aged eighty-five, after spending his later years living in the most northern tip of Scotland, near Durness. Having been initially reluctant to speak directly at any length about the day, he did consult his diaries to help verify the chronology of what happened. 'I expect you want to ask about the liquorice allsort?' he said. 'It's true. And I ate it. I liked liquorice allsorts. And please also remember one other thing. Beryl caught and passed ninety-eight other men that day. Not just me.' One of those was Keith Lambert, a future triple British professional men's road race champion. Beryl had started 18 minutes behind Lambert before reeling him in. 'I think she said something like, "C'mon lad, what are you doing?",' says Lambert, shaking his head. 'What a day! Goodness me! Unbelievable. She was as hard as nails. A phenomenon.'

Beryl would also see McNamara at hundreds of events in the years that followed. He was invited into the Burton home for an impromptu pot of tea after they had cycled back together from one race, and at the Rockingham Club dinner three years later Beryl was actually called on stage to present McNamara with a giant liquorice allsort. But they never once discussed a duel that transformed how men viewed women cyclists and which, seven years before the famous 'Battle of the Sexes' in tennis between Billie Jean King and Bobby Riggs, actually did involve two supreme athletes at the absolute peak of their powers. 'People regularly do still ask me how good Beryl was, and the best way I can put it is this,' says John McNamara. 'Just imagine that Serena Williams played Roger Federer at Wimbledon. And then imagine that she beat him. That's how good Beryl was.'

2

The Charnock Way

Morley, 12 December 2018

A short walk through Morrison's car park, past Morley Town Hall, a right turn up the now pedestrianised Queen Street and there on your right is the entrance. Beryl Burton Gardens. A steel archway sign hangs over the walkway, and on the wall to the left is a round blue plaque. 'Beryl Burton OBE was a cycling phenomenon,' says the succinct opening sentence. Jeffrey Charnock is Beryl's younger brother by nine years and has accompanied me on what becomes an emotional tour through their early life. He pauses to reread the plaque before ushering us around the corner to the back wall of the Yorkshire Bank and what is a quite stunning 60-feet-wide mural. Morley is 3 miles south of Leeds city centre and, following her death in 1996, Beryl was depicted by a group of local artists just as most people will remember her: alone, crouched over the handlebars, resplendent in her pale blue and white Morley Cycling Club kit and time trialling along at an unfathomable speed. Even the idiosyncratic kink in her riding style – right hand always slightly higher than her left – is captured. The outline of the Town Hall's Grade I listed bell tower, where civic ceremonies would be staged in her honour, represents an appropriate backdrop to the rolling Yorkshire countryside. Some of the passers-by on this busy Wednesday lunchtime do glance up at a woman whose achievements have, in cycling circles, given this market town of 44,000 people a proud global resonance. Others hurry past. None is aware that the man dutifully clearing up a few nearby pieces of litter is her sibling.

Having ensured that the gardens are again spotless, Jeffrey does himself pause to silently absorb the mural. As they understandably do on several occasions throughout our day together, his eyes begin to moisten while he gathers his thoughts. An underlying sadness at the abrupt end to Beryl's life will never dissipate, even if some comfort is constantly taken from the knowledge that his sister died doing what she loved. 'People just see the cyclist,' Jeffrey finally says. 'I don't. I see the girl that she was. I see the woman that she became. And then I see all the achievements. I know what shaped her and what she went through to get there. People sometimes also get it wrong about Beryl. They focus on how she was so driven and single-minded. Which she was. Or they portray her as very stern. Which she could be. But there was so much more than that. Kind. Funny. Not always intentionally, but a dry sense of humour. She was complex. Unique.'

*

Over coffee later that afternoon in their immaculate semi-detached home in Garforth, just a few miles from where they grew up, Jeffrey and his wife, Elaine, then cast their minds back to what was not just another time but also a very different place. Beryl Charnock was born on 12 May 1937 in Halton, a working-class district to the east of Leeds. 'Times were really tough and so was Beryl – she had to be,' said Jeffrey. Within months of Beryl's second birthday, the Second World War had begun and rationing was introduced. Simply ensuring that Beryl and her sister Maureen, who is two years older, had enough to eat became the daily priority for their parents, John and Jessie. By the time that Beryl had turned four, Leeds had been subjected to nine air raids by Nazi Germany's Luftwaffe which killed seventy local people. The district of Armley, where Beryl's grandmother lived, was among the most severely disfigured, and the occasional unexploded bomb is still discovered in the streets and nearby fields in which Maureen, Beryl and Jeffrey would play.

Jessie drove ambulances around Leeds during the Second World War while John, who was an engineer, helped produce tanks. The family's upbringing was strict and essentially Victorian in its unemotional but community-focused outlook. It was also unsettled. They initially lived in Dorset Terrace, in Harehills – an inner-city area of Leeds that has subsequently experienced serious riots – before moving to Saxon Road in Moortown, further to the north of the city, where a new estate was built after the war. Having an indoor toilet, a porch and coalhouse was considered a luxury. Periods were also spent living with their grandmother on Salisbury Terrace in Armley, out playing in the factory dust around homes that were later decontaminated because of the asbestos. Their grandmother was widowed with six children of her own and, as a baby in her terraced house, space constraints meant that Jeffrey would literally sleep in a drawer. 'Looking back, you wonder how you survived – houses were there one minute and gone the next,' he said, pointing out various landmarks or places where they would play as he drove us back through communities that are now richly multicultural and quite severely deprived. In Harehills, where the family lived until Beryl was twelve, the rates of childhood poverty are among the highest in Europe.

The three Charnock children were close despite their spread in age and, with rationing in force for several years after the war and their parents working long hours to provide the basics, they quickly became self-sufficient. Rolling fields and a stream, which are now the location for a ring road and large superstore, faced their estate, and the children lived a largely outdoor existence. 'There were no shops, just a Co-op van once a week,' said Jeffrey. 'You would share cups of sugar with your neighbours and have your butter portioned out in greaseproof paper. There was no money. Buses were non-existent. If you needed to get somewhere, you walked. The difference is that everyone was basically in the same boat. Working class and a very strong sense of togetherness.'

6. Fierce determination and a head of curls were lifelong characteristics.

Discipline was also paramount. 'Nowadays it would probably be classed as cruelty but we were taught the difference between right and wrong. You were frightened of authority. There are things that stay in your memory and you shudder to think what would happen today. Our dad was a tough man. You were on time. You were never cheeky to your teachers. You toed the line. Our upbringing wasn't all good, but it gave us this straightforward life and a certain mindset.' School dinners could not stretch to every pupil and, with Beryl and Maureen not making what was an arbitrary list, they would run just under a mile home every lunchtime. Beryl loved swimming and would walk the 3 miles to the Meanwood Road Baths. Jeffrey developed a particular passion for cricket and has spent much of his retirement watching Yorkshire at Headingley.

Growing up at the same time as Beryl in the nearby mining village of Fitzwilliam was Sir Geoffrey Boycott, who remains convinced that the shared values of post-war Yorkshire communities were crucial to their future sporting success. 'You had terraced houses and so there was a closeness,' he says. 'That is what Beryl grew up in. Flats have isolated people. The kids were safe in the street and you knew where they were. We'd play marbles under a gas lamp. Football on the wasteland. Or cricket down the ginnels of the terraced houses. The manhole cover was the wicket. If you hit it in someone's garden you were out … and you'd better get it quick before Mrs Brown's dog bit you on the arse!'

Boycott believes that the realities of daily life – where men worked long hours in coal mines or factories and there were no electrical appliances or supermarkets to help with running a household – were what most restricted women's access to sport. 'I don't think people were anti-women, but circumstances made it an impossibility for many. My mother went every day to the butcher's, baker's, grocer's and candlestick maker's. No fridges or freezers. She would then clean and wash. Get the carpets up. Use a copper to heat water. Boil the clothes. Put them through a wringer machine. Hang them out to dry. Then prepare lunch and dinner. My dad's gross weekly wage was £10. We had no money, but we had food on the table. And we had discipline and values. The mantra was simple: "If you want something, you better go out and work for it."'

That ethos was ingrained in Beryl, and to this day Jeffrey refers to what he calls the 'Charnock Way'. By that he means a streak of stubborn and resolute determination. Jeffrey still saw this daily in their older sister, Maureen, who continued to live independently through the Covid-19 pandemic despite some loss of memory before her death in February 2022. Beryl always loved competing, often in solitude and against herself. Childhood friends say that she would spend hours in front of a wall with an old tennis ball. She would set herself targets. Ten catches off the wall. Then twenty. Next twenty-five. And thirty. She would introduce a second ball and try the same. 'I was setting myself exacting standards,' she told Yorkshire Television in 1986. And what if she fell short? 'I would be filled with inner rage. I would pick the ball up and bite it with anger. Competitiveness is bred in you. It has to be brought out, but it's there. As far back as I remember, it was there, no matter what I was doing. Knitting, shaking a rug, washing up. Anything. It comes out in all forms.'

An intrinsic need both to achieve and not to waste time meant that she enjoyed formal education and disliked the holiday periods. An early school report described her as a 'stubborn little mule', and a perfectionist streak was evident in her reaction to a tutor who once disfigured her English book with corrections in red ink. 'I went berserk,' said Beryl. The eleven-plus examination was introduced across England in 1944 and, while ostensibly a means to divide children according to their most appropriate educational path, whether grammar, secondary modern or technical school, it was soon viewed rather differently. David Kynaston, the author of *Austerity Britain, 1945–1951*, described education as 'the silver bullet for enhanced social mobility' and, with a binary pass/fail outcome, the impact of this one examination became potentially life-defining. The eleven-plus was only in its fourth year by the time Beryl sat her assessment, at the age of just ten, at the Cold-cotes Primary School in October 1947. It was a paper that would evolve into more of an IQ test after it became accepted that the early mixture of maths, English and verbal reasoning could generally only be passed by those children specifically prepared for the particular nature of the exam.

Beryl was academically at the top of her class but had no such advantage and, unable to harness her burning desire to succeed, froze once the test had begun. 'Even papers which should not have caused me any great problem might just as well have been printed in Urdu,' she later said. The shock and disappointment at not answering even a single question was crushing. Within hours of the ordeal finishing, she had developed a high fever, collapsed and was rushed to St James's Hospital in Leeds, where she was diagnosed with Sydenham's Chorea and rheumatic fever. She had suffered a life-threatening attack of her nervous system. 'I was shattered – an abject failure,' she said bluntly.

Paralysed down one side of her body, barely able to speak and unable to control sudden involuntary movements, Beryl did not leave Ward 19 of the hospital for nine long months. The one stroke of good fortune was that St James's was less than a mile from their home in Harehills, and Beryl would always look out towards the main gate at visiting time and share waves with two-year-old Jeffrey, whom she desperately missed. Beryl's fever eventually subsided, but it was months before her mobility and movement extended beyond the use of one arm and one leg. She would literally hop to the bathroom and, under the doctors' instruction, was wrapped tightly in blankets so that she stayed warm. It was intensely uncomfortable and, even though Beryl struggled to sleep and would soak the blankets in sweat, they would not be changed unless she got a chill. An independent mind that could stray into outright rebellion became evident. Beryl refused point-blank to take the prescribed sleeping pills and was also in constant trouble for sticking her legs out of the bed to gain some respite from the heat. She began to steadily recover but was not judged well enough to go home even after being discharged from hospital.

The next fifteen months of Beryl's rehabilitation were spent in Southport in a convalescent home run by nuns. Beryl would later provide scant detail about this period of her life beyond noting a daily routine of morning church followed by a walk near the sea. The smell of the church incense made her feel sick. Convent life during the late 1940s typically began with 5 a.m. prayers followed by a rigid and largely silent routine of meditation, study, dishwashing, ironing, sewing and darning – all timed by the clang of a bell – before lights out by 9 p.m. Christian teaching meant always eating fish on a Friday, a routine Beryl continued throughout her life. Leaving the convent without permission was out of the question. Family visits were not allowed, even over Christmas 1948, and writing or receiving letters was restricted to a monthly activity. The darning would at least later come in useful, and the family still have some of Beryl's original old Morley woollen cycling jerseys on which any holes or worn areas were meticulously

7. Back home in Leeds following two traumatic years.

hand-repaired. Finally, after spending her twelfth birthday some 73 miles away from her family back in Leeds, Beryl was declared physically fit enough to go home.

She had missed two full years of school and, with no second chance in her eleven-plus, returned afresh in October 1949 to the Stainbeck High School in Moortown, where the family had since moved. Pam Hodson was a classmate and, although she has no memory of Beryl standing out in PE, she does vividly recall their English teacher, Miss Bellington – 'strict, with half-moon-shaped glasses' – and how Beryl would report any noisy or distracting classmate. 'Beryl wanted to get on and would always be, "Misssss, they're talking",' says Hodson. 'She was a loner. You tried to be her mate but you gave up eventually.' Beryl had spent two of her most critical developmental years with adult nuns, doctors and nurses rather than interacting with children. There was no psychological support, and a general lack of sympathy is summed up by Hodson. 'You get on with it, don't you?' Beryl would never

expect pity, much less worry about fickle playground popularity contests, and had instead returned with something far more
powerful: a raging desire to succeed. 'My whole future had been
placed in jeopardy by a silly examination,' she said. 'I knew that I
was quite bright. I felt as though I had been cheated. I was determined there and then that somehow I would make my mark. I was
going to be somebody.'

*

There is an evolving and growing body of academic literature
and research that draws a correlation between childhood trauma
and exceptional achievement. It was a thesis that first emerged
through the work of Victor and Mildred Goertzel, who in 1962
studied more than 400 super-high achievers. They selected people
about whom at least two biographies had been written, including
Louis Armstrong, Henry Ford and Eleanor Roosevelt, and found
that 75 per cent of their subjects faced unusually severe difficulties
during their formative years, such as the loss of a parent, abuse,
serious illness or extreme poverty. This thesis has subsequently
been further explored by the American clinical psychologist Meg
Jay, who argues that society often misunderstands the word 'resilience' and views it as an elastic quality that allows an individual
to bounce back to normality following a setback. 'What they do
is much more complicated and courageous,' she says. 'For them,
resilience is an ongoing battle, a way of approaching life.' What
can become a permanent mindset derives from the most basic
'fight or flight' brain science. 'The threat or danger of our situation floods the brain and body with stress hormones, such as
adrenalin or cortisol, and we kick into survival mode,' explains
Jay. In later interviews, in which the line of questioning would
inevitably involve trying to fathom how she remained so obsessively determined to keep winning, Beryl would invariably refer
both to her childhood illness and to her eleven-plus ordeal. It was

something that she often thought about while cycling, especially during moments of physical discomfort and historic achievement. She even predicted in her 1986 autobiography that 'psychiatrists and educationalists may read something into what happened to me'.

It would take more than thirty years for this thesis to be examined in a purely sporting context, but the Great British Medalists Project of 2016, a collaboration between UK Sport and universities in Exeter, Cardiff and Bangor, did just that. The results were striking. The starting point had been the desire of Chelsea Warr, UK Sport's then director of performance, to find what differentiated the sporting elite and what she defined as the 'super-elite'. This meant those who had not just reached an Olympics, or even once stood on a podium, but those who repeatedly won the major medals. Chris Boardman and Darren Tudor, who were both working at this time with British Olympic cyclists, were also involved in conceiving the project. Boardman believes that natural physiology is often overstated in explaining sporting greatness and instead he wanted to identify common traits that fuel a relentless commitment. 'Measuring how many hours you did, I think, is looking down the wrong path,' he said. 'It's what made you do thousands of hours. I thought you would find a psychological profile. For a lot of people it's about self-esteem. They needed something that made them special. They become fanatical. You get extreme people. I don't think it's healthy. It involves so many sacrifices. But it's effective.'

Longevity and repeated success among the world's absolute best were what defined the super-elites in Warr's study. Beryl may have been denied her chance in the Olympics, but there can be no doubt that she sits in this category alongside people like Sir Andy Murray, Dame Sarah Storey, Sir Steve Redgrave, Dame Tanni Grey-Thompson, Sir A. P. McCoy and Jonny Wilkinson. Warr's study took three and a half years and involved 1,400 hours of interviews with athletes who between them had won more than a hundred world and Olympic medals. The academics had paired sixteen sets of 'super-elite' athletes with a mere 'elite'. The idea was to find the closest possible equivalent when they were competing at a young age and try to establish why their paths diverged and the 'super-elite' achieved such sustained dominance.

The findings were anonymous, but what quickly became more noticeable than predictable factors such as opportunity, hours spent practising or quality of coaching was their respective description of critical life experiences. Every single one of the sixteen 'super-elites' reported a significant negative event during their primary developmental years. Only four of the 'elites' experienced the same. The accompanying written responses confirmed the profound importance of this event. 'I think every sportsperson will have something in their past that gives them the need to win,' said one respondent. Another added that 'When I lose, I will torture myself over it. I needed it more than others.' In Chelsea Warr and Owen Slot's book *The Talent Lab,* one of the study's authors, Professor Lew Hardy, described his interviews with the super-elites. 'Often with the parents, there was a moment of realisation that something they had done somewhere in their child's upbringing had a major impact,' he said. 'Some athletes cried in the interview, but a larger number of the parents did. Super-elites are amazing but they aren't necessarily the most well-adjusted, happy people. If they were, they wouldn't do what they do.'

What then follows in the super-elites compared with the elites, who are themselves outliers by conventional definitions of achievement, is an utterly ruthless and selfish need to succeed. It becomes a permanent pursuit of excellence. The super-elites can be difficult to be around. They rarely take time to enjoy a victory, and contentment is generally fleeting. Simply winning once was never enough. Getting the absolute best out of themselves was the benchmark that held greater importance than any narrow comparison with their opposition. For fifteen of the sixteen super-elites their sport itself was said to hold a greater relative attraction than the benefits of a normal life. That compares with just three of the sixteen elites, who also faced a significant daily battle to make the huge sacrifices that were necessary to compete at anything approaching a world level. This was again subtly but crucially different for the super-elites. Sacrifice did not enter their thinking. They did not question their lifestyle. It was simply who they were and what they did. As Dame Katherine Grainger, an Olympic medallist at five Olympics, explains: 'When people say, "How do you motivate yourself when it was raining, snowing, freezing and you are exhausted?" it feels almost like that is giving too much credit. You don't introduce choice. So you don't wrestle with it. I don't think cycling dominated Beryl Burton's life. It was her life.'

Sports psychology was almost non-existent in Beryl's time, but just the outline of her story now intrigues many of those practising in the field. Dave Collins, the former performance director at UK Athletics and a professor of coaching and performance, co-authored a paper called 'The Rocky Road to the Top: Why Talent Needs Trauma'. As the title suggests, his research also asserts that challenges, stress, setbacks and a non-linear path of progression are prerequisites to extraordinary achievement. Collins regards what he calls 'snowplough parents' – those who proactively remove all obstacles in their child's path – as detrimental. He now advises Chelsea's football academy, a talent centre that has dominated youth football in Britain since 2009, and he will even counterbalance clear signs of a 'snowplough' influence with challenges that deliberately 'discombobulate' a child and help them learn to overcome difficulties. 'I create speed bumps,' he says.

Collins makes a nuanced but important observation, however, about the much more significant and lasting trauma that Beryl endured. He agrees that a particularly upsetting childhood event can be enormously important in driving people to extraordinary feats and developing a certain mindset, but he stresses that it depends on the individual's interpretation of that event, their existing character, experiences and the subsequent support network around them. Emphatically, it is not something that he recommends. 'There's a saying that what doesn't kill you makes you stronger,' says Collins. 'Fine. But actually it might kill you as well. There are more kids screwed up by childhood trauma than made by childhood trauma. A key quote for me is by Aldous Huxley. He said, "Experience is not what happens to a man. It is what he does with what happens to him." What we found in our research is that post-traumatic growth is not inevitable but that it is something which some people do on their own or with someone. What counts is what you take into that trauma and what you then take out of it.'

Without knowing the detail of Beryl's life, he then confidently and correctly predicts that she would already have been a very driven person and would later also discover a strong surrounding support network. 'I think there were a variety of things happening with Beryl,' says Collins. 'I think you are talking about someone who went in with great strengths. Already strong-willed. Already quite athletic. Failed – for reasons outside her control. And the impact of that was big. Immensely frustrated. Really pissed off. And she said, "Blow that. I'll show them." She had to find a way to show them and she discovered cycling. It became her identity.' Meg Jay, who wrote the bestselling book *Supernormal: Childhood Adversity and the Untold Story of Resilience*, agrees and particularly stresses the importance of Beryl's immediate community and family. She then tells me that a trio of factors can invariably be identified among the highest achievers and that, alongside some activating event or circumstance, there is also a powerful inherent inner characteristic, such as perfectionism, as well as some subsequent environmental advantage. 'Adversity + nature + nurture = supernormal success,' she concludes.

Jeffrey is fascinated to hear this assessment. The explanations for his sister's success are something that he has thought long and hard about. He agrees that Beryl's childhood illness should be seen as one large part of an explanatory jigsaw rather than the sole piece, and confirmed that a fierce inner competitive drive was part of her character – and a family trait – for as long as anyone could remember. The need to be self-dependent would also only intensify shortly after Beryl had returned from convalescing in Southport and resumed school following a twenty-four-month absence. Their mother Jessie, who was a heavy smoker, fell ill with a serious respiratory sickness, and the children became responsible for the domestic chores. That resilience and a certain stress-fuelled 'fight' outlook would soon extend into every aspect of her life. Even when Beryl had a family of her own, was working full-time and had become the best cyclist in the world, she would still visit her mother and father's house 10 miles across Leeds late into the evening to do their ironing. 'I remember that vividly,' says her sister-in-law Elaine Charnock. 'She would have been on her feet all day picking fruit, cycled maybe 60 miles for her training and then called in with all her kit on. Beryl had to be productive. She never stopped.' Beryl would also always prepare and cook all of her food from the basic ingredients that were available to the family. 'She would never waste anything,' says Elaine. 'I think that stays with some people. Beryl was careful in some respects but very generous in others. I can still picture her sitting on our living room floor, eating a sandwich. She would always ask who had made the bread. I'd say, "Hovis." She would say, "But don't you bake your own bread? You ought to." I'd reply that I found it hard to slice, and she would then be, "If you bake your own bread, I'll buy you a bread slicer."'

*

Shortly before leaving Beryl Burton Gardens, Jeffrey proudly tells me about how his big sister once entered him into a local challenge to cycle 100 miles around Leeds and the surrounding Yorkshire Dales within 8 hours. Jeffrey was only fifteen, and so it was a considerable task. Beryl duly took him on some training rides, and he once crashed quite spectacularly after getting his front wheel caught in the city centre tramlines. 'She rolled over to me, took one look down, burst out laughing and just said, "Get up." I got up. I eventually did do this 100-mile ride inside 8 hours and, at the end, Beryl was there waiting. Happier than I was. She was the world champion at the time.' Jeffrey's eyes again well up as he recalls how his sister also taught him how to swim, and with the rain lashing down there is something somehow even more evocative about her mural. Beryl would never cancel a training session regardless of the weather and, after a last glance up at his big sister, there is one final observation. 'See the man pictured on a bench at the roadside,' says Jeffrey, pointing at the slender silhouette of an onlooker with a flat cap. 'I think of Charlie whenever I look at it. It's just like him. Charlie was incredible. A catalyst. When she started out, he promised Beryl that he would always be there at the start and finish of every race. And he was. You have to go and see Charlie.'

3

Charlie

On the windowsill of a bedroom in a sheltered housing complex in the Yorkshire cathedral city of Ripon stands a small brass picture frame in the style of a bicycle. There are spaces to display a round photograph in each of the two wheels, and pictures of Beryl Burton and her husband Charlie out riding their bicycles have been carefully cut out and placed in either circle. The frame is no more than 8 inches in diameter and represents the one small visual indication inside Charlie's home of one of sport's most extraordinary marital partnerships. The choice of photographs feels significant. There are no medals. No prize presentations. No victory salutes. There is not even a cursory nod towards literally thousands of shared wins. Charlie and Beryl are instead out touring and enjoying cycling in the simplest possible sense. Perhaps intentionally, and certainly appropriately, the photograph of Charlie is positioned at the rear of this particular brass bicycle. In his wife's slipstream – but an indispensable part of the machine.

Beryl was not herself prone to excessive shows of emotion or gratitude but, in some heartfelt words on the inside sleeve of her autobiography, *Personal Best*, she expressed her feelings: 'To Charlie, without whom none of this would have been possible. BB.' Laughter and tears are still never far away whenever Charlie talks about Beryl and, while his memory is inevitably more erratic, the strength of feeling is easily sensed. Charlie only stopped riding a bike himself in 2013, when he was eighty-four – 'I were getting a bit wobbly' – and, as he clasps his mug of tea, I find myself wondering how many hundreds of bikes those fingers must have built and how many thousands of tyres they must have changed. He then adjusts his spectacles, sinks back into his patched armchair, closes his eyes and thinks of Beryl. 'I still speak to her,' he says. 'She were wonderful. The love of my life.'

When I point out the photograph of them both and ask whether there were many other memorabilia from his wife's career, he simply lets out a chuckle. 'Beryl wasn't really one for keeping things or showing them off,' he says, before weighing up whether he should reveal what she really did with several of the coveted rainbow jerseys that were presented for her seven world championship wins. 'Shall I say?' he asks, looking across to the kitchenette. Their daughter, Denise Burton-Cole, had been quietly brewing another pot of tea and also instantly smiles at a memory that is just as vivid as all the cycling. 'She used them to scrub the floor,' continues Charlie, before his daughter has answered. 'She thought that they made good dusters.' Beryl would even mistakenly tell people she had won fourteen world championships medals until counting up the contents of an old canvas bag during a clear-out in 1984 and discovering that there were actually fifteen.

At least two rainbow jerseys were preserved, and one does now hang on public display at the Manchester Velodrome next to all the major medals from her career. Another is still lovingly (and slightly secretly) looked after by Beryl's friend Malcolm Cowgill, who has been the secretary of the Morley Cycling Club since 1959. Cowgill lives on the outskirts of Leeds, and keeps the jersey folded in a protective bag under his bed. It was presented to Beryl in 1960 but still looks no more than a few weeks old. When Beryl gave Cowgill the jersey, it came with an instruction – 'Mind you never wear it, because you didn't earn it' – that has evidently been followed to the letter. 'Is that the one with the pointed collar? I wondered where that was,' says Denise, before again smiling when the mention of Cowgill prompts her to recall the frankly ludicrous carry-on before each of the RTTC's annual dinner-dance prize presentations.

This was once the social night of the year in British cycling. With entertainment including acrobats, fire-eaters and live orchestras, and special guests ranging from Eddy Merckx, Fausto Coppi and Jacques Anquetil to Roger Bannister, Tommy Trinder and Herb Elliott, it would be attended by as many as 6,000 people and held in venues like the Royal Albert Hall. Beryl ended her career with ninety-seven individual victories across the RTTC's various distances and so, for a good quarter of a century, the main women's silverware had a virtual permanent home. Not that any visitor would have actually known. 'She was given a big cardboard box for all these trophies,' says Denise. 'We'd lug this box back every year and she'd then just put it straight into the loft or under the stairs.' And did she ever get the box out? 'Not until about a week before the presentation evening the following year. She would polish the trophies so they looked nice on the top table. We'd then take them back down on the bus from Yorkshire in the same box, unpack it and she'd be presented with them all over again. This went on for years. She told them to keep them in the end.' Charlie then interjects to casually reveal that he melted down some of Beryl's numerous medals so that he could sell the metal – invariably a small slab of gold – to help fund her racing.

*

After the trauma of her eleven-plus exam and then serious illness, Beryl was fifteen when she left school in 1952 and began work at Montague Burton, a tailor's business with a large factory in the centre of Leeds. Her first job was in an office 'half the size of a football pitch', where she read and sorted the punched Hollerith cards that stored numerical data about the firm's operations. She had been provided with a long list of medical 'dos and don'ts' following her convalescence in Southport. A further medical check provided by her new employers again starkly outlined the risk. Beryl's pulse was irregular and a scar had formed on her heart. The doctor concluded that she would be risking her life by pushing herself too severely. Should she ride a bike, the specific guidance was to walk up any hills and avoid getting out of breath. Rarely in medical history has a piece of advice been so emphatically ignored.

Charlie, who was already a member of what was then the Morley Road Club, also worked at Montague Burton and had been on a cycling holiday in Spain when Beryl began work. He would ride 7 miles into the office and, knowing nothing about the clunky metal shoe-plates that cyclists wore to provide a stable base from which to pedal, Beryl's first instinct was to be attracted by this older man's bronzed physique but wonder why he hobbled. She concluded that he must have a foot deformity. 'She thought, "That's a shame but nice, smart-looking lad," and she were a good-looking lass,' says Charlie. Beryl preferred swimming at this time but was persuaded out dancing by Charlie one Friday evening in 1952 with other members of the Morley Road Club. They had become disenchanted with being wallflowers at the club dinner dances, she later said. Beryl's only passing comprehension of cycling as a sport had come through being overtaken by club riders early on a Sunday morning when she borrowed a second-hand 'roadster' to clean houses for extra family funds. She then noticed Charlie's racing bike as they left work. 'I'm going to get one,' she promptly said. 'I thought, "Oh, are you?"' says Charlie. 'But she was very certain, so I ended up loaning her the bike. We moved forward from there.'

'Moving forward' was meant quite literally. Charlie had noticed that Beryl kept up with the men when they ran a quarter of a mile from their factory to the restaurant for lunch and asked if she would like to join him on their weekly Sunday club rides. Beryl immediately agreed, despite having no idea what she was getting herself into. Weekend 'club runs' all across Great Britain continue to follow many of the same informal conventions. They are generally upwards of 40 miles, punctuated with a stop or two for tea, cake and perhaps some sandwiches. Groups now often fragment in order to cater for the demands of different distances or speeds, but mostly still adhere to the unwritten rule that no one is left behind.

Beryl was living with her parents in Moortown when the invitation came but, intrigued, she rode in alone to the main post office in Leeds City Square, where the cyclists met for a 9 a.m. start. What were largely 4 downhill miles into the city centre became a dreaded slog later in the day. Between long hours pedalling through the Yorkshire lanes, Charlie literally pushed Beryl up the hills to begin with, and she returned home so exhausted on a Sunday evening that she had no idea when her mother asked where they had ridden. Beryl was equally unaware when it came to cycling etiquette and was the cause of chaos on an early club run when she decided to blow her nose while riding in the middle of a group of twelve riders. 'I dropped the hanky and immediately stopped to pick it up – a perfectly normal reaction I thought,' she said. 'The lads behind weren't impressed. Two disappeared into a ditch to the left and two shot up the banking into a telegraph pole on my right.'

Morley club rides could last from dawn to dusk and regularly surpassed 100 miles. They would go out in all weather conditions, even though cycling clothing was much more basic than now: knitted woolly jumpers, cardigans and hats for the cold, long nylon socks tucked into several pairs of trousers and a makeshift clear plastic sheet in the wet. Beryl would scoop up rainwater in the plastic sheet and take sips when she felt particularly dehydrated. It was an extraordinarily tough apprenticeship and, in what was a largely male and adult group of around twenty-five regular riders, few allowances were made. 'We – the lasses, that is – used to ride as hard as the lads and neither gave or received any quarter,' said Beryl. 'They had no mercy. I made up my mind early on that I just wasn't going to be left.'

The unspoken expectation was that Beryl would soon find rather more comfortable ways to spend her Sundays. 'I would see Charlie during the week, but had no contact with other members,' she said. 'As I left them on Sunday evening I would manage to gasp, "See you next week". I am sure they were quite surprised when I kept turning out.' Beryl was never comfortable in a group of riders and, despite Charlie's early guidance, would also crash regularly. It even became a joke among club members to acknowledge her with the greeting, 'Haven't you fallen off yet?' But did she enjoy it? Her response in an interview some thirty years later was instructive. 'I can't recall,' she said. 'What I do remember is that I wasn't going to be beaten by anything.' Her father did not stand in her way but made it clear that there would be no compromise to the weekly household chores. She did not argue. In a show of self-discipline and determination that was already staggering, Beryl simply got up at 6 a.m. to dust and polish the floors before departing at around 8 a.m. for an all-day ride. She was not yet sixteen.

Charlie was seven years older and naturally more worldly. He had been cycling since receiving a racing bike on his twelfth birthday from his parents, Abraham and Florence Burton. Abraham worked down the Askern Main Colliery, a coal mine that was open between 1911 and 1991, but was left bedridden following a serious work accident. Charlie had also already spent two years completing national service in Germany for the Royal Air Force when he met Beryl. This had helped him become a hugely accomplished mechanic and, as well as setting up Beryl with her first proper bike, he was already the go-to man in Morley for any sort of technical help.

Beryl's tenacity and liking for Charlie were what initially ensured that she kept returning to the weekly club runs and, if there is one sport that eventually rewards persistence, it is cycling. Having begun with no comprehension of racing, she was persuaded in 1953 to start taking part in the 10-mile time trials that would be staged out on the Bradford Road near Morley on a

8. Beryl, aged sixteen, being held up by boyfriend
Charlie before her first race.

Wednesday evening. With the memory of her eleven-plus ordeal etched in her mind, Beryl was privately terrified by the prospect of being timed for her efforts and hated the idea of anyone watching her. She was also too proud to say 'No' and so rode her first few races with her hands on the tops of the curved handlebars so that she did not look like she was trying. Urged on by Charlie to get down on to the 'drops', she immediately displayed the distinctive trait whereby her right hand was always higher than the left. A first 10-mile time of 33 minutes – well outside the 20 mph average speed known by cyclists as a respectable but mediocre 'evens' – hardly signposted what would follow. A first cycling certificate would arrive several weeks later, however, and certainly does feel significant. It is dated 12 July 1953. Beryl, who had just turned sixteen, had sped up considerably to record a time of 42 min. 27 sec. over 15 miles. When she then saved up for an Armstrong

Moth Sports, paying £7 12s. 6d. for her first handmade frame, it was evident that something had permanently changed. The key to a feeling of self-achievement had been discovered, and it was not about to be misplaced.

*

In understanding how Charlie and the Morley cyclists so quickly became the focal points around whom Beryl's entire existence revolved, it is also essential to appreciate the significance of what was a rapidly expanding club scene. It was only after the Second World War that it became normal to work five rather than six days a week, and, with none of the technological distractions of today, it was a time of rapid recreational growth. Priorities had also changed following the hardships of war, and cycling clubs became something much more than just sporting organisations. As well as their evening time trials and Sunday club runs, dozens of members from the Morley group would gather socially on a Friday night. It was initially in an attic room above the Co-op, which was hired for two shillings a week, and then latterly in a barn on the rhubarb farm owned by Nim Carline, one of Yorkshire cycling's most legendary riders. Carline's barn would be transformed each week and stored a table tennis table, a dartboard, free weights and stationary wooden cycling rollers on which riders could train indoors. Speaking decades later in a talk to other club cyclists, Beryl recalled what was the benchmark for an acceptable indoor session. 'There had to be a pool of sweat on the floor and a cloud of steam about the rider before it counted,' she said. 'It might not have been to the scientific Chris Boardman standard but it seemed to work.'

Beryl would bake cakes to share, there was a stove to make tea and, on special occasions, they would host beetle drives, complete with pea and pie suppers. Few people even had landline phones, and so club nights were also when logistical arrangements would be made for the weekend cycling. Beryl instantly loved the camaraderie and sense of liberty that went with getting out into the countryside after a working week inside a factory. With car ownership still rare, cycling also represented a wonderful low-cost opportunity to see and explore parts of the region that were otherwise inaccessible. 'You'd spend one-and-six on your tea and have had a marvellous full day's outing,' Beryl told the *Sunday Times* in 1975. In that same interview she also recalled special all-night club runs that would start on a Saturday evening and involve riding 100 miles to the Lake District before early morning breakfast near Haweswater Reservoir and then cycling another 100 miles back to Leeds.

The Morley cyclists were progressive in their attitudes towards women. Sheila Broadbent was among the committee members of the Morley Wheelers before it amalgamated with the Morley Road Club and actually beat Beryl in her first 10-mile time trial. 'But Beryl was always on her bike and soon got much faster,' she says. Another lifelong friend was Kathleen Mitchell, who was born to a mining family in Shafton two months before Beryl, and also began cycling seriously in 1953, when she was sixteen. 'I knew her when she was Beryl Charnock,' says Mitchell. 'It wasn't a case of thrashing down the road for 50 miles and back for tea. We worked all week and lived for Sundays, when we'd be out from first light until after dark. We would go to the Dales or the Yorkshire Moors and might do 120 miles. Beryl loved the reservoirs and scenery. We were experiencing a freedom that didn't exist in our lives before. Beryl had a great sense of humour. I had just got married and Beryl had met Charlie. One day we decided to cycle off to the family planning clinic in Sheffield. We giggled all the way there and back. The jokes were not printable.' Their early racing was also all about fun. In one off-road winter cyclo-cross race, Mitchell got stuck in a bog while Beryl was leading. In a gesture that would later have been utterly unthinkable, Beryl stopped as she lapped Mitchell to lift her out of the mud and pull up her shorts in the process. 'We were doubled over in laughter,' says Mitchell.

A bigger problem in time trials than sharing the roads with cars was the likelihood of having to weave through a herd of cows.

Beryl's love for the club scene would never recede, but cycling did also awaken a competitive streak that, over time, hardened like cement. 'I was smitten by the "go faster" bug,' she later said. This would manifest itself not just on the bike but also in often quite comical other situations. The musical chairs at Morley Cycling Club's Christmas party was a regular example. 'It started nicely but she would do anything to win – trip you up, push you out of the way,' says Mitchell, smiling. There was once also a fiercely contested rhubarb-baking competition. 'My husband and father worked with a lot of farmers and so I entered a rhubarb pie,' says Mitchell. 'Beryl also baked a pie, but mine won. She didn't like it. She really thought hers was the best.' Club run stops would sometimes turn into informal football matches, and Beryl had no hesitation in getting stuck in among the men. She often also bet a shilling with male members of the club on the evening 10-mile time trials – 'I make sure of collecting t'lads' bobs,' she told the *Morley Observer* – and would write down the times of the best men and use them as her target. Beryl later admitted to feeling an actual physical change whenever some form of comparison or competition arose. She eventually even had to consciously restrict her visits to a cycling café in Bawtry called the Lighthouse because her 'ears would start twitching' once the conversation turned to racing. 'I call in there and get so excited … I hammer home,' she said. 'It's the middle of winter and I'm lathered with sweat when I come in.'

*

Other all-time British greats were discovering cycling at this time in Yorkshire. These included Barry Hoban, who was working as an electrician down a coal mine and would later win eight Tour de France stages, and Brian Robinson, who was the first Briton both to complete the Tour de France and to win a stage. Hoban, Robinson and Denise became ambassadors for the annual four-day Tour de Yorkshire professional race and would be driven ahead of the race to mingle with fans in any town or village. An invitation for the final 175-km final stage between Halifax and Leeds in May 2019, which took in a spectacular loop through the Dales on their old training roads, allowed them to paint an alluring picture of the post-war cycling scene that Beryl had discovered. 'Just look at it,' said Denise, gazing across endless miles of spectacular scenery. 'Mum and Dad would be out here every Sunday. Dad would say that this was their church.' As the peloton made its way through Skipton, Hoban recalled how he and Tom Simpson would ride this sharply undulating road on a single-cog fixed wheel. 'If someone had gears in the 1950s it was like they were from outer space,' he said. Just a club run to an event like the York Rally would attract as many as 100 riders. 'You were more likely to be hit by a bike than a car – it was a sport of the working class,' said Hoban, a rider who was among Beryl's notable scalps when she set the first of her 12-hour records in 1959.

Although Robinson raced largely in Europe after finishing the first of his seven Tours de France in 1955, he soon heard tales of Beryl and her shared thirst to cycle copious distances. 'We were taught to be self-sufficient – Beryl was the same,' he said. 'We had two pigs, forty rabbits, a garden and no car. The bike was how we got around.' Robinson's Huddersfield Road Club would often see Beryl's Morley group on a winter Sunday, typically during a café stop at Tommy's in Otley, from where they would all race home after having the house special, tomato on toast. Yorkshire was a cycling heartland and numerous unpretentious cafés and tea rooms became woven into the club fabric. From the Stables family in Grassington – and Mrs Stables's hot pasties and Mr Stables's pipe, fiddle and storytelling – to Mrs Ambler's rabbit pie in Thirsk and Tom's Tea Gardens in Knaresborough with its miniature golf course, each had its own charm and resident characters. 'The golf could get more competitive than the cycling,' says Malcolm Cowgill. The sight of dozens of bikes, often four or five deep, lined up against the café walls would be a fixture of a Sunday lunchtime and, with few motorists on the roads, it was the cycling community that sustained these businesses.

Some clubs or cafés even had their own accommodation, where cyclists would ride out to meet on a weekend and share a few drinks before racing the following morning and then returning for a bacon sandwich. The prefabricated clubs huts in Ugley, Essex, were built in the 1920s and are largely still standing a century later. The closest equivalent to the Yorkshire cyclists was in Blyth, just inside the Nottinghamshire border, at an establishment called the Bridge Tea Rooms. It was known simply as 'The Ranch', and people would come from all over Yorkshire and Nottinghamshire to sit and talk with like-minded folk over a mug of tea or coffee. It was owned by a man called Walt Hall, who, for all his popularity with the cyclists, was perhaps fortunate to live in an era before Tripadvisor.

'The Ranch was like nothing on earth,' says Mike Williams, a great stalwart of Yorkshire cycling. 'You would all sleep in a big room with bedsteads resting on beer crates. Walt once said that he had got showers fitted. It turned out to be a hosepipe connected to biscuit tins. No one minded. People arrived on a Friday or Saturday, walked to the pubs in Blyth and staggered back before racing the next day. They came for the atmosphere and fun.' Walt's wife, Lilly, was an accomplished pianist and would play for the customers. There was a games room with a full-size snooker table and beautifully maintained gardens, where the cyclists would sit out on benches. Williams says that the pies – 'a hint of meat but otherwise full of potato and gravy' – were notorious. Beryl was always scrupulous about her food and not about to take any chances. 'I remember Walt offering Beryl a pie. She just looked up and said, "I'll stick with my wholemeal bread and raspberry jam, thanks."'

Morley was renowned even in Yorkshire as a club that rode

unusually long distances, and Robinson, who combined the world's biggest cycling races with winters back home, immediately saw that Beryl stood apart. 'You have to be focused, dedicated and selfish,' he said. 'She was unique among the women. Charlie had no chance of being as good. They complemented each other.' Robinson then smiled before adding: 'He must have been very pliable.' It was an observation loaded with understatement. Although Charlie did indeed have little chance of making his mark in national, let alone global, competition, he was an accomplished club cyclist who could win local hill climb events. It was also exceptionally rare for any man to compromise his own sporting passions for those of his wife. The television advertisements of the time provide a flavour of what was expected. 'This woman is alone, yet not alone,' says the Persil classic. 'Even though her family may be apart from her, they are still a part of her. Being judged by the care she takes of them, being judged by how clean and white she keeps their clothes, just as she is judged by that same whiteness.' Substitute the clothes for Beryl's always immaculate bikes, and Charlie would become Persil man.

While spending time with Charlie before the Covid-19 lockdowns of 2020, it soon became clear that the decision to move selflessly into a support role was not some conscious stand for gender equality but an entirely pragmatic calculation. Beryl's progress was rapid and, far from being threatened by her superior speed, Charlie took immense pride in his girlfriend's talent. It was this role reversal and a lack of interest in social norms that particularly fascinated the actor and writer Maxine Peake. 'I initially thought it would be this story about a woman in the 1950s and her struggle with a husband saying, "You can't do that", but not at all,' she says. 'It was working-class but not in the sense, "I'm a man, I work hard, tea on the table love." It was working class in the sense of doing things together. I fell in love with Charlie when I met him.' Charlie simply shrugs at the compliment. 'Beryl became so fast in comparison to me that I backed off. I just said,

9. Beryl Charnock becomes Beryl Burton.

"I'll get you to the events and make sure your bike is OK and you race." In the first year, we were waiting for her. In the second year, she were riding with us. By the third, she were leaving us behind.' That third year also carried a special significance. Beryl and Charlie got married a month before Beryl's eighteenth birthday in April 1955 at St John's Church in Moortown. They took their wedding vows at midday, and Beryl raced in a 10-mile time trial the next day in Hull. Their wedding night was spent in a nearby youth hostel and, as was customary, in segregated male and female dormitories. Charlie was only marginally taller than Beryl (5 ft 7 in. to 5 ft 6½ in.) – a fact of enormous practical help whenever cycling equipment needed to be interchanged – and they bought each other a bike as a wedding present. 'You can never say that we weren't practical,' said Beryl.

After an initial fortnight with Charlie's parents in Morley, they found their own one-up-one-down council accommodation in nearby Cross Street. Beryl would fall pregnant within a month of their wedding but continued racing throughout 1955, simply adjusting her handlebars to accommodate the growing bump. Her only recorded public response to expecting a baby was typically frank. 'I was happy at the prospect of becoming a mother, but a little disappointed that I would not be able to carry on with my racing,' she said. Her full-time work was also seen through the prism of her sport. 'It had to be employment which I could perform conscientiously but whose main purpose was additional income, mainly used to support my unpaid cycling activities,' she said. Beryl had left Montague Burton and now started work at the Forgrove Machinery Company in Dewsbury Road.

One of her colleagues in the wages department was Marjorie Dunn, who just happens to be the grandmother of the 2015 world road race champion, Lizzie Deignan. Beryl continued to cycle in to work until the day before she gave birth to Denise on 24 January 1956. 'The bump was virtually on the crossbar,' says Dunn. It was a major talking point in the office. 'The older women would say, "That child will be deformed." Women didn't ride bikes when they were pregnant then. She was coming in from Morley and had to contend with a very steep hill. She was very chatty. She'd come to work on a Monday and amaze us because she'd say something like they had been to Lancashire. And that they had cycled there, raced and then cycled back.' Beryl spent a fortnight in Morley Hall maternity hospital after giving birth but, with Charlie promptly acquiring a side-trailer in which their new daughter would sleep next to a bike, she was back training within a month. She was also ready to race in time for the start of the season a few weeks later in March. By the end of that summer, aged only eighteen and with a young baby and a full-time job, Beryl had recorded times that were in the top fifteen women in the country at every time trial distance up to 50 miles.

How was she possibly able to juggle all of this? The answer, quite simply, was that cycling was now so intrinsic to everything they did that it was a question of bending parenthood and work

10. The Morley cyclists, from left: Chris Pell, Denise,
Charlie and Beryl Burton, Sheila Broadbent, Shirley Pell,
Dave Robertson, Nim Carline and Laurie Morse.

to suit their passion. Any other order of priorities simply did not
enter Beryl's mind. 'They rode as a family but sometimes Charlie
was working and, if that was the case, Beryl would just take
Denise,' says Kathleen Mitchell. 'That could be more than 100
miles with a small child. We would stop every so often and Denise
would fall asleep. Beryl took everything in her stride.' Beryl would
tell friends that the country air was good for her baby despite a
minor panic on one club-run stop when the two-year-old Denise
disappeared, only to be found playing beneath a nearby bush.
By toddler age, Denise would also startle shoppers in Leeds city
centre by abruptly standing up inside the sidecar and shouting
at the top of her voice. She soon graduated to a seat behind her
mother's saddle, even if Beryl's outlook on matters of health and
safety was summed up during a club run when she was challenged
by one of the male riders to a race down Pendle Hill, 40 miles west

11. Beryl Burton and her new training partner.

of Morley in Lancashire. 'She had Denise on the back but she just shot off,' says Shirley Pell, another Morley cyclist. 'We were, "My God, if anything happens, that child is dead." She just went … and she beat this boy.' Mitchell's sister, Maureen Pearson, says that Beryl was like 'a proper mother hen' and would amaze her rivals by bringing Denise to races before simply handing her over to Charlie at the start.

While Beryl would soon decide every detail about her training and racing schedule, Charlie's entire life outside of work became devoted to fulfilling a range of jobs for which Team Ineos now have a sixty-four-strong staff. In her prime, Beryl had separate bikes for road racing, track racing, time trialling and winter riding. Denise would later also have the same, meaning that Charlie, including the bike he used to dart around courses to hand over food and drink, had nine machines to maintain. Beryl would still insist that the unavoidably mucky job of cleaning and repairing these bikes rarely crossed a line into their home. While utterly unconventional in so many ways, she was firmly traditional in her approach to household tasks and a perfectionist whirlwind in taking charge of all the cooking, shopping, cleaning and washing.

Any bike parts that encroached into the warmth of the house would be immediately placed back outside the front door. Their first home did not have an indoor bathroom, and a shortage of space was especially challenging early in the Burton marriage. Once they had moved into a two-bedroom council flat in Elmfield Court in 1959, Charlie could at least then work on the bikes in the relative shelter of an unheated communal corridor. Outside was a tiny bricked block of shared sheds, each large enough to store one bike. Charlie was not upgraded to an easily accessible single garage until they relocated to a house in the village of Woodlesford in 1964, which Beryl would name Five Farthings. She had won five of her seven world championships by then. 'He lived in the corridor and then the garage when he was not at work,' says Denise. 'He was a master mechanic and she trusted him totally.' Charlie's devotion evoked no shortage of jealousy or of raised eyebrows among Beryl's competitors, but, once his wife's needs were met, it would extend to any stranger who required mechanical help. 'Beryl could have ridden a race through a swamp in pouring rain, but her bike would still be immaculate the next week,' says Cowgill.

The expectations surrounding women in sport during this era were as much about how they presented themselves and behaved as about how good they were. Magazine and newspaper reports of women's cycling focused as much on the maintenance of 'feminine qualities' and their appearance as on the outcome of races. It was another sphere in which Charlie and Beryl would never conform and cared little for what people thought. Onlookers could be left shocked – but still greatly amused – by some of the tirades that Charlie absorbed. For all his skill and expertise, he was always very audibly blamed in the inevitable event of a mishap and, to his long list of other duties – chief mechanic, cheerleader, chauffeur, masseur, speech-writer and confidant – came another critical role: that of human sponge. Stories of successful athletes who are difficult and demanding to be around, especially in close proximity to a competition, are hardly unusual, but it remains striking how this is far more readily accepted in men.

Sidney and Eileen Cropper would often take Beryl to races and sometimes looked on open-mouthed at a husband–wife dynamic that had shifted from those early years when she was being guided by her older boyfriend. 'She could treat Charlie like a dog,' says Eileen, who would herself become an international cyclist. 'She would rant and rave – make him look stupid. I remember there being some issue about her back wheel. It was all, "Why have you done that! I told you I wanted it doing like this and not like that." Sidney was there and he said, "If you'd spoken to me like that, I'd have picked up your bike and wrapped it around your head."' But how did Charlie react? 'She got away with it because he was such a calm and placid man. He just let her do exactly what she wanted to.'

No outsider would gain such an intimate insight into the workings of the Burton family as Denise's best friend, Ann Pallister, who would travel regularly with them all over the country to races. She offers more context. 'Once we arrived, Beryl would stretch out and want to be waited on a bit,' she says. 'And she wanted things done by Charlie, not by me or Denise. Charlie would get the bikes together for everyone. Beryl might sometimes get worked up, but Charlie would just say "Shut up" and carry on. Perfect for Beryl. I never saw Charlie stressed out.' Denise says that her father was like the swan who could seemingly glide along serenely while absorbing plenty of stress beneath the surface. 'My mum could wipe the floor with somebody, turn around and totally forget about it a few minutes later,' says Denise. 'It was quite shocking if people weren't used to it.' Beryl, though, would never swear and generally just expressed exasperation with the words 'For crying out loud!' Her favoured description of those people who irritated her was concise. 'Berk,' she would say.

Beryl insisted on Charlie being present at virtually every race and, as she always readily acknowledged, he was vital not just practically but also for her psychological equilibrium. 'Without Charlie at hand I could rarely bring out my best – I feel as if half of me has been left behind,' she said. 'All I get is lots of encouragement and the occasional comment. That is all I need or want.' If the distance precluded simply arriving at a race by bike, they would either camp, youth hostel or stay with another hospitable club rider in the vicinity. Bed and breakfast and hotel accommodation were luxuries deemed completely out of the question. The Burtons were also constantly on the lookout for lifts, and almost every other cycling family of that time who had a car can recall transporting them to one race or another.

As Beryl flourished, other riders would increasingly see it as an honour to host her or the family on the evening before a race. If they could offer only one bed, then Beryl would of course have priority. Camping out became routine for Charlie, as well as for the Morley teammates who often joined him in support of their emerging star member. Charlie thought nothing of sleeping in the back of someone's car or quite literally under a hedge in a random field. At the age of twenty, Beryl began competing for national titles and later described the scene at the 1957 100-mile championships in a speech to the Cyclists' Touring Club. 'Up to Grandma's went babe [Denise] because I needed my helpers. On the Saturday Charlie, Nim [Carline], Tad [the Morley cyclist Trevor Noble] and myself all set off on the bikes to Bingham, about 80 miles away, where I had a bed fixed. My intrepid helpers, with their saddlebags stuffed with everything required for the weekend, were left to their own devices. I don't know which ditch they slept in, but there they were the next morning – bottles and watches at the ready.' Already showing her strength over long distances, Beryl finished second.

For the national 25-mile championships that year, Beryl and Charlie cycled the 85 miles to Grantham on the day before the race and camped out. She then rode the entire course once in preparation, completed her race in 1 hr 6 min. 50 sec. before riding back to Yorkshire. 'Trim and neat, a stylish rider, good-looking and bubbling over with exuberant personality' was how Beryl was described in *Cycling* by the reporter Dick Snowden. Beryl finished sixth, but her reaction to this particular experience was telling. She was dejected – 'I had a good cry' – but also inspired by finishing within 2 minutes of Millie Robinson, who was completing a hat-trick of '25' wins and had just beaten some of the world's best women in a rare international race in France. 'I remember Beryl after that race,' says Mitchell. 'She said to me: "It's Millie this, and Millie that. I'm going to make it Beryl this and Beryl that." She went from having a good laugh to being very serious and a winner.' Beryl offered Robinson her congratulations but also bluntly warned the champion that there would be a different outcome the following year. When you consider that Beryl would return and not just beat Robinson by 17 seconds in 1958 but then go undefeated in the event until 1983, we can hardly list this as an idle boast.

*

Our conversation has run into its third hour and, as Charlie then also starts talking about races much later in Beryl's life, the most extraordinary aspect of all becomes apparent. This was how he still approached his support role with the same dutiful care when his wife was in her late fifties and could no longer win. A likeness between the Burtons and the success of another phenomenal endurance athlete, Paula Radcliffe, is easy to make. Radcliffe was formally coached by her husband, Gary Lough, who willingly sacrificed his own competitive running to support his wife. One crucial difference, however, was that Charlie was still providing cycling's version of silver service more than forty years after his wife's first race. It would be like Lough accompanying Radcliffe to their local parkrun in the year 2035 and still attending to her every need as if it was an Olympic final. It was a level of sporting devotion beyond compare but, for the Burtons, nothing more complicated than what they did. And what they always wanted to keep doing. As I begin to thank Charlie for the afternoon we have shared, he interrupts. 'No,' he says. 'Thank you for visiting.' He then stands before offering a concise three-word appraisal of his wife: 'She were good.' Denise gives her father a prolonged hug before we leave and, as we then walk back towards the main market square in Ripon, turns to me. 'It was his life, too,' she says, poignantly. 'And he was as much a champion as my mum.'

4

It's Men Only Here

There are certain people who seem almost to belong in the grainy black-and-white prism through which they became famous, and so to then encounter them up close, in full Technicolor flesh, feels somehow impossible. That might go some way to explaining why, when Eileen Sheridan opened the front door of her home on the banks of the River Thames in 2021, the thought that this smiling ninety-eight-year-old woman had once pedalled 870 miles from Land's End to John O'Groats in 2 days, 11 hours and 7 minutes seemed mildly incomprehensible. She bought the house in 1952 as a base from which to attack a series of place-to-place records and, almost seventy years on, many of the records – as well as the property – remain hers. Standing just 4 ft 11 in. tall, Sheridan is an authentic giant of British cycling but is still convinced that Beryl Burton was the greatest sportswoman who ever lived. Sheridan is also very personally relevant to Beryl's story. She was once Britain's most famous female cyclist. She accompanied Beryl to the world championships in Milan in 1962, and they remained firm friends thereafter.

The history of women's cycling has only recently begun to be documented in any depth, and the stories of many great champions are thus destined to remain buried out of reach. Scratch gently beneath the surface, however, and you are at least left in no doubt that a rich tapestry exists. The American nineteenth-century social activist Susan B. Anthony said that cycling, and the associated 'feeling of freedom and self-reliance', had done more to emancipate women than any other activity and particularly championed the feats of her compatriot Tillie Anderson. She attracted crowds in their thousands and was hailed as the unofficial world champion from 1895 until 1902. Another Leeds cyclist, Nellie Rodgers, was fêted in Britain after rides of 168 miles in 12 hours in 1898 and then 356 miles in 24 hours in 1908, all while wearing an ankle-length dress. Social norms meant that it was deemed unfeminine and boastful for a woman to talk of her cycling passion, and, when journalists have since tried to trace those original pioneers, they have discovered that even some of the families knew nothing of their accomplishments. Significant change came in the decades either side of the Second World War and, by shredding the myth that women somehow lacked the physical and mental resilience to thrive in endurance sport, Sheridan helped lay the path on which Beryl would follow.

Having swum regularly at the open-air pool in Coventry throughout her childhood, Sheridan was given a bike for her fourteenth birthday, which she rode throughout the war years and Luftwaffe air raids, which killed 1,236 local people. 'Our house was hit by an incendiary bomb one night and we hid under the stairs,' she says. 'And the next morning I had to carry my bike over red-hot rubble.' As often the only girl in their Coventry Cycling Club rides, Sheridan was expected to pour the men's teas during their café stops – 'and they ate all the cake', she says, laughing – but would then make them suffer out on the road. She was soon accumulating domestic titles, and her 1949 landmark of 237.62 miles for the distance cycled in 12 hours became a catalyst for the records that followed. It was a day that she has always savoured. Women were not permitted to race directly against men in open time trials until 1970, and so Sheridan was made to circle the course in the opposite direction. She eclipsed the women's record by 17 miles, even if her most treasured memory was the journey home in the back of a van with the other Coventry cyclists. 'We were all piled in and everyone was singing in celebration – such happy times.'

12. Eileen Sheridan is passed a drink by her husband, Ken.

The Hercules bike company sensed an opportunity and, with no world championship for women, persuaded Sheridan to instead turn professional and attack those place-to-place records which had been set between 1938 and 1941 by the great Bournemouth cyclist Marguerite Wilson. Sheridan became nationally famous. She was known as 'The Mighty Atom' and quickly inspired a sales boom. Followed at 100 metres by a support caravan, which even included a toilet and bed, the pinnacle was her Land's End to John O'Groats odyssey in 1954, during which she slept for less than an hour across three nights. Her account of then being persuaded to get back on her bike and cycle another 130 miles to beat the women's record for 1,000 miles remains startlingly lucid. 'I began seeing people and animals. I then started seeing cars and I kept swerving into the verge. It was only when people asked me what I was doing that I realised that I was hallucinating.' It sounds terrifying, but Sheridan simply lets out a chuckle. Somehow she kept going to set a women's record for 1,000 miles of 3 days and 1 hour, which was itself only 2 hours and 20 minutes slower than the men's record.

The tribute written by her manager, Frank Southall, in Sheridan's 1956 autobiography, *Wonder Wheels*, rather captured the time. 'Her helpers remarked that through those three gruelling days she never lost her femininity,' he wrote. A BBC documentary also reflected the era, with the narrator concluding that 'No wonder she wins races ... she has to – to get back in time to catch up with the housework.' The revolution was still at an embryonic stage and, while Sheridan's exploits were critical athletically, Beryl would ultimately owe an even bigger debt to another remarkable lady called Eileen.

*

When the London Olympic flame passed through the United Kingdom in 2012, one torchbearer was living just a few miles down the River Thames from Sheridan. Eileen Gray, yet another wonderful advert for the lifelong health benefits of cycling, was ninety-two when the Games returned to London. She had also been among the volunteers at the Herne Hill cycling track sixty-four years earlier, when London's oldest velodrome was among the Olympic venues. Gray became the driving force not just behind women being permitted in the world championships in 1958 but also the Olympics itself in 1984. She remains the only ever female president of the British Cycling Federation, a former mayor of Kingston and, as the women's national team manager during Beryl's peak years, central to her historic international achievements. She also kept a diary – which she titled 'Rebel With a Cause' – that detailed both her campaigning and her front-row seat for many of Beryl's greatest victories.

With Stella Farrell and Joan Simmons, Gray had been part of Britain's first international women's team in 1946 during races at the Odrup track in Copenhagen. The riders were all given silk vests on which to sew a Union Jack and, although there were no formal competitions, Gray regarded this as a game-changing moment. 'Women had to wait to be invited, never mind they'd kept the whole country and the war effort going for six years,' she said. 'What the men didn't realise was that they'd given us a platform, visibility, and a chance to show what we could do. Something started that they couldn't stop.' While sports like tennis, athletics and swimming had included women in their most important competitions for decades, cycling was lodged in the dark ages, and Gray's first formal bid to have female races at the 1957 world championships was rejected by the male committee of the Union Cycliste Internationale (UCI). Rather than again virtually beg for inclusion, Gray issued a 'statement of policy', declaring that the Women's Cycle Racing Association (WCRA), which she founded, would organise their own world championships if their request was turned down the following year. Gray again appeared personally at the UCI Congress at the Palais d'Orsay to make her case and, with the support of a growing number of other nations, notably the Soviet Union, returned triumphant. Writing in *Sporting Cyclist*, Sidney Saltmarsh summed up the UCI's attitude: 'All right girlies anything for peace and quiet – we'll let you come and play at our championships but don't blame us if you make yourselves look ridiculous.' It was sixty-five years since the first men's world championships, but the global stage that had been denied Sheridan and Gray now existed. Women would be part of the 1958 world cycling championships. The next job was to find some British riders.

*

Eileen Cropper had been waiting patiently on Platform 1 of Leominster station in rural Herefordshire and, having identified herself by waving a copy of the latest *Cycling* magazine, her greeting was memorable. 'Lovely to meet you,' she said, smiling. 'It has taken a little while for anyone to notice we existed. You're sixty-one years late.' Cropper was eighty-four in the summer of 2019 but still walking with a brisk spring, and did not break stride before ushering me into her car and revealing the detail behind her own part in a moment of sports history. As with Beryl in Morley, her cycling apprenticeship 20 miles away in Bradford amounted to keeping up with the men. The experience was not always so welcoming. 'The lads would goad me and sneak bricks into my saddlebag,' she said. 'Some of them hated me. I remember catching one in a time trial and, as I approached, he shouted, "Please don't pass me, Eileen".' And did she take pity on him? 'I just looked at him and said, "Sod off, I'm passing you".'

Many British clubs still banned women. Val Baxendine, who would represent Great Britain with Beryl at the 1960 world championships, even received a rejection letter from the Norwood Paragon Cycling Club, which, having informed her that it was an 'all-male club', did invite her to make the teas at their next event. 'I thought, "Get lost, do it yourself",' she says. Prizes for women's races even well into the 1970s were items like hair-curling tongs or pouches of washing powder. At a time when women in England were even banned from playing organised football, the wider backdrop was described by Richard Holt, a professor in sports history. 'Animals were more readily accepted than women as the objects of sporting admiration,' he wrote. 'Men did not want their women to appropriate the grit, competitiveness and guile that they saw as belonging to themselves.'

Beryl had just turned twenty-one, and 1958 would be her breakthrough season in domestic time trialling. Charlie and Beryl had camped out with Kathleen Mitchell and her parents the night before the national 50-mile championships in Stratford-upon-Avon, and they had all enjoyed a supper of chip sandwiches. 'One of the men scoffed at her for eating these sandwiches,' says

Mitchell. 'Beryl then went out the next morning, won her first national title and made a point of finding the man to say, "See what you can do on chip sandwiches." It came out of the blue. She had suddenly gone from taking part to being very, very good. That was it, then. Nobody could beat her for twenty-five years.'

Beryl also won the 25- and 100-mile national time trial championships that summer but, with no track- or road-racing experience, was overlooked for the three inaugural women's world championships events: the 3,000 m individual pursuit, the road race and the sprint. Although Beryl's omission was understandable, hindsight suggests that she was already capable of winning either the road race or the pursuit, which was effectively a 1.86-mile-track time trial. Cropper was more clearly established among the best women's road racers in the county and did receive an official letter from Gray to say that she had been selected. 'We were given a joint passport and a GB vest but had to provide everything else,' she said. One unexpected benefit was that three local shops offered to donate the bike on which Cropper would ride the first women's world championship. 'I said "yes" to them all – they never did find out,' she said, grinning. The British Cycling Federation (BCF) had told Gray to send a reduced women's team and offered only £100 towards the costs. Gray's diary registers 'horror' at the suggestion, and through a series of raffles she raised enough money for a full complement of six riders. The road race was held on the motor-racing circuit of Reims-Gueux, 90 miles east of Paris, on Sunday, 31 August 1958. Cropper had set off on the Thursday by train from Bradford and, after changing at Leeds and then London, taken an overnight ferry from Folkestone before further trains to Paris and finally Reims. It all left just enough time for a quick look at the circuit on the Saturday afternoon. Benny Foster, the men's British team manager, immediately made his presence felt with a doomed mission to prevent the men and women's teams from interacting in any way. 'You were supposed to do what Benny said, but when the lads got to France they soon turned up where we were staying and were trying to seduce us,' said Cropper. Gray's diary describes Foster's presence as the cause of 'a great deal of aggravation' and, despite his public denials, she says that he was always opposed to the women's inclusion.

Italian cycling legend Fausto Coppi and his friend Raphaël Géminiani also made a point of personally introducing themselves to all the women's teams on the Saturday. 'Coppi had a brown pinstriped suit on,' recalled Cropper. 'Strange-looking. He looked like he might open this suit and say, "Stockings?"' Cropper, who was already married, says that the wider pre-race preparation was chaotic. 'They put us up in a dosshouse. Three beds in one tiny room and three in another. Nowhere to put your clothes. The only choice of food was horse meat full of garlic. I felt poorly and went to lie down. Other people were on my bed. One of the male participants with one of the ladies. I went bananas and kicked them out.' Things did not much improve the following day, when Cropper says doping was clearly evident. 'Some of the riders were quite openly popping pills. They had it in their back pockets and were doped to the eyeballs.' The race, which was run over 59 km (compared with 277 km for the men), was won by Elsy Jacobs of Luxembourg. She had broken clear of the main bunch, and Cropper says that the officials then just guessed at the remaining positions. 'It was an absolute shambles. We didn't go to any presentation. It was straight back on a train to Paris. No seats were booked and it was heaving. We were sat on dirty floors all the way home on the boat and train.'

There was further uproar at the 1958 track events in Paris, where Foster, Bill Shillibeer and Reg Harris were overseeing the British men's team. They had left the women to their own devices throughout the competition but, when Stella Ball reached the pursuit final and was assured a rare British medal, Foster and Shillibeer somehow made their way into the inner circle for the gold medal ride-off. Shillibeer even pushed Ball off on the start line. 'Our whole routine that had worked so well went to pot,' said Gray, who felt that the disruption cost Ball victory. The UCI had also provided the women with no schedule throughout the track events and simply jammed their races into whatever spaces appeared in the men's programme. That had meant 15-hour days in often sweltering trackside conditions while waiting to be called at what might be just a few minutes' notice.

Obstruction from male administrators remained a feature of preparations for the next world championships in 1959 and, with the Netherlands still only recognising men's cycling, the women's events were staged separately in Belgium rather than Amsterdam. Despite the British women having won a silver and two bronze medals the previous year in France (compared with no medals for the British men), the BCF again offered only £100 towards their costs. They also ruled that even this funding was contingent on their selectors choosing the riders. With no real knowledge of women's cycling, they picked Jean Dunn (who had won bronze in 1958) for the sprint and Millie Robinson for the pursuit. They then suggested that these two riders simply doubled up and both also rode the road race. That would again mean no place for Beryl, who had not only defended her 25-, 50- and 100-mile national championships but also added the British road race and BAR titles. The 100 victory inspired a particularly breathless report in *Cycling*, which described her performance as 'dizzying, dazzling and dumbfounding' and 'the most perfect combination of style and power in a woman'. With Gray's crucial encouragement – 'I persuaded her that it was just another time trial' – Beryl had also begun track pursuiting and beaten Robinson comfortably in both their head-to-heads, including a British record ride at Herne Hill.

Gray was furious at the BCF's 'staggering' ignorance and, refusing to stand for such nonsense, eventually secured Beryl's inclusion in the travelling party, ostensibly as 'a reserve', on the strict basis that the women absorbed the additional expense. It meant that the Burtons had to finance Beryl's train from Leeds to

London, whereupon the WCRA arranged the rest of the journey by road and ferry. The late change of selection meant that Beryl arrived in Belgium without knowing whether her entry had been accepted. The furthest she had ever previously travelled was to Ireland on a cycle-camping holiday the previous summer, when, with a two-year-old Denise in the seat behind her, 'it pumped it down for a fortnight'.

Gray also still needed a cheap travel solution to get the British girls to Liège and, to the eternal appreciation of women's cycling, they found a lifelong friend in Tom Feargrieve, who had previously been the men's team mechanic. In the winter of 1958 Feargrieve had randomly passed a second-hand car dealership, where he had stumbled upon a huge three-litre V8 Ford Estate. The vehicle had three gears and a top speed of 45 mph but could chug along reliably over vast distances at 14 miles to the gallon. Most importantly, it had space for a roof rack which could hold six bikes, and two rows of seats behind the driver which also folded into a bed. The car had cost Feargrieve £75, which amounted to ten weeks' wages, and it would become the unofficial transport for the British women's team over subsequent years. With the riders resting up in whatever accommodation Gray managed to secure, Feargrieve and fellow mechanic Ian Thackeray would always sleep inside what was affectionately known as 'Britannia'. Beryl travelled to Liège with Feargrieve and the rest of the team. Charlie made his own arrangements, camping out in a nearby field and, in return for a few cigarettes, was granted free daily trackside access by one of the stewards.

Although Beryl might well have added to her world titles if she had been selected in 1958, there was a certain benefit to missing the 'shambles' that Cropper had so eloquently described. Gray no longer trusted the BCF to make their logistical arrangements and, while money was scarce and options were limited, she was attentive to her team's needs and also adept at handling Beryl's occasionally volatile temperament. The team stayed at the Hôtel

13. The pioneer Eileen Gray, Tom Feargrieve and the
ever reliable 'Britannia' women's team car.

Duc d'Anjou in the centre of Liège and faced a daily 6-km cycle to
the velodrome in the suburb of Rocourt, which involved crossing
various tramlines and a steep cobbled hill. It rained frequently,
and the cyclists would often ride to the track carrying umbrel-
las. The BCF team kit again amounted to the loan of one single
jersey to each female rider and, with the Burton family finances so
restricted that Beryl could not afford her own tracksuit, she wore a
pair of plaid trousers and a green cycling jacket over the top of her
team jersey and wool cycling shorts. Beryl rarely bought clothes,
especially at this stage of her life, and relied either on garments
that had been handed down through her family or on those she
had made herself. When Denise started school three years later,
the very same plaid trousers that Beryl wore during these world

championships were shortened so that the spare material could be used to make her daughter a shoe bag.

Beryl had also arrived in Belgium with only the second-hand pair of wheels on her bike that she had bought earlier that year for 10 shillings – the equivalent of 50p. Dunlop had at least loaned the team new tyres for the event, although their gesture did not extend to providing anything with which to attach them to the wheel rim. Charlie was duly dispatched into Liège to specifically source some shellac adhesive and, despite linguistic skills that did not extend beyond speaking English in a broad Yorkshire accent, returned triumphantly with the right glue for the team.

The women's track pursuit is an event where two riders simply start from stationary positions on opposite sides of the track and the winner is either the person who catches their opponent or who crosses their finishing line first after 3 km. Beryl barely slept the night before her first world championship appearance and, having arrived as a complete unknown to the other cycling nations, qualified fastest in what was only her fifth race over the distance. In the quarter-finals she then defeated Belgium's Yvonne Reynders – their first head-to-head race in what became an exceptional rivalry – before beating the Soviet Union's Lyubov Jogina by only 0.6 seconds in a tense semi-final. The final was against Elsy Jacobs, the reigning world road race champion.

It was a hot evening, and Beryl, who had decided to base herself in the shadows beneath the track tunnel, was so tense at the prospect of riding for gold that her shaking hands failed to peel an orange. She even faltered as she reached for her shoelaces. Robinson had been defeated in the quarter-finals by Jogina and provided timely encouragement by donating Beryl her lighter specialist race wheels. Charlie attempted to tie up Beryl's shoes but a small error provoked a furious outburst and he was promptly instructed to watch from the stands rather than inside the track. 'I was wound up, well coiled – I couldn't relax,' Beryl later said. Feargrieve also tried with limited success to calm her.

It was only ten years since Beryl had suffered a nervous break-down at the prospect of taking a school exam. Now she was about to ride for the chance to become Britain's first world women's cycling champion. Charlie was a virtual non-smoker but so jittery that he went through an entire packet of cigarettes as he waited. Beryl was again teetering on the edge. Her thoughts flashed back to her eleven-plus exam, but, just as Dave Collins had explained, she was now ready to turn that painful memory into an extraordinary surge of motivation. 'My competitive urge came to the fore and I sought some kind of retribution against the gods for that damned eleven-plus and my childhood ill health – I settled down and the adrenalin began to flow,' she said. The race was still dramatically close and came down to the final 500 metres, when Beryl, through force of willpower and stamina, held out to win by 0.2 sec.

The subsequent presentation produced a wonderful photograph, with Beryl clutching a bouquet of flowers and looking supremely satisfied as she glances down towards Gray. These two women would barely stop for another quarter of a century, but in that fleeting moment the realisation of both their dreams was captured. The entire British women's team, as well as Charlie, Gray and Feargrieve, celebrated together that night over a meal of mussels and chips. With the WCRA only able to provide £2 a day for each rider towards their accommodation and food, it was a considerable extravagance. 'British cyclists had to dig deep into their pockets to win medals for their country,' Beryl said.

The crowd had also left a lasting impression. Beryl now knew that, far from being the sideshow it was in England, cycling was a massive international sport. 'We are conditioned to think of cycling as a lower sport but over there it's *the* sport – it's indescribable, absolute magic,' she said. The owner of the hotel was so proud to have Beryl staying that he hung her rainbow jersey in the centre of his restaurant. A large crowd joined the celebrations. Beryl was then also invited to travel direct to France and Luxembourg for additional track exhibition races in front of thousands of spectators. Charlie needed to return for work, but Beryl did not hesitate to accept. 'It was a thrill to be part of all this and to realise that I, a girl from Yorkshire with a small club, was a world champion recognised beyond Britain,' she said. Robinson was also invited, and they took turns during their travels through Europe by train and bike to carry a shared bag of spanners and tools on a piece of string around their neck.

There would be an even more uncomfortable finale for Gray. In addition to her duties as British team manager, the UCI had asked her to work as a *commissaire* (the cycling equivalent of an umpire or referee) during the championships. Gray had naturally assumed that there would be a place for her at the officials' banquet following the final night of racing, but what happened next even outraged the *Daily Mail* of 1959. Amid 'much back-slapping, wining, dining, bowing and scraping', they reported that Gray was turned away from the 'male-only' gathering at the door. When she protested, she was bluntly told that it's 'men only here'. The *Mail* reported that 'Mrs Gray was angry, hurt and humiliated' and that she 'quietly' returned to her hotel. It was an experience that she never forgot.

Beryl's arrival back home alone at Leeds railway station a week later would also provide a stark reality check. She had been competing in front of huge crowds abroad and was curious to discover the local reaction to her exploits. 'There was barely even a mention in the local paper,' says Malcolm Cowgill, the Morley club secretary. Indeed, with Charlie looking after Denise and the Burtons unable to afford a car, Beryl actually walked the remaining 5 miles home from Leeds station to Morley with two bikes, a bag of luggage and the coveted gold medal and rainbow jersey. Oblivious to the fact that the hitch-hiker he was passing had just become Britain's first world cycling pursuit champion, a passing lorry driver did at least give her a lift up Churwell Hill.

14. Beryl glances down to Eileen Gray after being crowned Britain's first women's world cycling champion.

5

Yorkshire Forever!

Beryl Burton was the champion of the world. She was twenty-two years old and arguably already the best cyclist that Britain had ever produced. Competition, however, was still as much about some of the pompous administrators as about the increasingly full-time female riders she was now competing with for international supremacy. Even after delivering so spectacularly the previous year, the diary of women's team manager Eileen Gray again solemnly recounted British cycling's priorities. The women had won five medals, including Beryl's gold, since being admitted into the world championships two years earlier. The men had more than double the number of events but managed only one medal. So where did the BCF direct almost all of its budget for the 1960 world championships in East Germany? To the men, of course, who also had the additional opportunity of competing that year at the Rome Olympics. Gray did again manage to get a £100 contribution from the national association and was determined that Great Britain would field a full complement of six women for the road race and five for the track events. Her solution to the funding shortfall was further raffles and what they called a 'Send a Girl to the Worlds' campaign that would involve collections at sporting events throughout the year.

There was also crucial support for Beryl within Morley, where the influential former mayor, Norrie Ward, was a keen cyclist and advocate for her achievements. A civic reception to celebrate her world championship victory had attracted a crowd of 500 people outside the town hall in 1959, and an appeal fund was created the following year to help support her cycling ambitions abroad. Beryl said that she had felt 'Queen-like' and deeply moved as she stood on the steps to acknowledge all the applause. The notes of the civic speech made by the mayor, Robert Pumphrey, have been preserved by the town council. 'Despite her brilliance, success has not gone to her head,' he said. 'She is modest, retiring and has carried herself with perfect calm and dignity.' Mayor Pumphrey presented Beryl with the gift of a handbag 'on behalf of the townspeople', and coordinated letters, largely to the textile mills that once drove Morley's economy, as well as working men's clubs, to raise money. The overwhelmingly positive response demonstrated the vast local pride that was felt in her achievements.

The 1960 world cycling championships in Leipzig was among the first major sporting events to be held in an Eastern European country following the Second World War. There was an immediate logistical challenge. The domestic 100-mile time trial championships was scheduled for the Monday bank holiday just two days before the start of the track world championships where Beryl would defend her 3,000 m pursuit title. The BCF repeatedly told her to miss the 100-mile event – organised by the rival RTTC – and leave for East Germany the previous week. Beryl was not about to forgo a title and had devised an alternative plan that would involve flying to Berlin. Demonstrating an absolute willingness to resist external pressure, she then simply threatened to withdraw from the world championships if they did not accept her solution. The BCF 'hummed and hawed', said Beryl, but reluctantly agreed on condition that she paid for her own air travel. As well as the chance to defend her national title, Beryl also actually wanted the three additional days between the Wednesday and Friday so that she could train specifically on her pursuit speed around her usual roads in Yorkshire. The appeal fund, which was also supported by riders from the Morley Cycling Club, helped with the airfare.

The team's mechanic, Tom Feargrieve, was again also ready to rev up 'Britannia' for what was a 1,300-mile round trip to Leipzig. With Beryl flying, there was even the rare bonus of a space in the car for Charlie. Ann Sturgess and Val Baxendine were among another group who met in central London and travelled by train to the Karl Marx Station in Berlin. It was exactly one year before the Berlin Wall was very suddenly built, but East and West were already divided by a border that was patrolled by officers of the Stasi, East Germany's state police. As their train finally crossed into the East, it suddenly ground to a halt in the middle of fields that were surrounded by steep embankments. Armed soldiers examined all of the passengers' passports. 'They took some people off the train whose paperwork they didn't like, which shook everyone up, and made the group very conscious that they were in a Communist country,' says Sturgess. The bikes were also stripped down and searched before the riders were taken to their accommodation at a local boarding school.

Beryl's immediate priorities were rather different. She was now aiming for a hat-trick of hat-tricks over the domestic 25-, 50- and 100-mile time trial distances. The national '100' course travelled along the Bath Road, then barely more than a country lane, adjacent to a single airfield that is now Heathrow Airport. Beryl was due to fly at 4.10 p.m., less than 4 hours after she would complete her ride. She had travelled to London with some Morley clubmates, but the biggest complication was that her racing bikes had been transported to East Germany on top of 'Britannia'. Riding one of Charlie's bikes with only a front brake affixed to the left side of the handlebars, Beryl had built a predictably big lead after 80 miles when disaster almost struck. A car pulled out in front of her and, as she tried to feather beneath the fingers of her left hand, nothing happened. The cable had slipped and she only just managed to swerve clear of the car. She had no brakes for the remaining corners, roundabouts and junctions but still barely slowed and, on a bike one size too big, finished in a new record time of 4 hrs 18 min. 19 sec. She was respectively 11 min. 19 sec.

and 21 min. 46 sec. ahead of the second- and third-placed women. 'Berylyzed' was the one-word headline in *Cycling* magazine.

Charlie had already arrived in Leipzig, but then travelled a further 115 miles on the train to meet his wife at East Berlin Airport off what was a delayed plane. They hurried to the main central station, but the hold-up meant that they missed the last train to Leipzig. Stranded, Beryl and Charlie began walking the deserted streets of East Berlin in search of somewhere to stay. 'Eerie' was how Beryl described the experience. With the time soon passing 1 a.m., and Beryl having been awake for more than 20 hours following her earlier 100-mile record, the only sign of life was from inside a police station. Beryl and Charlie cautiously knocked, reasoning that even a police cell would be better than sleeping on the street, and communicated through a series of words and gestures that they were in East Germany for cycling's world championships. It is hard to overstate the suspicion that was embedded at that time in Germany society. A fifth of the Eastern population had moved to the West over the previous fifteen years, and secret government plans were already afoot for the construction of a physical blockade through the middle of the city.

Beryl and Charlie were instantly told to hand over their passports and wait in a spartan room from which they could hear the police making telephone calls. 'The tone of the officer seemed to us, even with our lack of German, to become ever more deferential,' said Beryl. The officer had actually been speaking with the East German Ministry for Sport, where the member of staff instantly recognised the name Beryl Burton. Beryl may have been largely unknown in England but, as Charlie puts it, 'the high men in the German parliament soon found us a room'. Beryl was finally asleep shortly after 2 a.m. Unaware originally that the Ministry for Sport were also covering the cost of their lodging, Beryl and Charlie politely turned down the offer of breakfast the following morning out of fear that it would blow their entire budget for the week ahead, which was their combined weekly wage of

£25. Charlie also had another idea. He had heard that there was a sizeable profit to be made if you changed your pounds into West German marks before buying East German currency. They duly travelled across the border on an elevated overland railway before returning to East Berlin for an afternoon train to Leipzig. The legality of the transaction is unclear, but it more than trebled the value of their cash and ensured that Charlie would have sufficient funds to cover his train journey back to England.

The Burtons would always need to take extreme care over their spending, even if some of the more eccentric stories of Beryl's thriftiness have become the stuff of legend among other cyclists. As well as collecting any coins beside the road while out training, she always stopped if she caught sight of anything useful, such as spanners or even handkerchiefs. 'She would clean her bikes with the mucky ones but wash the good ones and then give them to Charlie,' said her friend Brenda Robins. After one time trial Beryl promptly turned back down the road when she had finished after noticing that a farm on the course was selling potatoes at a bargain price. Dead pheasants or rabbits would frequently also make their way into her saddlebag for that night's meal or sandwiches the following day. Beryl always refused to join the Yorkshire Ladies' Cycling Association in protest at a 3p membership fee, although, as Christine Minto pointed out, that at least gave other riders the chance to win something. Margaret Allen is convinced that, for Beryl, one further attraction of cycling was the saving on buses or trains for everyday social or shopping trips. As Beryl explained in a BBC interview in 1994, there was also a serious practical side to all this. 'I had to work full-time for twenty-five years,' she said. 'If I didn't work, I didn't do the cycling. When you were racing, you just prayed that you didn't puncture because you knew that you didn't have enough money out of the next week's wages to buy a new tyre. But I think, if you want to do something so badly, you will always manage to cope.'

Beryl began the defence of her world 3,000 m pursuit

15. Recovering between rounds at the
1960 world championships in Leipzig.

championships around a 400 m velodrome named after Alfred
Rosch, a communist official who ran a bike repair shop and was
shot dead by looters in 1945. Cycling was a huge sport in East
Germany, and the annual two-week Peace Race, which would
route its way between Prague, Berlin and Warsaw, was already the
biggest amateur race in the world. The road to the outdoor velodrome was covered in flags and bunting and, with the men's and
women's events again being staged together, there was a capacity
crowd all week. The British riders had never experienced anything
like it. 'The stadium was packed and the noise had to be heard to
be believed,' Beryl said. The racing was not televised in the UK, but
Charlie and Denise were given documentary film in 2012 that had
been shot by a team from the German Democratic Republic. With
excited fans crammed into the stadium – mostly men and largely
wearing flat caps or silver paper hats to protect themselves from

the sun – the footage has the feel of an early FA Cup final. Beryl, wearing her plain blue British national team jersey and immaculate white socks, looked magnificent as she powered around the packed velodrome in her qualifying ride against Elsy Jacobs to set a new world record of 4 min. 12.9 sec.

All the world championships of that time were held on open-air tracks and, when persistent rain wiped out Thursday's racing, the pursuit series was extended across three days. Charlie and Beryl tried to relax by getting a tram into Leipzig and soon received another reminder of their growing continental fame. The tram inspector instantly recognised Beryl and simply refused all offers to pay. Beryl greatly benefited from the day off and, now fully rested after the stresses of the previous days, was in sparkling form for her quarter-final against Lubow Kotchetova, the Soviet Union rider who had won the first world pursuit championships in Beryl's absence two years earlier. Beryl's subsequent description of her mindset was telling. 'I thought of the evening "10s" on the Morley–Bradford road, the room over Morley Co-op, and all the British cyclists back home, and placed that in my mind against the might of the Russian sports machine. "Yorkshire forever," I thought. I let everything rip.' Beryl won in another new world record time of 4 min. 10.4 sec.

She was again dominant in the semi-final against the local East German champion, Andrea Elle, a rider she had befriended during a rare training opportunity in Berlin that was organised by Gray at the start of the year. Beryl developed a passion for opera singing during this trip and, after seeing the indoor tracks on which the East Germans rode through the winter, would often describe riders like Elle and Kotchetova as 'shamateurs' or 'state professionals'. Elle had a daughter of a similar age to Denise, who would spend five days a week in a nursery funded by the East German government so that her mother could train full-time. When Beryl was told about this, she said that her 'thoughts kept returning to the mound of washing awaiting me in Morley'. Beryl, though, was always hugely respected by the Eastern Europeans, and this worked to her advantage in Leipzig, when the Soviet Union team made an unexpected gesture and allowed her to use the stationary rollers they had set up in a trackside cabin to warm up for the race against Elle. 'It was a show of sportsmanship from a quarter I least expected,' said Beryl, who was blunt in describing her semi-final win against Elle. 'I crushed her in front of her home crowd.' The final, against Marie-Thérèse Naessens of Belgium, is also captured in the German documentary film and shows Charlie, dressed in trousers, a white shirt and sandals, roaring his wife to victory from the side of the track in another world record time of 4 min. 6.1 sec. Beryl later described that race as the most extraordinary atmosphere of her career, and the footage – with flags waving, a band playing and 25,000 spectators rising to deliver a rapturous standing ovation – confirms this memory.

*

There were several clear days after the pursuit series before the women's world road race championship, which was held a further 65 miles south of Leipzig at the Sachsenring motor-racing circuit. As well as Beryl, the road team comprised Baxendine, Sturgess, Sheila Holmes, Kay Ray and Joan Kershaw. Ray drove to East Germany with her future husband, Les Scales, and had been locked in a room at one of the checkpoints while armed police searched their car. The women's team were again kept separate from the men in what was very basic boarding-school accommodation. The toilet was simply a hole in the ground, and they were all woken up in the middle of the night for a random passport inspection. The fruit that was provided as part of their meals was considered such a luxury that they were asked to share any uneaten produce with the local children who would gather outside their accommodation.

Baxendine was also struck by the poverty once you moved

outside the bubble that had formed around the world cycling championships. 'I thought we were going through allotments to begin with when we got into East Germany because there were all these plots of land and little sheds,' she says. 'Eventually someone said, "No, that's where people live."' Each of the competing nations had been assigned its own local helper to provide logistical assistance, even if this very welcome touch of hospitality was rather counterbalanced by the constant sight of a Stasi officer. The British team's helper was a teenage East German called Renata, whom the riders all befriended to the extent that there were tears when they said their final goodbyes on the last day. It was even suggested that Renata should secretly return to England with the team inside 'Britannia' but, according to Baxendine, Renata told them that 'they would take it out on my family' if she tried to defect.

What was only the third ever world women's road race championship began at 9 a.m. on 13 August 1960. It would take in seven circuits of an 8.7-km course that circled not just the motor-racing track but also public roads running through the nearby village of Hohenstein-Ernstthal. The key obstacle was a cobbled climb of almost a mile that averaged a very testing 10 per cent gradient. At just over 38 miles, the race was sufficiently challenging to suit Beryl and, having crossed the line at the very front of the bunch after each of the first three laps, she increased the pace during the fourth lap. It was not a sudden burst of effort but, rather like a boa constrictor slowly shutting down the life of its prey, the cumulative impact proved deadly. Jacobs was the last rider able to follow, but a gap would gradually begin to open and the records show that, with three laps remaining, Beryl had established clear daylight and a 6-second lead. Fully committed, and trying simply to imagine that she was now riding a lone 25-mile time trial, Beryl could hardly have been happier. There had been no plan or tactical preparation among the British riders. Baxendine had not even known that there was a cobbled hill until the morning of the race and, following a downpour of rain, found that her back wheel kept slipping. 'I didn't see much of Beryl. She went to the front and rode away. It was easy for people to say, "Just sit on her wheel." Most of the men couldn't do that. She probably needed that hill to get a gap but, once she was gone, that was it. I never saw Beryl fail to win a road race once she was away from the field.'

The photograph in *Cycling* magazine captured the moment of Beryl's breakaway – she is riding on the drops when she attacks on the cobbled climb and the hollow expression on Jacobs's face is sufficient to know that she will never regain contact. 'There was nothing else to do then but keep going on my own – I took a sip of water from my bottle and poured the rest over my face as I was getting rather hot,' Beryl told *Sporting Cyclist*. What happened next was extraordinary. Beryl increased her speed and, according to the official records, actually rode the final three laps faster than the opening three laps of the race by a margin of 3 min. 27 sec. The speed of the peloton by contrast barely changed, and so the final gap to the rest of the field was a colossal 3 min. 37 sec. In the space of just over 16 miles she had single-handedly demolished a bunch of the very best women's riders in the world, many of whom had trained full-time for the race. 'Beryl toyed with them,' said the headline in *Cycling*.

The final lap amounted to a victory procession and, amid another noisy carnival atmosphere with bands and flags all over a circuit packed with 65,000 fans, Beryl's thoughts once again veered between her childhood illness and her close friends and family. 'I felt tremendous,' she said. 'I knew I was licking the world's best, and I had a fleeting thought of the doctors who had told me to take things easy.' There was no two- or even one-armed victory salute as Beryl crossed the finishing line. Unlike almost any other cyclist, it was something she never did. The old footage simply confirms Beryl's modest smile of satisfaction at getting the job done, before reaching down to loosen her toe-straps and freewheeling to a halt. When she returned to the 'pits', a piece

16. Beryl simply destroyed the best women in
the world by almost 4 minutes.

of glass was found in her rear tyre, which she actually brought
back to Yorkshire as a reminder both of the race and her good
fortune. Beryl was then whisked around the Sachsenring circuit
to the cheers of the crowd in a black open car, complete with an
enormous bouquet of gladioli. 'Berlin walls and differing nation-
alities didn't count,' she said. 'They were cheering me – double
world champion – and I loved it.' An elderly man broke out from
the crowd to hand Beryl a specially engraved plate that had been
made in one of the local villages and which she hung in the living
room of all her subsequent homes.

George Pearson, the editor of *Cycling*, was also in East
Germany and himself became the unexpected centre of attention. Journalists, coaches and officials from across Europe, but
most notably East Germany, the Soviet Union, the Netherlands
and Belgium, peppered him with questions about Beryl and her
training methods. Baxendine also discovered the extent of Beryl's
international fame when she competed later that year at a track

17. *Cycling* magazine cleared their front cover for the historic achievement.
She is photographed being congratulated by Tom Simpson.

meeting in Liège. 'I went over as the replacement for Beryl but her
name was still listed in the programme,' she says. 'I've never signed
so many autographs or seen so many disappointed faces. She was
just Beryl to us, but she was like a film star on the continent.'

Beryl's achievements at the 1960 world championships were
unprecedented. No cyclist, male or female, had previously won
gold medals on both the road and the track at the same world
championships. She had also won two-thirds of the titles on offer
to women. One of those had been achieved by setting three world
records and the other by a winning margin that even the most
celebrated male riders of the era such as Fausto Coppi or Eddy
Merckx could never emulate over much longer distances. It was
also Britain's first elite win on the road and remains quite plausibly the most dominant display by any rider of either sex at any
world cycling championship. The impact on British cycling was
profound. 'Beryl's double gold and immense popularity persuaded
the powers at home that women's racing had to be taken seriously,

for which succeeding generations have much to be thankful,' said Gray when Beryl died in 1996. 'Her victories in 1960 felt like the pinnacle of all we had worked for. Winning gold medals in the early days meant riders having to grin and bear it, apart from needing outstanding ability, tenacity and dedication. She put British women on the world stage.' In her diaries Gray later pointedly noted that the British women's team had again surpassed the men – Jean Dunn also came third in the sprint, whereas the men won a solitary bronze and would then return empty-handed from the Rome Olympics.

Gray was also infuriated in Leipzig by how a member of the men's staff left the track championships once their events had been completed and took with him the spare tubes and tyres that the women had brought for themselves. Speaking more than fifty years later, at the age of ninety, Gray said that the incident 'still makes my blood boil'. Baxendine also says that Reg Harris, the former world champion sprinter, immediately removed the tyres from the women's bikes at the end of the road race – 'a pair of Dunlop Twos' – to ensure that they would become the permanent property of the men's team. 'The men had all the kit and support,' said Baxendine. 'We were the poor relation. We had nothing – but we were in it for the right reasons.' The lack of money was highlighted that year in *Sporting Cyclist* magazine. The reporter, Peter Bryan, wrote that the British teams are 'becoming scroungers'. There were even stories of requests direct to the UCI for an advance on each team's 'cut' from the event's income and of British riders being lent money by anyone willing to help facilitate their participation. 'The present badly-designed BCF badge should be changed to a more appropriate penny-farthing,' wrote Bryan. The women's team began their journey back to England immediately after the road race inside 'Britannia', while Beryl, who had booked a return flight, was asked to stay behind until the next day for a reception. Driven as ever by Feargrieve, 'Britannia' was followed to the East German border by a Stasi officer on a motorbike and, at every checkpoint, the British team would proudly display Beryl's gold medals. The journey back to England took two days – 'it was like a cattle truck,' says Baxendine – and yet who was waiting on Feargrieve's doorstep as he finally pulled into his home? A certain Beryl Burton, who was desperate to reclaim her bike and resume training.

Prize money or sponsorship remained out of the question, but there was one major personal bonus from becoming a double world champion. The Cycle Industries Association was so taken by this self-funded and self-coached rider that they awarded Beryl and Charlie a three-wheeled car. Beryl said that the new car 'seemed to us like owning a Rolls-Royce' and that they could now 'travel in style' to more events. This was before even the days of the Reliant Robin, and a full licence was not needed to drive a three-wheeler out on the roads. Although the Burton family would move on to other vehicles in the coming years, the memory of that first three-wheeled car has recently prompted Denise to ask her father a question. 'When did you actually pass your driving test?' With Charlie having been off the road for over a decade – but having safely driven them literally hundreds of thousands of miles in the preceding fifty years – his response in simply pointing to his nose and saying, 'Never you mind,' was hardly the most reassuring. The three-wheeler, with its 50 mph maximum speed and lightweight frame, which would wobble in the wind, duly also became the focus for a whole series of new adventures. Family members, neighbours and other cyclists all tell stories about being enlisted to help with a jump-start. Charlie virtually cries with laughter at the memory of the car toppling sideways into a ditch after he had hastily parked it on the road and got out to wait for Beryl during a 100-mile time trial. As Beryl powered by and grabbed her drink, there was no time for explanations as she did a double take back over her shoulder and saw the family car capsized by the edge of the road.

*

The scale of Beryl's achievements in East Germany was sufficient to prompt comment and respect from even the misogynistic male cyclists. The BCF upped their funding and provided their own team manager, even if that often caused far more aggravation than leaving Gray to her own devices. Reg Harris, the four-times world sprint champion, had previously opposed women riding on his track at Fallowfield in Manchester but now took a particular interest in Beryl and wrote an extraordinary column about her in *Cycling* in September 1960. In an article entitled 'A Star Who Needs a Spotlight', Harris rightly asserted that Beryl would have been a certainty that year for Olympic gold had women cyclists been permitted, and wrote that she had 'put numerous male cycling stars to shame in a manner never before achieved by one of the fair sex'. Having already achieved every available feat in her sport by the age of twenty-three, Harris concluded that there were now two options. The first, which he counselled against, was to keep setting new records and winning the same titles. Harris instead advocated effective retirement and an ambassadorial role that would include 'numerous public appearances' and 'panel games alongside well-known celebrities of the sparkling screen'. He also suggested a future of 'newspaper columns, interviews, receptions and trade shows'.

It is almost impossible to imagine a set of suggestions that could misjudge Beryl's character more spectacularly. Whether Harris wanted to be her agent or perhaps did not like the thought of her surpassing his own four world championship victories is unclear, but it was a nonsensical proposition for an athlete who derived such fulfilment from competition. The television suggestion was especially laughable in the context of Beryl's lifelong refusal to have a set in her house for fear that it would interrupt a lifestyle that would continue to revolve around racing for another thirty-six years. Harris, though, was correct in one important aspect. Beryl Burton had become 'a name to conjure with throughout the countries of Europe' and yet remained deeply underappreciated in her homeland. *Cycling* had itself carried the front-page headline 'Beryl Burton World Champion Again' but preferred a photograph of Dave Handley, who finished third in the men's sprint, on its front-cover report of the track championships. She only received her due billing after adding the road race title a week later and then in a photograph with Tom Simpson, who had not finished the men's event. *Sporting Cyclist* also put Beryl on the cover, even if the inside coverage consisted of fourteen sentences within nine pages focused on the men. Upon returning home with two more rainbow jerseys, Beryl again scanned the newspapers for some recognition of achievements that were genuinely seismic in her sport. 'The local Morley weekly paper printed a short piece about me in their next edition and the three Yorkshire daily papers printed in Leeds gave my success a cursory mention,' she said. 'National papers managed varying degrees of short reports. I was not seeking personal adulation, but a little more recognition would not have gone amiss. I was a double world champion in an international sport and it might as well have been the ladies' darts final down at the local as far as Britain was concerned.'

6

Rhubarb and Miles

Beryl Burton always had a succinct five-word answer whenever someone asked for her secret. 'Miles,' she would say. 'And plenty of 'em.' There was no sports science, no dietary restrictions, no fancy periodisation or interval training and, unusually for such a dedicated athlete, she kept no detailed records or diaries. Her approach was instead underpinned by two beliefs: that the hardest worker invariably wins, and that just a few days off the bike would set her back several weeks. Cycling also helped Beryl to unwind psychologically and so, right from when the bug first bit in the mid-1950s until her death four decades later, there was scarce deviation from a training routine that would average around 400 miles a week. It was a time, quite simply, when the generally lone sight of Beryl Burton was as much a fixture of the landscape through the Yorkshire Dales as the sweeping valleys or rugged climbs. Add in that a bicycle was always also her means of day-to-day transport, and it is quite plausible that she would have cycled somewhere close to a million miles during her life.

These eye-watering distances were not just the foundation for Beryl's prodigious success but also became the stuff of legend within the cycling community. She was once fined £3 after not realising that a stretch of the A1, which she had long used to cycle to and from events in London, had become a motorway. Having been stopped by the police, and duly received a summons to which she pleaded 'guilty', she was left to scramble up a steep road-side bank with her bike before crossing some fields to the nearest

B-road. Much of what she did was unthinkable even to other long-distance riders, and yet the characterisation of Beryl as an uncomplicated soul who simply rode far and fast remains facile. Without always consciously knowing it, her entire lifestyle and ethos contained much in their fundamentals and subtleties that were well ahead of their time. And, although 'miles' were indeed her holy grail, it was a humble vegetable that would come to have the most improbably vast influence on her career.

*

Just over a mile from Beryl and Charlie's first flat on the edge of Morley is King George Avenue. There is now a housing estate at the end of this row of semi-detached houses, but it once led to the 40-acre site of the farm and market gardens that were owned by Nim Carline. He was another member of the Morley Cycling Club and an extraordinary local character. Just about everyone who was involved with British time trialling during this era has an anecdote about Carline and his no-nonsense approach to life. The old photographs somehow only embellish the descriptions. Carline had the slightly crimson cheeks of a man who could most definitely hold his ale, complemented by narrow eyes and the sort of creased, sandpaper skin texture that suggested he had been riding directly into a headwind for most of his life. Carline was never short of money, but never left the council house in Tingley that he shared with his mother. He would rarely buy any of his own clothes, and the photographs also confirm a tendency to wear borrowed old jumpers, trousers and hats. He would sometimes end up racing in cycling shoes that did not necessarily even match, let alone fit.

'You've never met a man like Nim in your life – more Yorkshire than tea,' says Eileen Cropper. 'He was first to the bar to buy a drink for everybody but could not bring himself to buy anything for himself. I danced with him once at a club dinner in all my finery. He looked me up and down and said, "Here, lass.

18. Nim Carline while winning the 1963 national 24-hour championships.

Where have they been hiding you?" An absolute man's man.' One of Carline's barns would invariably host club social events, and he would also act as an informal bouncer at the door. When Carline was not working or training, he would set off through the Dales or Lake District on wild camping expeditions. He would also travel abroad from the late 1940s on extreme mountaineering or cycling holidays that included scaling parts of the Himalayas, riding across Turkey, Iraq, Iran, Yugoslavia and Afghanistan en route to Delhi, and winter camping trips in the Alps. On one summer hike up Mount Teide in Tenerife, his cagoule melted and he suffered severe altitude sickness after falling asleep at the volcano's 12,198 ft summit. Before leaving Yorkshire ahead of any foreign excursion he would chain his bikes to the floor and board up all the windows and doors to ensure that his house – which he steadfastly always refused to buy – could not be modernised in any way by the local authority.

Carline was also an exceptional long-distance cyclist and

between 1962 and 1973 won what remains an all-time record six titles in the most gruelling and feared national time trial championship for the distance cycled in 24 hours. He was twice also the men's national 12-hour champion. His riding style was founded on brute power and bloody-minded effort – and the way that he would rock from side to side to keep a huge gear turning became a trademark. 'You would know that it was Nim even if all you could see was his silhouette, lurching from side to side,' says Morley secretary Malcolm Cowgill. The experience of riding team time trials with Carline is understandably also etched in Cowgill's memory. Carline would push himself so hard that he would often vomit – a habit that was tolerable if he was riding behind your back wheel but an unforgettably disgusting experience if you were in his slipstream. Cowgill once suffered a particularly unpleasant double whammy when, as well as being splattered, the sick also went down the shorts he had lent Carline for the event.

Preparations for any time trial were often interrupted by Carline's urgent requests for help in finding a missing garment of clothing or the mudguards he had removed after riding to the start. 'We would all be crawling around in a grass verge looking for Nim's sock,' says Beryl's brother Jeffrey. Carline rode one national championship – and won a bronze medal – in a jumper that had been knitted by his friend's mother after he misplaced his usual club top shortly before the start. When he won the C. A. Rhodes Memorial Award in 1963 for the outstanding Yorkshire cyclist of the year, the tribute recorded stories of his unannounced arrival in Muslim villages in the Middle East. It also said that 'this rugged, rough, tough, hard' rider could be heard singing Gilbert and Sullivan to keep himself going on the finishing circuit of a 12- or 24-hour time trial.

*

Carline was nine years older than Beryl and, after Charlie, easily the biggest influence on her cycling career. It could not be described as a coaching relationship. Denise simply snorts at the idea of anyone instructing her mother, but their general outlook was closely aligned and, shortly after giving birth in 1956, Beryl also started labouring at his farm. She much preferred working outdoors, and Carline, who had known Charlie long before Beryl, was relaxed about baby Denise accompanying her. Carline's farm was part of Yorkshire's rhubarb triangle, a 30-square-mile area between Leeds, Bradford and Wakefield that once produced 90 per cent of the world's winter rhubarb. The cold wet winters were particularly well suited to the production of rhubarb, but it was hugely labour-intensive and required teams of physically strong individuals who were willing to work long hours in the elements. A *Cycling* interview with Carline in 1965 reported that he worked 72 hours a weeks on his farm, although that would drop to 44 in the middle of the time-trialling season.

Laurie Morse also worked on the farm and laughed when I suggested that Carline and Beryl must have got along well. They would in fact have the most blazing rows in front of other staff, usually after a small disagreement over the correct way to do something at the farm. 'Neither backed down – they were too similar – but it always sort of passed,' says Morse. Carline's approach to work was structured and uncompromising, and, even for a world champion among his employees, no exceptions were made. The working day began at 8 a.m. and, if you were late, you were docked some of your wages. There was a 10-minute break at 10 a.m., an hour for lunch and another 10 minutes in the afternoon before finishing between 4 and 5 p.m. The rhubarb production cycle begins with planting a fresh crop in the fields, filling the sheds with lines of beds before splitting the roots, lifting the rhubarb on to a trailer and packing it into the soil. The warm darkness inside the shed is only compromised by the candlelight of someone watering the crops until it has grown sufficiently to then be pulled out and packed up. Once the rhubarb shoots were emptied, the beds on Carline's farm were also used to produce broccoli, mushrooms and cauliflowers. Competition over tasks like turning enormous stacks of manure, or packing hundreds of huge trays of vegetables, was intense. 'It was back-breaking,' says Morse. And how did Beryl fit in among the men? 'Beryl was accepted – she was strong and a perfectionist.'

Beryl would initially push Denise to Carline's farm in a pram. If she was due to be working on a tractor or somewhere she could not watch Denise, she would take her to Charlie's parents' home in Fountain Street – bike in one hand, pram in the other – before cycling to work. It was just under 2 miles to Carline's farm, but Beryl, says Morse, would often arrive wet through with sweat after adding a morning training loop. She would get changed and then do the same on the way home, regularly riding for several more hours immediately after work and sometimes also again later in the evening once the family had eaten. Beryl would initially finish work aching from head to toe but, just as with those early club runs on a bike, she was not about to give up. 'There were no passengers,' she said. 'I worked alongside young men, lifting heavy boxes on and off vehicles, digging holes for the roots of whatever was being planted, and you had to be finished by the time the lorry arrived with more. Carrying, lifting, bending, digging, all day long, in all weathers until my back ached, my arms ached, my shoulders ached, my legs ached. It was not only crops I was planting ... but the seed of my success.'

There is some delightful old ITV footage of Beryl at Carline's farm. She is filmed arriving past the houses down a wet, muddy path on a bike with mudguards and a saddlebag. Her trousers are tucked into her long socks and she then works under candlelight at considerable speed, stacking the crop under her left arm while bending down and using her right hand, metronome-like, to pick the rhubarb. Beryl is later interviewed and, having been asked what makes her so good at cycling, there is a telling insight. 'You have

19. A crop of rhubarb and the seeds of Beryl's success.

to have that bit of bitterness,' she said, before pausing and then adding, 'I think you need that to make yourself go ... and beat them'. The source of that 'bit of bitterness' is not revealed, but the steel in her eyes and utter certainty in her voice are unmistakable.

Within a few weeks of working on the farm, Beryl noticed something that would be hugely significant to her cycling. She was more supple and yet also more powerful through her lower back and core. It is striking in photographs of her first few years in cycling that she was of a slighter build and higher in her position on the bike. Beryl later came to hold an unusually crouched and stable posture that was perfect for time trials. Even after later moving to Harrogate in 1976, Beryl still offered her services at a fruit farm in nearby Knaresborough. It was partly because she enjoyed the work but also because she intuitively knew that it made her faster. 'Being flexible, bending and stretching all day long is good for the bike game,' she told Yorkshire Television. 'I find it easier when I have been working here to get down on the drops. I'd stay outside 24 hours a day if they allowed. There must be a bit of gypsy in me.'

Two other Yorkshire women, Dorothy Hyman and Anita

Lonsborough, were also blazing a sporting trail and would win four Olympic medals in athletics and swimming during the 1960s. They would meet up with Beryl at various ceremonies and invariably discussed their respective training. 'Beryl would always say, "I don't believe in all this newfangled stuff like weights",' says Hyman. 'I would then look at her and say, "Beryl you do it every day in the rhubarb shed. That's your weight training." She really was an exceptionally hard worker even though there was no real glamour or recognition. She never did any training beyond riding her bike and all the lifting at work, but that made her stronger than anyone. There was nobody to touch her.'

*

As well as Beryl's output on the farm, Carline was delighted by the emergence of another Morley cyclist who could match and later even exceed his capabilities. The early stage of their training, however, left painful memories. 'I would wait in the house wishing there was some way I could avoid it,' said Beryl. 'I was in and out of the lavatory and perspiring even before I sat on the bike. I had to match him side by side, tears in my eyes, but determined I would not drop behind.' Carline would generally train on a single fixed gear, regardless of whether he was riding on the flat, climbing one of the many steep ascents through the Dales or going back down the other side. Beryl initially did the same. A 'fixed' means that you have only one gear and, just as long as the bike is moving, the pedals must rotate. It therefore eliminates freewheeling pauses and is a wonderful way both to develop power and to learn how to pedal quickly and smoothly.

Carline soon became the only person with whom Beryl would sometimes train, and she did not like outsiders joining them. Margaret Allen, another Morley club member who was eleven when she first met Beryl, can remember trying. 'We had just raced and were in "The Ranch" having a cup of tea,' she says.

'I had been out with them probably three Sundays and she very suddenly said that she didn't want me to go any more. Nim turned to her and said, "You shouldn't have said that," but that was it. I never went again.' There was an equally abrupt incident when Allen unexpectedly finished second to Beryl in the 1964 national 100-mile time trial. 'I was on a good ride and, although she caught me, it wasn't as quickly as she expected,' says Allen. 'I was still about 11 minutes behind but Beryl couldn't bite her tongue. She came up and said, "Don't you think that was silly, you riding as hard as you did?" You stand back now and think "Wow!" I idolised her. Still do. But there it was. I don't care what Beryl went into, business or another sport, she would have got to the top. She had a lovely side but she was a hard person and had that cutting edge.'

That cutting edge eventually extended even to Carline and from the late 1960s Beryl had progressed to the point where he could find training with her too much. 'It was early January and there were four of us riding back from Otley,' says Graham Barker, a rider from the nearby Rockingham club. 'Nim and Beryl were at the front next to each other. But every time Nim got level with her wheel, she increased the speed another notch. And she did this repeatedly. I could see Nim suffering. After a while, me and Pete [Holden] said, "We'll take you off the front, Nim, give you a break [from the wind]." You wouldn't say that to Beryl. She wouldn't like that. We rode down to Leeds and Beryl peeled off home. Once she was gone, Nim looked across to me and said: "Thank God you took us off. That's what she's like all the time."' It is worth repeating that Carline was among the greatest men's long-distance time triallists of all time. Beryl became similarly competitive with Roy Caspell, then the reigning men's national 12-hour champion, after he had narrowly beaten her when they both rode under 4 hours in a 100-mile time trial in 1972. Rather than congratulate Caspell on his victory, Beryl immediately challenged him to an additional ride through the Dales that would take their tally that day to almost 200 miles. 'Roy was a 6 ft 1 in. man at the absolute top of his game, Beryl was an 8-and-a-half stone woman,' says Barker. 'And I just remember Roy returning absolutely exhausted. He looked at me and said: "She's knocked seven bells out of me."'

Alongside this huge volume of miles, it is the sheer variety that also stands out. Beryl would simultaneously do around four or five different types of cycling. There were those all-day rides, which would actually combine periods of steady riding and rest with extreme effort, either up a hill or in the sprint for place signs on terrain that was as unremitting and unpredictable as any in the world. Although the Dales provided the bedrock for her training, the Yorkshire Moors or Wolds, the Peak District and even the Pennines and Lake District contained plenty of familiar roads. As well as these longer rides, Beryl would also spend many evenings whizzing up and down the A1 to Doncaster or the A64 to York with lorries, wagons and trucks for company. She would generally move along the roads at speeds of between 30 mph and 50 mph and draft behind these vehicles for as long as possible before resting and then repeating the exercise. 'We all thought she was mad,' says Pam Hodson, her former classmate and another international cyclist. 'There were no slip roads for bikes, and there would be two lanes of traffic. The other cyclists would joke that she would rather go out and do "bit and bit with lorries" than ride with them.' 'Bit and bit' is the phrase used in cycling to describe sharing the workload by taking turns to pedal into the wind. Although Beryl rarely trained with other women, Sheila Broadbent, a colleague from Carline's farm and a Morley teammate, once accompanied her down the A1. 'She was at the front and by the time we got near Doncaster [25 miles south of Morley] I was done,' says Broadbent. 'She carried on past Doncaster. The cars and trucks would chug up the hills, but Beryl wouldn't change gear and just powered past them. It was the fastest and hardest I have ever ridden.' Beryl was once even stopped by police and told to ease off during one of these rides because she was breaking the 30 mph speed limit as she entered Leeds.

Beryl would always try to tailor her training to whatever main race was approaching. A long-distance time trial would mean packing in rides of much greater distance, but ahead of each year's world track pursuit championship she would attempt to replicate these conditions with short timed efforts on a nearby country road called the Methley Straight. Charlie was always there, stopwatch in hand, even if the training simply involved repeating the standard 3,000 m distance and trying to hold a straight line next to the kerb. Beryl also went to considerable lengths to get regular track-racing experience, and every Wednesday she would ride 15 miles to Maureen Pearson's house in Shafton. They would then cycle a further 50 miles together to Nottingham, where there was a weekly track league. 'My dad would follow in the car with our track bikes and then we would race all evening,' says Pearson. 'Only a few of the men could keep up with her and we'd laugh all the way home. Charlie would then collect her after work from Shafton.' Beryl would also travel to the Herne Hill track in London whenever there were big meetings. 'She'd put Denise in a carrycot, get on her bike and this long string of male riders would form behind her while she was warming up,' says Alf Engers. 'It was like the Pied Piper had arrived.'

Another essential strand of Beryl's cycling was the vast number of leisurely 'easy' miles. She never learned to drive and so travelled everywhere by bike, whether that was to the shops, to work, to races, to visit friends or even on holidays, which were invariably also spent touring new places by bike. 'That is the big difference to a lot of the cyclists now,' says Christine Minto, the first women's national 24-hour champion. It also meant that, although Beryl generally only resumed training in January in serious preparation for a competition season that stretched between April and September, she had retained considerable fitness. Her autumn and winter cycling would invariably just be done on a much heavier bike and in a much smaller gear (generally a 70-inch fixed). 'I can switch mentally from competition to pleasure riding,' she said. 'People would say, "I saw you out training the other day," and I would be, "No, you didn't." I would just be drifting along, only maybe 1 or 2 miles per hour slower, but completely relaxed.' When Beryl did start serious training in the new year, she believed that she needed at least two or three consistent months of averaging 400 miles a week to be ready to race. She was never in any great hurry to switch back to a light race machine and had few greater pleasures in life than riding past serious male cyclists on her winter bike complete with mudguards and saddlebag.

Beryl's competitive urge ensured that her routine during the season would also involve plenty of racing. Two midweek time trials in addition to whatever events most appealed each weekend – whether time trials, track racing or a road race – was normal throughout the main six-month period. Beryl would compete over almost any distance or terrain and, although she was world champion five times at just 3,000 m, her longest-standing records would be set in efforts that were more than fifty times longer. She would also enter regional grass track sprint competitions in Roundhay Park in Leeds, which was just over 1 mile from where she had grown up and pretty much the only venue at which her parents, John and Jessie, might watch. There is even old footage of Beryl competing in – and, of course, winning – Yorkshire cyclo-cross races, which would take in some quite savage off-road courses through the mud and over the streams of the Dales.

*

The compound impact of Beryl's routine is a source of fascination to contemporary sports scientists. Many of the greatest endurance runners had a similarly laborious foundation of farm work in the fields of the Great Rift Valley in Africa. This would be interspersed with vast amounts of walking and running during their formative years, often simply for practical purposes like going to school or gathering crops. As they got more serious about their running, they would generally also train twice a day and include plenty of the sort of 'easy' miles that were part of Beryl's daily life. From his experience working with Olympic swimmers and rowers, and as head coach at Team Sky, where he oversaw the Tour de France victories of Sir Bradley Wiggins, Chris Froome and Geraint Thomas, Tim Kerrison repeatedly stresses that the first priority is to do the 'simple things better than anyone else'. That extends to a series of relatively obvious and non-negotiable fundamentals, which, in cycling, does include plenty of miles on the bike.

'Never mind the marginal gains, manage the big losses – minimise the obvious mistakes,' agrees Jamie Pringle, who was the lead physiologist in support of British Olympic athletes between 2008 and 2016. Pringle cites research that examined the accumulated training times and distances of eighty-five world-class endurance athletes and found that total volume remained the single greatest determinant of performance. He identifies two key attributes in Beryl's training. The first is what he calls her 'robustness' to absorb an unusually high volume and variety of training. 'It's one thing to do the training but another thing that your body adapts and does not break down,' he says. The second is a precise understanding of her own training needs. 'It's what you might call athletic self-awareness – somebody who knows with a degree of realism how their body responds,' he says. 'Beryl's mindset might have been "I'm going to ride my bike and not even think about the hours" but, if you are doing that much, maybe 30 or 40 hours a week, you have to be judging it right. If she wasn't, she would have cracked.'

Philippa York, who as Robert Millar was the Tour de France's King of the Mountains and finished fourth overall in 1984, also emphasises this capacity to physically absorb increased training and racing loads without getting ill or injured. She found that this was one of the biggest restricting factors whenever an athlete tries to move up a level, whether that is progressing beyond club races or, in her case, trying to win a Grand Tour. Denise agrees and is adamant that her mother's approach would destroy many riders, including herself. 'Beryl Burton was undoubtedly of a strong constitution – the type of person, male or female, who rain, wind, cold or hot doesn't affect,' says York, who lived in France for sixteen years and noticed a special reverence for those working-class riders who were 'strong, uncomplicated, sane' and could 'dig holes all day and then go off and beat everyone'. The great Bernard Hinault, who rose from a farming background to become a five-times Tour de France champion, epitomised this caricature. 'BB also seems to fit that description,' says York.

Kerrison challenged many previously accepted conventions after joining Team Sky in 2009 and gets irritated by the characterisation of his work as essentially about statistics, numbers and mystical 'marginal gains'. As well as consistently 'nailing the basics', he particularly highlights the environment that surrounds his riders. The decision, for example, to create a base in Monaco was made to allow key riders to train together on a daily basis. Certain signings were partly also made to spur another individual. 'The longer I do this, the more all the non-science stuff, all the human stuff, has climbed up my priority list,' he says. 'You have to understand what you are trying to do and accept what sacrifices it takes. As a coach, your job is to then create an environment and culture conducive to what it takes. We are social architects.'

All that might appear quite abstract, and remote to Beryl Burton and Yorkshire in the 1950s and 1960s, but then think about the vast variety in her training and the wider environment. A hotbed of cycling. Wonderfully mixed and testing routes. A thriving cycling community on her doorstep who provided both competition and absolute support. A husband, in Charlie, who was ready to commit every spare second of his life to facilitate her ambitions. And then a boss in Carline, who not only loved cycling and understood its demands but saw Beryl as something of a protégée. For all the low wages and exacting standards, it meant that there would never be any employer pettiness about holding Beryl back from major races and, whenever the seasonal demands of the farm allowed, she was encouraged to train or simply go off on cycling holidays.

With all this in mind, we can perhaps now also tailor and complete Meg Jay's earlier equation from the generic 'Adversity + nature + nurture = supernormal success' to a 'Beryl formula' of 'Childhood illness + the Charnock Way + Charlie and the Morley cyclists = supernormal success'.

*

The post-war generation was also the first to understand fully that consistent training rather than innate ability was key to improvement. Formal coaching was initially non-existent for the best women, but Beryl thought deeply about how she could advance and, in 1964, spent a weekend in Rugby being assessed by C. R. Woodard, a leading sports scientist of the time. He recorded Beryl's pulse rate at forty-eight beats per minute and, in a report which the Burtons kept, described her 'exceptional' physique and 'wonderfully supple' muscles. Beryl's achievements would also strongly reinforce Woodard's belief that sporting gender differences were largely explained by the historic lack of opportunity afforded to women. Another doctor, Rod Goodfellow, who with wife, Chris, would host the Burtons if Beryl was ever racing in the Midlands, highlights a fascinating conversation at this time. 'Beryl told me that she never felt any pain in her legs,' says Goodfellow. 'I think she had some sort of mental or physical block which would enable her to push herself harder.' Woodard was also intrigued by Beryl's psychology and, during the interview that also formed part of her assessment, she emphasised how cycling helped her mental health. 'It is the most relaxing pastime on earth,' she said. 'I often get wound up with people and circumstances but, once on the bike, I unload it all.' She also repeatedly stressed that she rode every race with the sole intention of winning.

Beryl's biggest documented concern in her conversation with Woodard was how time constraints could impact her diet and sleep. She said that shortcuts in either area would be 'disastrous' and, in an era when sport had little nutritional expertise, she was again instinctively well ahead of her time. Beryl ate basic, fresh produce and, with the exceptions of tinned beans, peas, rice pudding and peaches, nothing that was pre-packed or pre-produced. 'A lot of meat and vegetables, especially steaks, liver and chicken,' says Denise. As a thank you for transporting his daughter all around the country, Ann Pallister's father, who was a butcher, would often give the Burtons fresh joints of meat. She would always prepare fish on a Friday, and would cycle off each day to Carline's farm with several rounds of wholemeal sandwiches in her saddlebag. 'She loved her food – we used to say, "She can't half trough",' says Kathleen Mitchell.

Beryl would even take a Primus stove with her to races and, especially if she was waiting around all day at a track meeting, would be seen cooking a steak or piece of liver near to the start line. For particularly long-distance rides she took on food like flapjacks, fruitcakes and dates or sandwiches with jam, banana, honey or peanut butter. She would usually drink only water or weak squash while racing, although sometimes warm tea or coffee for rides of 100 miles or more. She avoided milk, as she thought it caused phlegm to form in her throat. 'As soon as she finished, she'd eat and tell us to do the same,' says Pallister. 'A lot of stuff that she was doing is what they tell riders to do now.' The fact that Beryl completed such long miles on a protein-rich diet suggests that her metabolism had adapted to burning fat before carbohydrates, a state that all the best long-distance cyclists now try to teach their bodies. According to Tim Kerrison, Chris Froome's greatness is partly founded on how efficiently his body burns fat and consequently how little stored glycogen he will use during less arduous moments of a three-week Grand Tour.

Thursday was Beryl's only day off from serious cycling, and she would always spend her rest day doing washing and baking for the week. As the letters she sent out to friends would repeatedly confirm, she had a weakness for most types of cake and would share her three specialities – flapjack, Victoria sponge and chocolate, coconut and cherry – at club events or her regular 'garage sales', where she would sell items from home to raise funds for her cycling. 'She had a lot of pride in making her cakes and would put on these beautiful spreads outside her house,' says Margaret Allen. Many of the best riders would drink and smoke during the off season and certainly enjoy a few glasses of wine at their winter club dinners. Beryl attended numerous such events as the guest of honour but would treat an orange or apple juice as a genuine extravagance. She would, however, always be near the front of the queue for second helpings of food. 'I find the things I like to eat are the ones that do me most good, such as plenty of fresh vegetables and fruit,' she said in 1985. 'My advice? Eat what you want and stay clear of fancy diets. The way to get fit for cycling is on the bike.'

The extent to which Beryl's success was down to innate physiology or simply hard work was one source of disagreement with husband Charlie. He still contrasts his wife's speed on a bike to his own moderate results and remains adamant that genetics played their part. 'She shopped at Harrods – I made do with Woolworths,' he says. Beryl's counterargument was her 'terribly slow' first 10-mile time trial of more than 30 minutes. She was certain that her edge lay in a willingness to outwork every rival and, speaking in 1994, still sounded baffled by the idea that it was possible to overtrain. 'I wasn't as natural as everyone thinks,' she said. 'Some people say they couldn't do the amount of miles I do but I need miles to get speed. Ability on its own can never replace hard work. I think as a nation we are basically rather lazy. Things are too easy now.'

Far from being mutually incompatible, Beryl also believed that there was a direct correlation between training hard and being productive in everyday life. 'It's just as though someone switches me on – all the little things which I have been promising to do (like writing to you) start getting done,' she wrote in a letter to the *Cycling* photographer Bernard Thompson and his wife, Ethel, after resuming training one January. In that same letter Beryl said she had been out at 6 a.m. in snow that was heavy enough to leave a line of lorries stranded on Knaresborough High Street. She also described how, while waiting for a railway level crossing on another ride, she had nipped into a hairdresser's for a cut that was completed just as the barrier went up. 'I finished about five miles per hour faster than I started,' she said, clearly thrilled at the efficiency of her decision. A big race would invariably prompt her to cycle out to see Margaret Allen and Maureen Pearson, two sisters with a salon 15 miles away, in Shafton. 'She had really beautiful curly hair – but she liked it cropped short when she was racing,' says Pearson. 'She would have her hair done, we would go through three or four pots of black tea, and then she always went to the fish and chip shop a few doors from us. It was the highlight of our week.'

Interviews in *Cycling* magazine would provide further insight into how Beryl derived a definite psychological edge from her tough Yorkshire upbringing. 'Life is much harder up north – it's cold and damp and you have to work to get anywhere in anything,' she said in 1966. 'I think southerners give in too easily and haven't the same fighting spirit.' She later added: 'The main reason I was able to beat the other girls was that they simply weren't doing enough. I don't mean just in training, but in everyday life. Many parents of racing girls think that if they do a lot for their girls they will make them better riders. Girls have to do some grafting. A lazy mind produces a lazy rider.' When Reg Harris tried to counsel a twenty-three-year-old Beryl in 1960 to take 'absolute rest' between training rides, she simply dismissed the advice of Britain's multi-world champion as 'irksome'.

Beryl even believed that still assiduously attending to all the household tasks was part of the reason she could beat the best men over longer distances. 'Men are softer,' she declared. 'Women might be better suited to longer distances because they are used to keeping up the pressures in their domestic life. You develop more of a drive, because so much more has to be fitted into the day.' This whole ethos, which stretched far beyond cycling, is critical, says Pallister, to understanding what made Beryl unique. 'I think you also have to consider what Beryl did at home in the evenings and weekends,' she says. 'She used to look at people paying others to do their cleaning or gardening and shake her head. It was the same when gyms came along. Beryl would say that they could get the same benefit by doing all their own housework and gardening. Her house was always spotless. I clean houses now and I think that she is right. It does keep you fit. Still now, I often say to myself, "What would Beryl Burton think? What would Beryl do?" Her influence has stayed with me. She was a different breed. Not just in what she said, or how she trained or raced, but in how she approached every single day of her life.'

7

Dear Yvonne

A scorching Sunday in the beer garden of the Hotel De Heide-
bloem near Antwerp, and the Affligem Blond – alcohol content
6.7 per cent – is flowing almost as readily as the memories and
anecdotes. My drinking partner for the afternoon is an eighty-
three-year-old woman who, as you pull into Brussels Eurostar
station, is depicted alongside Eddy Merckx on a giant mural that
was unveiled to mark the 2019 Tour de France's Grand Départ.
With four world road race titles, Yvonne Reynders is one up even
on Merckx, and her enduring local fame quickly becomes apparent from the number of times our conversation is interrupted by
random well-wishers. An afternoon full of smiles and laughter is
twice punctuated, however, by glimpses of genuine sadness.

The first is when Reynders vehemently protests her innocence
about a failed drugs test in 1967 that prompted her to abruptly
retire from cycling shortly after her thirtieth birthday. The second
is when our conversation turns to Beryl Burton, with whom she
shared fourteen world titles and against whom she raced directly
eight times in the world championships of the most gladiatorial
of all cycling events – the individual track pursuit. This included
five out of the six finals between 1961 and 1966.

Reynders has brought with her a small holdall of photograph
albums from her cycling career and, when I reciprocate with a
copy of Beryl's autobiography, *Personal Best*, her eyes light up.
She immediately flicks to the photographs section, and just seeing
so many pictures again of her greatest rival immediately has a

profound physical impact. 'Beryl,' she simply whispers under her breath, nodding, while carefully examining the set of black-and-white photographs. These include them riding side by side along a heavily gravelled road in 1961, and then sharing numerous world championships podiums. After Reynders carefully studies these grainy old photographs of herself and Beryl, there is about 30 seconds of silent contemplation before she slowly removes her glasses and reaches for a tissue. Tears are rolling down her cheeks.

*

It is difficult to overstate the importance and lasting impact on a great sportsperson of their biggest rival, especially those who are destined to have the peak years of their career collide with someone of comparable stature. Where once it must have been distressing to find that your dominance of a sport has been diluted by a similarly unusual talent, an appreciation does often then build of what the rivalry gave as well as took. And, whether you are talking about Martina Navratilova and Chris Evert on a tennis court in the 1970s and 1980s, Muhammad Ali and Joe Frazier in the boxing ring or how tennis in the twenty-first century has been so dominated by three men – Roger Federer, Rafael Nadal and Novak Djokovic – great rivalries are invariably a gift that elevates performance to heights that would otherwise remain out of grasp. They also create deep emotional bonds and, for all the linguistic barriers between Beryl's broad Yorkshire English and Reynders's purely Flemish dialect, early tensions did give way to empathy. Reynders eventually even bought herself an English dictionary specifically so that she could translate some words and try them out on Beryl.

What neither woman had previously ever known was some of the similarities in their upbringing. Having been born just eleven weeks after Beryl in 1937, Reynders endured a very different but hugely significant childhood trauma. Her mother fell seriously ill from tuberculosis, and she was forced to grow up on the outskirts of Antwerp with her alcoholic stepfather, Maurice van de Vyver, whose dark presence in her early life is still cited as the reason she never married. And, just as Beryl developed such physical strength from rhubarb farming, so Reynders also has an unexpected explanation for her success. 'Charbon,' she simply says. Coal. It was what she delivered to houses and factories to help with her parents' business on a cargo bike that was specially designed to support a large wooden box and space for 10 kg sacks. And how many would she carry at a time? 'Around twenty – sometimes twenty-five,' she says, grimacing at the memory of pedalling 250 kg around the streets of Antwerp. It was also a teenage Yvonne's job to carry the sacks of coal to the front door of people's homes. There were no lifts back then in Antwerp's apartment blocks, and so she would regularly take as many as five bags, under her arms or on her back, up countless flights of stairs during working days that spanned 13 hours. When a friend's father later gave her an old steel frame, she saved, borrowed and literally begged for the remaining parts and built herself a first proper racing bike. Cycling for pleasure and subsequent criterium races on short road circuits would then provide a crucial evening and weekend release from her deeply unhappy home life.

Reynders dreamed of racing at the Antwerp Sports Palace, a concert hall and indoor track cycling arena that staged the prestigious men's six-day race. There was an advert prior to the series in 1954 which stated 'everybody welcome' for a one-hour chance to ride on the track. This actually only meant men (women were banned), but Reynders sensed an opportunity. She had her hair cut short – 'like a boy,' she says, grinning – and made her way on to the track on one of the bikes she had built. The track was steeply banked and, as she gradually grew in confidence and swooped up and down the boards, she was consumed by a feeling like no other. 'I felt like I was flying,' she says, shutting her eyes and momentarily again tasting that sensation. Suspicions were aroused. 'One of the supervisors of the track eventually recognised me and shouted at the top of his voice: "Yvonne, what are you doing!?"' Reynders ignored the voice and continued until the steward had stopped every other bike on the track and physically forced her off. The same advert appeared the following year, and she took her protests to the mayor's office in Antwerp. 'I told them, "Women are everybody." They relented, and eventually we were allowed on the track every week. This was a turning point.'

Reynders also rode increasingly with the leading Belgian men and would study their interval training. Rather like Beryl in Yorkshire, one of her favourite and most hazardous training sessions would involve cycling for as long as possible behind trucks on the A12 road between Antwerp and Brussels. Add in the regular use of an indoor track and she developed a rapid change of pace, astute tactical awareness and exceptional bike-handling skills. This was crucial in understanding her rivalry with Beryl, who, while athletically stronger, lacked this range of attributes. Under the direction of her stepfather, Reynders also developed a stage show on stationary cycling rollers that would include removing the handlebars and stem, or taking on and off a tracksuit, as she pedalled. Rollers are made up of three interconnected cylinders and require considerable balance. Weave off to either side by more than a few centimetres and you can end up in a big heap on the floor. Reynders would learn to perform these tricks on top of tables in front of crowds of cyclists, and her stepfather would individually sell photographs for five francs. There is a sadness in Reynders's eyes while she recounts this particular story, as if she had been reduced to the unwilling role of performing seal. 'I had a lot of fights with my father,' she says, before revealing that she finally severed all ties when she discovered that he had been secretly visiting her domestic rivals in an attempt to intimidate them.

After being well beaten by Beryl in the 1959 world pursuit quarter-finals, Reynders won her first world title in the road race later that week in Liège. She had arrived alone by train at the championships on the day before the track racing began with two bikes and no accommodation but was taken in by a local family. There was further good fortune during the road race when she benefited from a large crash 4 km from the finish. In the ensuing confusion she attacked down the right to win ahead of a bunch of riders who had been impeded, including Beryl in fifth. A year later and Beryl had proved that she was the best rider in the world by dominating both the 1960 pursuit and the road race in East Germany before a remarkable sequence of head-to-head show-downs. Reynders's face again lights up when I mention this streak. 'Sometimes I had the luck, sometimes she did. I'd love to do it all over again.' It is a nice thought but, with video footage so scarce, Reynders is at least willing to do the next best thing and help piece together a rivalry that was among the very best in sport.

Isle of Man, August 1961

The 1961 women's world cycling championships almost did not happen at all. For the second time in three years the UCI awarded its showpiece event to a country that did not recognise women's cycling. Wikipedia still records the women's events as being held with the men in Zurich and Bern, but they were actually staged some 1,300 km away. After the UCI had simply shrugged at Switzerland's refusal, Eileen Gray again stepped up where the men hid and organised for the races to be staged on the Isle of Man. Gray's diaries would later record embarrassment at how the British women's team took part in an opening parade of what were effectively a home world championships in their own assortment of tracksuits, jumpers and cardigans. Beryl had arrived agitated and deeply upset after an unnamed British official approached her to say that it was time to step aside and give others a chance. 'I wasn't wanted,' she said. 'All the fight and effort that Charlie and I had put into getting to the top of a hard sport – the joy and satisfaction that we thought we'd given to British cycling – all wasted.' Beryl, who was only twenty-four at the time, later told friends that the incident should have made her angry and more determined but that instead she felt dejected.

A further irritation was that the 3,000 m pursuit would actually be held over 2,828 m for the simple reason that the track was 404 m in circumference and the electronic timing system – which was being used for the first time in a women's world championship – could only deal with full laps. With the riders staying in shared accommodation, Charlie camped out alone in pouring rain showers. Reynders now had a dedicated coach in team manager Oscar Daemers and arrived on the Isle of Man as part of a Belgian team that had two masseurs and would all train together twice a day. She had also stopped work for the previous six months specifically in order to prepare and, looking visibly stronger, set the best qualifying time. Tom Feargrieve, the British mechanic, later said that he felt 'daggers in my back' from Beryl after he had sportingly applauded her rival's performance. Beryl qualified second before responding in the semi-finals with the quickest ride of the entire series – 3 min. 59.2 sec. – in beating Marie-Thérèse Naessens.

The final was scheduled for the next day but, with high winds and heavy rain, the riders spent long hours waiting for a break in the showers. Beryl was going for a hat-trick of world titles and what followed was, in the words of *Cycling* magazine, 'one of the greatest races ever known'. Reynders always tended to push a smaller gear, meaning that she was more likely to make a faster start before Beryl's vast time-trialling strength made her stronger over the second half. There was no excessive panic then as, from their starts on the opposite sides of the track, Reynders established a lead of six bike lengths after three of the seven laps. When this was reduced to two lengths at five laps, the odds appeared to be shifting in Beryl's favour. Reynders rallied and, still leading by a length at the bell, finished with a dramatic thrust of her bike

– sprint style – towards the line. No one knew who had won when they flashed across their respective starts almost simultaneously, but the final times showed Reynders first in 4 min. 0.7 sec. and Beryl losing by the narrowest possible margin at 4 min. 0.8 sec. Another 172 metres to the usual 3,000 m distance and she might well have won.

A further factor of even greater significance was observed by Val Rushworth, the national sprint champion and a deeply frustrated trackside spectator. She had noticed how Reynders remained fixed inches below the white race line on the bottom of the track whereas Beryl would weave up and down just above the line. It meant that she was covering a greater distance. Rushworth eventually even sourced photographs of the two women riding to prove her point. It was a decisive error and largely a consequence of Britain's scarce track-cycling facilities. Daemers, who also ran the track in Ghent, would later tell Beryl that he 'struggled to imagine a civilised country not having at least one indoor velodrome'.

Reynders's experience in regular track and closed-circuit road events in Belgium was also invaluable in the road race that followed. Despite needing to stop and change bikes after a broken gear cable, she brilliantly bridged the gap to a leading group containing Beryl, Elsy Jacobs and the Soviet riders Mariya Lukshina and Aino Pouronen. Beryl forced the pace and, although the two Soviets lost contact, Reynders and Jacobs clung on to form a select group of the only three previous winners of the race. It left Beryl in an impossible quandary. If she did not drive the pace, any chance of a medal was certain to disappear, given her relatively weak sprint finish. If she continued to ride hard, Reynders would probably stay right behind and still prevail. Knowing no other way, Beryl ultimately pressed on and, while Jacobs was exhausted, Reynders surged past at the finish to complete her own 'double' of road and pursuit titles. Sixty years later and, asked to rate the greatest moment of her career, Reynders does not hesitate before choosing her two golds on the Isle of Man. As for Beryl, the standards that she now set were evident in her assessment of 1961, with its multiple national titles and two world silvers, as a year 'I sometimes feel like wiping from my memory'.

Reynders and Beryl did meet again two months later for an invitational pursuit race at Herne Hill, and there was now a definite edge. 'I tried chatting to her, but she was her normal aloof self,' said Beryl, who, determined to exact a modicum of revenge, won by more than 3 seconds. Reynders had stopped delivering coal by 1961 and, with growing numbers of women's criteriums being staged in Belgium, was earning anything up to 2,000 francs a race. There were also none of the British amateur rules about sponsorship, and she was paid to advertise prominent local companies on her cycling kit. A similar revolution was under way in the Netherlands, whose vast ongoing success in women's cycling would begin with Keetie Hage's emergence in the late 1960s. The contrast with Britain, and the sort of prizes that Beryl might win, was summed up in what they received that day at Herne Hill following their race. 'We each got a puncture repair kit,' says Reynders, laughing.

Milan, August 1962

The next world championships were staged in Italy and represented a particular logistical challenge for Charlie, who, despite acting as an informal mechanic for the women's team, was always sidelined from the minimal official entourage. The riders travelled by train while Charlie made the 1,000-mile journey to Milan from Leeds on the back of Morley clubmate Dick Hudson's scooter. He had a spare bike for Beryl literally strapped to his back, and they camped out at random destinations en route. It was an eventful journey. They set their tent on fire one night, inadvertently pitched up in an Italian graveyard on another and suffered a tyre blowout while coming down the 2,000-metre Simplon Pass in the French Alps. Hudson, who was colour-blind and so needed shouted instructions from Charlie whenever they approached traffic lights, arrived in Milan so covered in mosquito bites that Beryl did not initially recognise him. They were also several hours late. 'I was so worked up with worry I gave them hell ... and then big hugs all round,' said Beryl.

The politics inside the administration of the BCF remained, and Gray, who had rescued the championships the previous year, was told that she could not attend. Eileen Sheridan, another trail-blazer but a more conciliatory personality to the British officials, was instead invited to take on the role of women's 'chaperone'. The subsequent diaries of Gray, who received a full debrief from the women's team, were illuminating. 'Reports confirmed that male bigotry had done little for their support,' she wrote. Also unknown to anyone but Charlie was the fact that Beryl had been unable to get a full night's sleep in the six weeks prior to these world championships following a serious crash while racing on the Fallowfield track in Manchester. As well as removing much of the skin from her back, it had left enduring pain both in her ver-tebrae and a hip that required assistance even to turn over in bed. It contributed to a major shock in the national 50-mile champion-ships a few days after the crash when, for the only British national time trial championship that Beryl completed between September 1957 and April 1982, she did not win. Liverpool's Joan Kershaw was the victor, beating Beryl into second by 32 seconds.

Beryl had another month to prepare for the world champion-ships and was back at something close to her best when she arrived at the Vigorelli Velodrome in Milan. She qualified third fastest in the pursuit, behind both Reynders and Pouronen, but improved as she adjusted to what was the fastest and most famous track in the world. Naessens, whom she had beaten in 1959 and 1961, was dispatched in the quarter-finals. Reynders and Beryl were then both victorious against riders from the Soviet Union in the semi-finals. The final was held a day later and pushed back until almost midnight, after a series of men's sprint events were delayed by tactical trackstands, where riders deliberately stall and dare the other to take the lead. With the women's events again being shunted around to suit the men, Beryl had spent the entire day not knowing when to eat or even whether to go for a short cycle on the road or just stick to the borrowed set of rollers that she had stationed beneath the stand. 'It was ridiculous,' said Sheridan.

The location and history of the Vigorelli track still added an extra dimension. Situated in the centre of Milan, and with a capacity crowd of 9,000, it was known as *pista magica*, or 'magic track', and was where greats such as Fausto Coppi, Jacques Anquetil and Roger Rivière had all set world hour records. This was a boom era for Italian cycling and, with capacity crowds as well as bands, flags and bunting in the surrounding streets, there was a carnival atmosphere. 'It was thronging with people and bursting with life,' said Beryl, who felt like 'Daniel going into the lions' den' by the day of the final. She repeatedly told herself that the growing advantages in coaches, facilities and technical support of the continental nations could be countered by 'Yorkshire grit'. Sheridan was trackside and, despite the late hour, had gathered as much vocal British support as possible, including even the contingent of journalists.

Beryl had resolved to start fast but was again fighting her nerves. 'What the hell was I doing?' she later said. 'I wanted to be at home in Yorkshire, not having thousands of bike-mad Italian fans staring at me. Who, in Britain, at 11 p.m. on a Monday knew that I was carrying their colours in a world final in Milan? "It doesn't matter," I thought. "I'm riding for Charlie, Denise and the lads and lasses in the Morley Cycling Club".' Beryl's plan was simple – 'Hit her with everything' – and she was unexpectedly three lengths up after only one lap. 'I pounded my 89-inch gear as though my life depended on it,' she said and, having shocked Reynders with such an aggressive start, would finish fully 100 m clear. It was, in the words of *Cycling* magazine, a 'slaughter'.

20. Flanked by Yvonne Reynders (left), Beryl celebrates another world
title and becomes the first woman pursuiter under 4 minutes.

Beryl's various descriptions of the ride – 'blinking in the flashlights
of the trackside photographers ... hazily aware of the roar that
accompanies you around the track ... sparkling chrome-plated
spokes and tightly fitted silk Great Britain jersey gleaming in the
arc lights' – always remained vivid. The time was also of monumental significance – a world record 3 min. 59.4 sec. – to become
the first woman inside 4 minutes for 3,000 m. *Cycling* called it
'the greatest ride in the history of women's pursuit racing'. As
well as another rainbow jersey and gold medal, Beryl was handed
a bouquet of deep red gladioli and there was rare emotion as she
wiped away a tear on the podium next to Reynders. Charlie was
weeping with joy in the track centre. Sheridan, Beryl and Charlie
later shared a bottle of wine at a hotel in the centre of Milan. And
Beryl slept that night with her fourth world championship gold
medal nestled beneath her pillow.

Liège, August 1963

Beryl's domestic dominance was such that her only real regular competition was either with the best British men or in her annual world championship showdown against rivals who were now training full-time. It was only four years since her first victory in Belgium, but the track championships were again held at the Rocourt Velodrome in Liège, where Reynders would be guaranteed partisan home support. Beryl had a heavy cold in the days leading up to the championships, as well as ongoing back and hip pain, but her mentality was always that it was possible to 'ride away' even the most significant ailment. Reynders was again fastest in pursuit qualifying but, with Beryl progressing comfortably through the lower half of the draw, the stage was set for their third consecutive final.

It was a calm, warm evening when, just after the floodlights were turned on at 8.30 p.m., Reynders began with a blistering start. With the winner having previously been decided by who took an early advantage, Beryl feared that her title was already lost. Reynders still held a comfortable lead as the race approached half-distance and was also on course to comfortably surpass Beryl's time of 4 min. 19 sec. on the same track in 1959. Beryl tried to rally and, although she was not initially making inroads, did stabilise the situation and stop the gap from growing. 'Reynders seemed phenomenal,' she later said. 'It called for an answer. I rode probably the best pursuit lap of my life. My eyeballs were hanging over my front wheel.' In the space just of 500 m Beryl drew level and would then maintain this increased pace over a glorious final kilometre to again win decisively in 4 min. 7.39 sec.

A crowd of some 40,000 briefly fell silent as they realised that their own champion was beaten but, according to *Cycling*, they then 'accepted the inevitable and found their voices to applaud the finest unpaced woman cycling has ever produced'.* The finishing

---

*The term 'unpaced' refers to races that are individually timed.

time was 12 seconds faster than Beryl's first world title at the same velodrome and, while slower than her Milan world record the previous year, it was the performance that she rated as the 'absolute pinnacle' of her track career. 'Rocourt is comparatively slow, Vigorelli smooth and fast and worth more than the 8 seconds, which separated the two rides,' she said. The celebratory photographs confirm how much it all meant to the Burton family. Now seven, Denise was present for the first time at one of her mother's world championships. A beaming family image was reproduced in the *Daily Mirror*, but Beryl was again disappointed to return home and find that her fifth world title in five years had merited only a cursory few lines in the *Yorkshire Evening Post*, next to a full report of a local athletics competition.

The world championship road race that year took place 100 miles to the east of Liège in the hilly Flemish Ardennes. It was the weekend after Beryl's pursuit triumph, and so she simply spent one of her 'rest' days cycling across Belgium for the race. Charlie and Denise followed in the family's three-wheeled car. The car was where Charlie and Denise would feast during the evenings on takeaway sausage and chips from a caravan in the village square. Denise would then lie across the back seat at night while Charlie, always willing to sacrifice his own comfort for his wife or daughter, would curl up in the front. 'He looked like Quasimodo in the morning,' said Beryl.

With no spare accreditation or tickets, one persistent problem facing the Burtons was how to smuggle Charlie into any world championship venue. When he was alone at a track, a bike on each shoulder and a cigarette behind his ear, which would be casually passed to the doorman by way of a gift, was the tried and trusted routine. Should that fail, the women's team would all go in together, and then one of Beryl's teammates would pop out with a spare pass, which Charlie would pin to his shirt. 'Fortunately no one bothered to really read the names,' said Beryl. But how would they also smuggle Denise and an unmissable three-wheeler

21. Charlie and Denise took the family's three-wheeled car and camped out en route to Belgium for the 1963 world championships.

into the venue? A plan was formulated whereby Charlie would drive a few inches behind the back of Tom Feargrieve's 'Britannia' team car. The riders were all seated at the back, speaking to Feargrieve in front and making hand signals to Charlie behind, as they approached a road with a barrier checkpoint and armed police. 'Our bus stopped at the barrier – official pass shown – and Charlie was waved on by the girls until he was about 6 inches from the bus rear and hidden from the gate,' Beryl later recounted. 'The girls at the front then urged the driver to go faster while we at the back waved Charlie on. We went through the barrier in tandem inches apart in a cloud of dust and the last we saw of the police was a waving of arms and revolvers. Shades of James Bond!'

22. Seven-year-old Denise reading in front of the car which doubled as her hotel in the Flemish Ardennes.

Having won the pursuit title so emphatically, Beryl was confident about her chances of distancing Reynders on what was a relatively hilly and testing course. Her race, however, lasted just 5 minutes. The driver of a service car, which was supposed to be at the front, was late arriving for the start and inadvertently set off behind the main field. In his haste to get to the front, the car brushed past the bunch and sent Beryl head first into a telegraph pole. She was knocked unconscious and rushed to hospital. The finishing sprint was ultimately contested by fifteen riders, with Reynders holding off the Soviet charge to win her third world road title.

Beryl

Paris, August 1964

Having won four of the past five world pursuit championships – and only been denied by one tenth of a second on the Isle of Man – Beryl arrived for the 1964 world championships as a heavy favourite for title number five. Harry Jackson, a men's team pursuiter, was among those who travelled with her to the Parc des Princes in Paris by train and says that she was engrossed in her knitting throughout the journey. They then all cycled across Paris from the Gare du Nord with their suitcases balanced on the front of their bikes. The women had still not been given so much as a team tracksuit by the BCF, but an unnamed sports manufacturer had posted Beryl one of their best branded tracksuits. This presented a significant problem. The rules governing amateur cycling meant that Beryl would instantly risk everything if any sort of commercial logo was on display, and so she carefully unpicked the company's name before stitching all the little holes back together.

Charlie, as ever, made his own arrangements and found a wooded area near the Parc des Princes to pitch his tent. Having been awoken in the night by a lively herd of pigs, he was found early the next morning in a sleeping bag in the doorway of the British team hotel. Taking pity on him, Tom Pinnington, who was a BCF committee member and naturally did have a hotel room, smuggled him on to a sofa in one of the corridors.

There had been a partial thaw in the fractious relationship between Eileen Gray and the BCF, which ensured that she again travelled with the women following a two-year exile. Her presence was vital to Beryl. She had been training on what was a pink concrete track with Val Rushworth when they were both brought down by a male rider who swerved as he adjusted his tracksuit bottoms. It was a heavy fall and, as well as the superficial blood and grazing, Beryl lost all movement in her right hand. Gray accompanied Beryl to the back of the Parc des Princes to seek treatment for a suspected broken wrist but was promptly informed that only a male team official could wait in that area of the arena. Annoyed by such nonsense, and with no British male representative available, Gray instead approached officials from the French team and sought out their doctors' advice. The first round of the pursuit was imminent and so a painkilling injection was suggested. Beryl declined and, riding in severe discomfort, qualified only third behind both Reynders and Pouronen.

As the adrenalin subsided and the extent of the injury became apparent, Beryl accepted a painkilling injection ahead of her semi-final the following day. The next problem was that she now had no feeling in her hand and lower arm. This meant that she could not pull on the bars as she rode – an essential source of power and balance – and so was effectively one-handed. Gray assumed that this would definitely be the end, but Beryl had a solution. She instructed Charlie to tie her numb right hand tight to the handlebars with a spare toe-strap. It made controlling the steering more challenging but, with the pain eased, she duly improved on her qualifying time by 3 seconds to narrowly beat Pouronen and guarantee at least a silver medal. 'It was one of the gutsiest things I ever saw on a bike,' says Rushworth. To even reach the final had been remarkable but, against an opponent as good as Reynders, it was a race too far. With her hand again discreetly strapped to the handlebars, Beryl was never ahead and ultimately well beaten as Reynders finished only 3 seconds outside her rival's world record. The severity of her wrist injury remained a mystery to all those outside Beryl's immediate entourage. When I relay the story to Reynders, she simply raises her eyebrows in surprise and reiterates admiration for Beryl before adding, 'It was me or her.'

San Sebastian, August 1965

It was again Reynders the following year, when, having arrived a full week before the racing, Beryl and the rest of the team fell sick with a severe bug. Gray had again been sidelined from the trip, but her diary does not spare the male administrators, and she was furious that the women's team had spent so long before their competition in what was particularly grim and cheap accommodation. With Beryl not even well enough to get through the qualifying rounds, Reynders swept to her third world pursuit title. She was now only one behind Beryl overall, and in their personal head-to-head in finals the score stood at 2–2.

This was also the one and only period when Beryl thought seriously about quitting competitive cycling. Denise was still under ten and, for all Beryl's blinkered focus on her sport, additional pressures clearly were being felt. She and Charlie were both working full-time and, although the award in 1964 of an MBE at Buckingham Palace represented timely recognition, the financial and practical challenges remained acute. She described her life as dominated by logistical planning and decisions like 'whether we could afford another pair of cycling shoes'. Charlie had even taken on a second job during weekday evenings that involved collecting rent and insurance payments. Just competing in the 1964 world championships had cost the family £100. That would equate to more than £2,000 today. In what was a rare public statement of complaint, Beryl pointedly noted that 'British women get more medals in world championships than British men, yet we always seem to be at the bottom of the list when it comes to help. Schoolboys get more attention.'

In trying to raise funds to move out of their two-bedroom Elmfield Court flat, Beryl had left employment at Carline's farm for several years during the mid-1960s and initially went back to working as an accounting machine operator. She would generally resign from any job a few weeks prior to any world championships before reapplying for work once she had returned. Employment with the Post Office did briefly provide rather more stability but all her holiday leave was unpaid. The BCF had also ruled that the remaining money (£100 12s. 8d.) from the appeal fund that had been organised in 1960 by the Morley Town Council could not simply be given to the Burtons to assist with their cycling. That was deemed to contravene her amateur status, and so some of the money was instead used to purchase a gift. Beryl chose a £50 radiogram – a furnished record player – that she would keep for the next thirty years. In a handwritten letter of thanks to the mayor of Morley's office, which has been preserved among the civic records, she said that it was something she has 'longed for, for many moons, but the money has always been required for more pressing means'. A specific donation of £30 was also made towards a winter training trip to the indoor velodrome in Berlin. Beryl again personally wrote to thank the mayor, Mr Finnigan, saying, 'I shall ride all the better, content in the knowledge that they [Denise and Charlie] are not having to struggle along at home on my behalf.'

Beryl was also becoming worn down by the historic rivalry between the BCF, which was responsible for road and track racing, and the RTTC, the governing body that oversaw time trialling. Even though Beryl was easily Britain's best cyclist, the BCF decided in 1965 to invent an arbitrary rule that seemed designed specifically to stop her racing in the main time trial events. The new regulation said that anyone taking part in a domestic time trial over the distance of 50 miles in the month before the world championships in Frankfurt the following year would not be considered. Never mind that Beryl's greatest previous achievement – her two gold medals in 1960 – were won in the days after winning the national 100-mile championships. Beryl's response was predictably unflinching. She ignored this diktat, obliterated her rivals by 19 minutes in the national 100-mile championships and let the selectors please themselves. Beryl's time of 4 hrs 8 min. 22 sec. had not only bettered her own British record but also beaten Keith Stacey, who had won the men's national championships only two weeks earlier in 4 hrs 9 min. 00 sec. It left the BCF in an embarrassing, if entirely self-made, dilemma. Could they seriously ignore a rider who had just gone faster than the British men?

Charlie, who was usually a quiet model of diplomacy, even took it upon himself to write to *Cycling* magazine and accuse the BCF of 'killing initiative with petty rules'. Another reader accused the national governing body of treating Beryl as 'an embarrassment and an encumbrance'. In a second rule change that would have affected Beryl far more than any other British rider, the BCF even threatened to stop track riders from doubling up in the world road race. In her diary Gray described the threats as a 'tyranny' and wrote a letter to complain about the BCF's 'bullying' behaviour.

Frankfurt, August 1966

The BCF eventually caved in, and Beryl travelled to Frankfurt rejuvenated and able to again combine the road race with the pursuit. Charlie travelled to Germany by a combination of train and bike and, after receiving a telegram with her husband's estimated time of arrival, Beryl was waiting at the central station with food. Speaking in 1995, Beryl described how happy she felt whenever Charlie arrived at a world championship. 'You'd think it was a year since I'd left him, rather than a week ... the relief and joy at seeing him riding up the road was almost indescribable,' she said. The hotel at which the British team were staying was surrounded by pine woods and, with just a sleeping bag for bedding, Charlie settled down on the first night under a large tree. He was awoken terrified by the rustlings of wildlife and debris dropping from the tree, and so moved his makeshift bed to a grass area adjacent to the hotel. The situation was explained to the hotel management. No, he was not a tramp and, yes, he was the husband of the world's greatest female cyclist. There were no spare beds, but they did at least turn a blind eye and so Charlie remained in his sleeping bag up against the hotel wall for the next fortnight.

Beryl qualified fastest in the pursuit, even despite the British administrators almost missing her start time. She had been told that she would be racing at 9 p.m. Only at 6 p.m. did they realise that the fastest riders were due off at 7 p.m., prompting a rapid dash to the track. Beryl's steak and salad meal had to be hastily stuffed into a plastic bag for later in the evening. 'This kind of thing never happened when Eileen Gray managed the women's team,' she said. Beryl was then further irritated when she discovered that her first ride of the competition was against Reynders. The UCI had bizarrely paired the only two winners of the event over the previous seven years in the same qualification race. After injury and illness the previous two years, Beryl arrived feeling that she had a personal point to prove. 'I had a score to settle with Dear Yvonne, and meant to show her who was boss,' she later wrote. Beryl won their heat, but Reynders also took her place among the top eight for the quarter-final ride-offs. Both then progressed to comfortable semi-finals wins. The stage was set for their fifth and last world pursuit final.

An extra spice had been added during the previous week's road race when Beryl rode with a strength and bravery that were typically in inverse proportionate to her tactical acumen. Over a ridiculously short course of just 28 miles along the Nürburgring motor circuit, she simply went straight to the front and tried to blow the field apart. This worked to the extent that only four riders could stay with her: Reynders, Pouronen, Jacobs and Hage. Beryl repeatedly urged the other riders to come through and take their turn into the wind but they ignored her. Beryl angrily called them 'leeches' and 'sheep' but was left in an invidious position. She knew that she would finish down the field in any sprint that involved the entire peloton and so decided that her best chance was at least to ensure that the breakaway succeeded. 'Even on the 2-mile hill, which we climbed five times, they were there, locked on – and I thought it a shame that riders of the class of Reynders and Pouronen should act in this way,' said Beryl. They duly did all beat her in the sprint, with Reynders winning and Beryl finishing fifth and making no attempt to disguise her disgust at the perceived breach of etiquette. 'If I was Reynders or Pouronen, I would not feel particularly proud of my medal,' she said. 'I'd rather have raced hard and come last than sat in and come first. I had to take what comfort I could from being the moral winner.'

There would be nowhere for Reynders to hide in the pursuit final and, as she inched to the start line on what was an unusually cool summer's night, Beryl kept telling herself that it was now one-on-one. She remained convinced that she was still the best unpaced rider in the world and, while that was certainly true in any road time trial, the odds were always narrowed over 3,000 m on a track that also required smooth bike handling. Charlie, wearing a smart jacket and polo-neck jumper, had cycled through Frankfurt on Beryl's road bike and took up his position in the home straight. The lights by the side of the track would flash as each rider passed her station and, with the race starting just after dark at 9 p.m., Beryl used these to judge her effort. The final was broadcast live on terrestrial television in Germany, France, Belgium and Italy, though not Great Britain. According to Graeme Obree, who would win two world men's titles in the 1990s, a pursuit is often as much about the pain threshold as pure athletic ability. 'It's who can hold their hand in a fire for the longest,' says Obree, who, after beating Italy's Andrea Collinelli in the 1995 final, felt like he could taste blood from his burning lungs. Beryl would enter a similar twilight world in Frankfurt and described what followed in her memoirs:

> It was relentless. Reynders was not giving an inch, but neither was I. How many more laps? I had lost count. I felt that I was wobbling. My eyes were misting. I felt my strength was ebbing, yet my legs were still pumping rhythmically as though they belonged to somebody else. The bell signalling the last lap sounded like an alarm clock waking me from a dream. I forced the last gram of effort from my body. I came down the straight as though demented. I hurled myself over the final

metres, clipping the inside of the track. There was one loud explosion as the line officials fired their pistols seemingly in the same instant. I was hanging over the bars. As I came into the trackside Charlie was running towards me. 'Have I won, have I won?' I shouted hoarsely. The naked eye could not separate us. The times? Burton 4 min. 10.47 sec. Reynders 4 min. 10.79 sec. Charlie had tears in his eyes. I could hardly stand. Sweat poured from my body. Then came the podium, the flowers, 'God Save the Queen'. I had notched up another victory for Morley and Great Britain.

It was Beryl's fifth world pursuit title. 'My only regret is that it did not appear on British television,' she said, before adding, 'but I was not swimming, running, jumping, playing with a ball or riding a horse, so I could hardly expect it.' Reynders remained magnanimous in defeat. 'By the end, there was such a strong understanding that we didn't need words to communicate,' she says. 'Just hand signals and the look on our faces was enough. We never fought.' Both women were still only aged twenty-nine – and, remarkably, they had won thirteen out of the sixteen world championship road and pursuit gold medals awarded between 1959 and 1966.

*

Reynders tested positive for an amphetamine called ephedrine in 1967 and, although she was only actually banned for three months, walked away from cycling entirely. Just the mention of the incident brings tears to her eyes and, while it raises obvious questions about her past victories, she remains absolute in denying any wrongdoing through her career. Reynders believes that the test was deliberately mixed up and that certain riders from Belgium were sabotaged during a race in the Netherlands. Her friend Jos Vekemans, who is a local politician in Zoersel, says Reynders had her suspicions confirmed decades later by an old acquaintance. She also did briefly make a spectacular comeback by regaining the 1976 Belgium national road race championships. The Belgian officials had planned to pick other riders for their world championship team but relented when Reynders refused to accept the national championship jersey in protest at the selection policy. Aged thirty-nine, she proved that she had lost none of the guile and class that made her one of the greatest one-day road racers by winning a bronze medal ahead of a field that contained Beryl's daughter Denise, who finished nineteenth.

Reynders promptly stopped racing again and, having worked as a dementia nurse and podiatrist, her retirement has been largely spent fishing for trout and caring for her thirty-two tortoises. One of them recently turned 100. 'I know them all by name, and they have their own villa that I built in the garden,' she says, with as much contented pride as while recounting any of her world championship wins. She also continues to cycle for pleasure. Reynders then asks how it was that Beryl should die so young and expresses regret that they did not reconnect in later life. As I explain the heart failure that Beryl suffered, and how she never actually stopped racing competitively, Reynders again sobs. She says that she often thought of trying to contact Beryl in the two decades between her own retirement from cycling and Beryl's death, but 'I could not write in English, I was doing two jobs, and had little time'. Reynders asks for her condolences to be specifically relayed to Denise and Charlie. When I tell Denise, she says that her mother would always refer to Reynders as 'one of the best cyclists who ever lived'. And how does Reynders feel when she thinks of Beryl? 'Affinity, compassion, understanding and huge respect. She was the best I raced against. Of course, I would have won much more if Beryl wasn't there, but I am happy that she was. It would not have been such fun.'

8

'La dame à bicyclette'

The biggest crossroads in Beryl Burton's cycling career would arrive just as she reached the absolute summit. A dramatic series of achievements in 1967 and 1968 surpassed even her six previous world titles and, as she finally edged into the nation's consciousness and even briefly the mainstream of international cycling, limited opportunities to monetise her success did emerge. Having just turned thirty, it was also the last period during which Beryl would sometimes still speak wistfully of a family life after competitive cycling. In a speech to the British Sports Journalists' Association (SJA) in 1967, she was clearly already resigned to retiring without the chance to compete in either the Olympics or the Commonwealth Games. It was a subject that Beryl did not often address publicly, but in a room full of national media and major stars from other sports she solemnly described it as one of her 'few regrets'. She even individually noted the years of each Olympics and Commonwealth Games since 1958 in which she could have competed. 'We women cyclists can only watch from afar,' she said. 'We do with admiration, tinged with envy, itching to get in there and compete but relegated to the position of spectator.' Beryl also declared that 'the time is coming, sooner or later, when I shall have to make way for some fast young females at international level ... and then I shall hang my serious racing wheels up with no regrets or backward glances'. She added that 'When I give up, I'll go back to being a housewife and cycling club life.'

The committee of Yorkshire cyclists who selected the annual C. A. Rhodes Memorial Award, however, were evidently sensing a rather different Beryl Burton. In the minutes of their deliberations for the 1967 prize they noted that 'a change appears to be overtaking her personal prestige and standing', before asserting: 'Her approach does seem to have shifted from that of the amateur who rides for fun ... other issues seem to have been clouded over by preoccupation with success for its own sake.' Descriptions of Beryl in the moments before a race seemed also gradually to evolve. Reports from the 1950s and 1960s would use words like 'bubbly' and 'vivacious' and might describe her brushing Denise's hair while Charlie pinned a number to her lower back. Later on, the anecdotal impression was of an increasingly serious, quiet and intense build-up. A *Sunday Times* feature depicted her pre-race preparation in the mid-1970s and how she simply sat alone in the back of a van while very deliberately unwrapping a boiled sweet. 'She was nervous,' was her reply to all inquiries after her health, and even that was said in an off-hand way, she was drawn so completely into herself,' it said.

One overriding problem for Beryl was the competitive limitations, which would always stretch far beyond just women's exclusion from the Olympics or Commonwealth Games. While British male contemporaries like Brian Robinson, Tom Simpson and Barry Hoban could all depart for cycling's Promised Land of continental Europe, where there were teams of full-time professionals competing across an illustrious calendar of races, no such option existed for Beryl. Turning professional for a British woman would largely mean following Eileen Sheridan in being paid by a bike manufacturing company to promote their goods. The company would support you for various individual Road Records Association place-to-place rides, which could be attempted by professional or club riders, but also demand plenty of your time for adverts and photo shoots. It would also mean an automatic end to competing in strictly amateur British time trial, road and track races – and therefore selection for the annual British world championship team. The straightforward choice, then, was earning from cycling or still regularly competing in cycling.

The French newspaper *Le Monde* reported in 1967 that an unnamed French firm had offered Beryl an 'interesting contract' that she refused. The rumour in Yorkshire, heard by several club cyclists of the time, was that she turned down the extraordinary sum of £25,000 to ride exhibition races on the continent against Yvonne Reynders. Beryl had previously joked during a 1960 appearance on the BBC *Sports Personality of the Year* show that she 'wouldn't say no to £20 a week and a £1 a mile' but has only ever publicly mentioned the persistent Raleigh overtures. She said that a representative of the Nottingham bike company 'made numerous visits trying to persuade me' and even brought a proposed contract to the Burtons' council flat. This included what Beryl called a long list of 'thou shalt nots that they wanted to hedge my life around'. Beryl was equally unimpressed by the contract's three-year duration and sufficiently far-sighted to see that she could be released by Raleigh and then, as Sheridan found, be left unable to compete again. Worst of all, she would also have to leave the Morley Cycling Club. The cheque that was being waved in front of her nose must still have been tempting, but Beryl's decision remained entirely consistent with her outlook and values. She flatly declined all offers, and the amateur club scene would remain the cornerstone of her life. 'It was a decision I have never regretted,' she said.

Beryl did benefit from her friendship with Ron Kitching, a Yorkshire entrepreneur who owned a thriving cycle business. Charlie accepted a job as his warehouse manager in Harrogate in 1976 and, with Beryl asked to officially open some of his chain of shops, their relationship evolved to the point where she had access to equipment and bikes. It was entirely informal but, with Beryl often photographed on a bike bearing the 'Kitching' name, it was an arrangement that benefited all sides. Beryl also struck up a friendship with Peter Salisbury, a shoemaker from Northampton who would custom-fit, design and then hand-produce what became her trademark – and somewhat sassy – leather red cycling shoes. The line between amateur and professional was otherwise so strictly enforced that she would carefully even conceal the labels of sportswear companies. She stitched two bees (to signify her BB initials) over one label and, on the tracksuit top for the British national team, started something of a trend by emblazoning the letters 'BB'.

*

The 1967 world championships were significant for a wider international shift in women's cycling, but there would be one final head-to-head pursuit against Yvonne Reynders. Beryl and Reynders were the only winners of the event since 1959 and again qualified for the semi-finals, but in the space of 10 era-changing minutes they were beaten by two Soviet Union riders who were, respectively, eleven and nine years their juniors. Beryl had already begun wondering whether her general focus on time trialling was blunting her 'zip' over 3,000 m, and the Soviet riders, while much improved, were not as yet challenging her world record. Her bronze-medal-winning time of 4 min. 8.93 sec. was within 4 seconds still of both Raisa Obodovskaya and new champion Tamara Garkushina and good enough to beat Reynders by 13 seconds in their ride-off. It was Beryl's sixth victory in their eight world championship pursuit head-to-heads, even if the main immediate emotion was evidently still fury at having lost her title.

The cycling journalist Les Woodland reported that Beryl arrived in Heerlen for the road race later that week from Amsterdam in 'a foul mood'. Eileen Gray had again been left at home, and Charles Messenger, the British road team manager, was among those who had been telling the BCF that Beryl should be excluded on account of her continued involvement in long-distance time trials. It was a farcical standpoint. Although Beryl had indeed suffered a slight loss of speed on the track over 4 minutes, she was getting stronger in longer road races and still light years ahead of any other British rival. Messenger initially tried to congratulate Beryl on her pursuit bronze but was bluntly told that 'there's only one medal that matters' and later said that 'it wouldn't have taken much for her to have sloshed me'. Seventeen British men had been taken to the world championships, compared with four women, and Beryl was also unhappy at all the pressure to stop time trialling. As tempers frayed, Messenger told Beryl that, if she wanted a stand-up row, she could have one. They duly exchanged points of view, and Beryl, who actually came to quite like Messenger, felt a whole lot better.

Although the women's road race was still only 33 miles, the course was unusually testing and included four ascents of the Ubachsberg hill. Messenger was so bullishly confident that he placed an order for champagne on ice at the team hotel before the race. Beryl checked the entry list and was intrigued to see a number of names from the Soviet Union that she did not recognise. Her tactics were entirely predictable, and after 5 miles she simply went to the front to find out whether anyone could stay with her. The answer was initially 'yes', but only one rider: Lyubov Zadorozhnaya, from the Soviet Union. Zadorozhnaya clung on behind Beryl's back wheel for 5 miles but then, as they climbed the Ubachsberg hill for a second time, a small gap appeared. 'I turned up the gas and kept it on full, letting the disappointment of the track find its way through my legs,' said Beryl. 'It was reminiscent of Leipzig seven years earlier, alone against the rest of the world. Could I, the oldest in the race, really solo away?' The answer was later provided by Zadorozhnaya herself. 'I had to let her go, or I would have done myself some damage,' she said.

The world championships were broadcast on BBC radio and, with Beryl increasing her lead every mile, the emotion in the commentator's description was audible:

23. 'In the manner of Coppi', said *Cycling*'s headline after
Beryl powered to her second world road race title.

Here she comes, around the corner, 400 yards to the finishing
line and of course it is ... Beryl Burton! The Russian girl went
first, Beryl went with her. On the second lap she jumped away.
She's crossed the line now. Beryl Burton of Great Britain,
the thirty-year-old housewife from Leeds, the mother of an
eleven-year-old daughter, wins her seventh gold medal. And
Charles Messenger, the British team manager, wearing his
red jersey, chasing after her. Wildly excited. Another gold for
Beryl Burton!

For all his previous awkwardness, Messenger was in tears. There
was, as ever, no victory salute as Beryl crossed the line, just a
satisfied smile before she leaned down very deliberately to release
her feet from the toe-straps. 'I've ridden harder races and finished

more shattered,' she said, nonchalantly. The result sheet made for remarkable reading. Zadorozhnaya had also stayed clear of the bunch and finished 1 min. 47 sec. behind Beryl. Third and fourth were another two riders from the Soviet Union – Anna Konkina and Galina Yudina – but they had both lost 5 min. 47 sec. in the 28 miles since Beryl attacked. It was another slaughter on two wheels. If the women's race had been run over a comparable distance to the 165 miles that the professional men would face the following day, it is not far-fetched to imagine that Beryl would have beaten the best riders in the world by at least 20 minutes. Alan Gayfer, reporting for *Cycling*, wrote that, 'had she gone on, she would have started to lap some of the field. For a Swiss, an Austrian and a West German finished 17 minutes behind.' The correspondent of the Italian newspaper *Gazzetta dello Sport* also paid their ultimate compliment. 'This was like one of Fausto Coppi's greatest victories,' he said. Beryl had won gold and bronze at the 1967 world championships and, with the Soviet Union winning another clean sweep in the sprint, she was the only cyclist from outside the USSR to win any of the nine medals on offer to women. Standing at the top of the road race podium, and flanked by Zadorozhnaya and Konkina, Beryl made a point of proudly wearing a tracksuit top that was all black but for a pristine white Yorkshire rose.

It was not the end of what was her finest season and, only a fortnight after being presented with a seventh rainbow jersey in Heerlen, Beryl returned to her home roads of Yorkshire to produce her 12-hour record. There had been relatively little media coverage for a seventh world title, but her achievement of catching Mike McNamara while beating a male world record did stir wider recognition. The SJA made Beryl their Sportswoman of the Year, and in a cartoon on the front of their programme she was depicted overtaking the motorcyclist Mike Hailwood and shouting, 'Shift over Mike and let someone pass who can really travel.' In collecting her award from the Earl of Harewood, Beryl's speech repeated a favourite maxim of the Morley Cycling Club: 'Smile when you

24. A kiss from Henry Cooper after being named
Sportswoman of the Year for 1967.

lose ... and laugh like hell when you win,' she said, before adding,
'and tonight, ladies and gentleman, I'm laughing, and thanking
all of you for considering me and the sport of cycling worthy.'

The BBC had not imagined that she was a realistic contender
for their coveted Sports Personality of the Year prize of 1967, but
the British public disagreed. Beryl was unexpectedly voted second
behind the boxer Henry Cooper, even though none of her races
had been broadcast on television and there was scarce coverage of
her achievements in any national newspaper. Unlike recent years,
where the runner-up is invited on stage and all the contenders are
extensively featured during the programme, there was no visible
sign of Beryl when Cooper collected the main award. She was,

however, present at BBC Television Centre, and her terse recollection was of being 'on screen for about 2 seconds and then, following due honour to Henry, the programme was filled with English football and cricket teams'. In Maxine Peake's play, the presenter Frank Bough is portrayed asking Beryl for her thoughts and, without waiting for an answer, simply saying 'remarkable' as he moves on to interview Cooper. Beryl was later told that there was relief among BBC producers when the votes were counted up and it was found that she had narrowly lost out to Cooper, a national treasure but only ever the British and Commonwealth champion. The show was watched by more than 10 million people and, as of January 2022, Beryl has remained the only British female cyclist to finish in the top three.

Further recognition followed in the Queen's birthday honours list of 1968 with an upgrade to OBE. Any winner can invite two guests to Buckingham Palace and, having been accompanied by Denise and Charlie when she received her MBE, Charlie offered his space to Denise's best friend, Ann Pallister. Denise was twelve and Pallister fourteen. Charlie drove them all down to London and, after dropping them off outside Buckingham Palace in his recently acquired Cortina estate, simply had a sleep in the back while he waited for their audience with the Queen to finish. It had been a travel upgrade on their MBE journey in 1964 in the family's three-wheeler. Pallister's parents bought her a red dress and leather jacket for the big day. 'You walked down a red carpet to get in and there was an orchestra playing,' she says. 'Then into another room, where Beryl got her OBE from the Queen and where there was another orchestra playing this beautiful music. I thought I had died and gone to heaven.' And what did Beryl make of it? 'I am sure she was thrilled but I don't really know,' says Pallister. 'She was the same if she'd had a really good victory. She wouldn't say anything. You would never know the difference. She would have just got the OBE and been, "C'mon, away, off. Where are we racing next weekend?"'

25. Accompanied by Denise (right) and her daughter's best friend
Ann Pallister outside Buckingham Palace for her OBE.

*

The answer was invariably a time trial of some description and, after becoming the first woman under an hour for 25 miles in 1963, and then under 2 hours for 50 miles in 1967, Beryl was targeting another slice of cycling history. It was only twelve years since Ray Booty had become the first man to cycle 100 miles in under 4 hours and, having already lowered the women's record by more than 30 minutes to 4 hrs 1 min. 41 sec., she was in sight of that landmark when she arrived in Essex for the 1968 national championships. Booty's brother, Gordon, was a similarly talented cyclist but had once made what Ray called 'the supremely chauvinistic' promise that, 'should Beryl Burton ever beat him, he would bury his bike'. Ray later wryly remarked that 'Both events came to pass.' Beryl stayed the night before the '100' championship race with her old friend Ann Illingworth and had relaxed by knitting while reminiscing with a rider who was among her teammates at the 1960 world championships in Leipzig. Knitting was the one activity aside from cycling that could keep the hyperactive Beryl occupied for any length of time and, just as for the diver Tom Daley, it was clearly an important form of relaxation. Brain scientists now believe that activities like knitting and Lego, which Mark Cavendish uses to unwind, have the same neurological impacts as meditation and mindfulness.

Individual start times in any time trial are generally spread at one-minute intervals over up to 2 hours and, as the fastest rider, Beryl was invariably seeded to set off last. She was always still among the very first to arrive. She liked to check the entire route and would do this on her bike if it was a shorter race of up to 25 miles or otherwise with Charlie driving. 'She would mostly check the road for potholes and sharp corners – but would be really taking it all in, surveying the scene and priming her body and mind,' says Pallister. As well as a long warm-up, Beryl would also always stretch. Pre-race was a time when she would only really speak if she needed something, and her rivals would get virtually no acknowledgement. The morning wind and rain did not stop Beryl from warming up for half an hour before the 1968 national '100', but, having been out along the A12 start near Brentwood and noted a series of traffic islands, she had privately dismissed the idea of lowering her own record below 4 hours.

Beryl then set off and, as she settled into a rhythm in her classic pale blue Morley club top, felt a pleasant surprise. It was one of those rare days that all cyclists savour. Rather than an incremental build-up of fatigue, she felt pent-up power and energy. Beryl usually rode with a basic stopwatch attached to her handlebars and, knowing that a mile would take 2 min. 24 sec. at an average speed of 25 mph, always had a relatively accurate idea of her progress. The rain did not cease and, as it rolled off the end of Beryl's nose down on to the gear cables that hung beneath her chin, the only movement in the top half of her body would come every few miles when she swept the timing display clear.

Beryl completed the first 25 miles in 59 min. 31 sec. No other woman had previously ridden under an hour over that distance. There were still 75 miles remaining, but as Beryl caught and passed the other women in the field she actually began to accelerate. She completed the second 25 miles in 59 min. 4 sec., and then the third in a scarcely believable 57 min. 4 sec. Charlie and Nim Carline, who had been darting all over the course between Romford and Marks Tey on their bikes, now knew that she was on schedule for another monumental achievement. Their point of reference was again not the other women or even the prospect of a competition record. It was the possibility of dipping below 4 hours and beating another men's course record. This stood at 4 hrs 2 min. and was held by John Greatwood, who had completed exactly the same route in the men's race earlier that day. The report in *Cycling* magazine described the exuberant Carline frequently breaking the Sunday morning quiet with raucous calls of 'Mek it crack!' every time Beryl whizzed by.

As the finish approached and her glistening wheels sliced through the morning layer of rain to create a relentless line of spray in her wake, Beryl had to blink before she could believe what her stopwatch was saying. She eased her body upright after passing the roadside chequered board to signify the finish and, as she noticed little coils of steam rising off her arms, a shiver went up her back. 'My time in retaining the title was 3 hrs 55 min. 5 sec. ... the first ride in less than 4 hours by a woman, and not by a slender margin at that,' she said. And how did she feel? 'Slightly annoyed at myself for not making it a 3.54 and at the weather gods for not giving us a better day. But there it was.' And there it stayed, too, lodged in the all-time record books for the rest of her life. It was the performance that she privately regarded as her athletic peak.

The final analysis showed that Beryl had bettered her own existing women's 100-mile record by more than 6 minutes and beaten Greatwood, the winner of the men's race that day, by 3 min. 23 sec. On a virtually identical bike she had also beaten Ray Booty's first ever sub-4-hour '100' by more than 3 minutes. Only three men had ever ridden 100 miles faster. In the final mile she had caught her friend and Morley teammate Maureen Pearson for 38 minutes.* Pearson, who would subsequently win the national 100-mile title, was initially confused at why people were cheering so loudly as she approached the finishing line. The answer was provided by the 'spine-tingling' sight of Beryl whizzing past her with a shout of encouragement. 'It must be hard for lay-folk, non-cyclists or others to appreciate what this performance means', wrote the *Cycling* reporter Mal Rees. 'It is comparable with the stupefaction that would result from a woman athlete beating the four-minute mile by a sizeable margin.'

*

It was a performance to compare with the 12-hour record she had set eleven months earlier, and Beryl was now increasingly in demand as a minor sporting celebrity. Shirley Pell became a close friend after first meeting the Burtons in 1954 and says that, by 1967, Beryl would get recognised and approached for an autograph during their occasional nights out to the opera at Leeds Grand Theatre. Beryl always felt duty-bound to represent her sport and would frequently also attend events that provided no personal benefit. In 1968, for example, she featured in a glossy

---

*Being 'caught for' is a phrase used commonly in time trialling. It refers to the amount of time that one rider had originally started before another competitor and has therefore lost as they are passed at that point of the race.

promotion for the AA magazine *Drive*, which involved a series of trips to Hertfordshire at her own expense. Beryl would also appear at various sporting dinners in London, and in her autobiography it is easy to sense a simmering resentment at how she was treated compared with most of the other leading sportspeople. 'The professionals were able to claim a fee for their time,' she noted. In only ever receiving expenses, she says that she 'always tried to play fair ... with Yorkshire thrift' and keep claims to a minimum. 'This meant that Charlie and I incurred personal costs which we did not mind doing in view of the occasions and the honour of being present,' she said. 'But I learned from experience that few, if any, acted as frugally as we.' This is all confirmed by some of Beryl's immaculately handwritten and calculated expenses claims, complete with receipts down to the last halfpenny, which have been retained in the Morley Town Hall and BBC archives.

Beryl was invited on to shows like the BBC's *Record Breakers*, where she was introduced by Roy Castle as perhaps 'the greatest sportswoman the world has ever known', and would usually stay in Kettering with her friends Brenda and Keith Robins whenever she was appearing in London. 'She was a great pal to me and had a wonderful sense of humour but she wasn't terribly chummy with her rivals – they were there to get beat,' says Brenda Robins, who was not herself a competitive cyclist. 'She didn't want to get involved with everyone she came into contact with. She would say, "I have got a private life as well and I am not going to give myself over". When she stayed, she always used to bring her own steak and cook it herself. She would have her knitting. I had hundreds of patterns and she would go through those. She didn't have a television but would always want to watch anything that was on, even if she did usually then talk all the way through.' Robins says that Beryl secretly 'loathed' many of the celebrity London events where she was required to make speeches, although she did like dressing up and 'looked magnificent, with amazing legs' in her evening outfits.

The social events that Beryl truly relished were, of course, those with fellow cyclists. Photographs from the annual RTTC prize presentation evenings confirm how she would wear a sparkling dress, earrings and necklace. She might also put on a wig or have her hair highlighted, straightened or styled in a bouffant. Denise and Ann Pallister would try to stay up the night before, with their curlers in, to keep their hair in place. Members of the Morley club would sleep on Beryl and Charlie's kitchen floor before being collected early on the Saturday morning by a club-hired minibus that would transport them all south. Beryl would always spend the entire evening dancing. She and her Morley friends would privately dismiss those cyclists who sat around the edges just talking about training as the 'pedal and crankers'.

During the winter months between November and January, Beryl would also spend almost every Saturday night at some club prize presentation dinner or other up and down the country. She was in huge demand as a guest of honour and rarely ever happier than in the company of other club cyclists, among whom she was also known as 'BB'. If the invite had come from far afield, Charlie would drive and often quietly depart mid-evening to have a sleep in the car before their late-night journey home. Had they stayed over, Beryl would then invariably cycle back in the morning regardless of the distance. If the dinner was within about 40 miles, she and Charlie would generally arrive on their bikes – with her evening dress folded in the saddlebag – and cycle home in the dark. As well as presenting the prizes and giving a short speech, Beryl would always be seen helping to wash the dishes and clear away tables and chairs at the end of the night. There was no payment for these appearances – although a bouquet of flowers was invariably presented – and such occasions became almost like an extended victory tour at the end of each season. If she had cycled, Beryl would simply place the bouquet under the jumper on her back as she pedalled home. She and Charlie were once stopped by police during one of these late-night journeys and, after discovering a trophy in Charlie's saddlebag, suspicions were only allayed by the sight of Beryl and her flowers. Clubmates would tell her that she looked like a flowerpot on two wheels.

For all her devotion to Yorkshire club life Beryl was always still attracted to different ways of testing herself, and with her fame at its peak during the 1960s she accepted several unusual international opportunities. Cyril Geoghegan, the manager of the men's South African team, had been struck by her world championship dominance and so invited her for a series of appearances and races. Charlie could not take this sort of time off work and, with Beryl jumping at the offer, he stayed behind with Denise. 'Six weeks of South African sunshine and cycling as opposed to an English winter required no deep thinking on my part,' she later said.

Beryl was treated like an A-list celebrity and, as well as long sunny days out on her bike and exhibition races against some of the best young male riders in South Africa, there were sight-seeing trips to safari parks and townships alongside barbecues with other notable sportspeople. It was several years before sporting sanctions were imposed on South Africa and, while Beryl described herself as 'not a political person', she was always interested in other cultures and became upset by an incident in Durban where she saw a group of black people rounded up and searched in the street by the police following reports of a theft. 'I thought it repugnant,' she said.

Another unique adventure arose in September 1968, when, four months after her sub-4-hour 100-mile time trial, Beryl was asked to compete in the Grand Prix des Nations race in France. It is hard to overstate the prestige at that time of an event that was regarded as the unofficial men's professional world time trial championships. In seventy editions of the race, which was won by the likes of Fausto Coppi, Eddy Merckx, Bernard Hinault and Jacques Anquetil, Beryl was both the only woman and the only amateur granted a starting place among the leading men's professionals.

It was the British cycling journalist Jock Wadley who first had the idea and, when he outlined some of Beryl's achievements, the organiser Félix Lévitan – who also co-directed the Tour de France – instantly agreed. The one caveat was that Beryl would start 12 minutes ahead of the men and, while not officially part of the 46-mile professional race, that meant showcasing herself in front of the packed closed roads around Paris before finishing at the Stade-Vélodrome Jacques Anquetil in Charenton-le-Pont. Ron Kitching had helped Beryl and Charlie with their travelling expenses to the French capital, where there was considerable media interest. France had limited history at this time of elite women's cycling (a solitary sprint bronze in 1964 was their only world championships medal), and the general expectation was that Beryl would be no more than a curiosity as the men's field swept past. 'When it was suggested that I would cover this tough course at a speed faster than 40 kph there was some shaking of heads and Gallic shrugs at the temerity of "L'Anglaise Burton" – I felt that the eyes of France were upon me,' said Beryl.

She stayed in a boarding house with Charlie and, after a steak and rice breakfast, rode the 10 miles to the commune of Auffargis. Her start time was 1.36 p.m., and at the registration she duly signed her name next to the misspelt words 'BURTON Berryl'. Beryl wore her pale blue and white Morley club jersey for the ride. Surrounded by a motorcade that included two gendarmes on motorbikes, a press car full of journalists and a support vehicle with spare wheels and the name 'Burton' on the top, Beryl later wrote that 'never have the Morley colours been carried with such an escort'. She was being treated like a leading men's professional in the Tour de France, and it was her most exhilarating day on a bike.

'Crowds of people collected in the villages, cheering and clapping and shouting encouragement,' she said. 'At every intersection along the route police were blowing their whistles. Some of them looked surprised, as though they had not expected me so soon.

I swung the bike about, picking my line at each corner, using as much road as I needed. What luxury! No cares about traffic or hazards. The streets were packed, mile after mile of cheering crowds, who lifted me along, a surge of sound in front and behind "Allez, la Britannique!" What a complete contrast to the reaction to our surreptitious events early on a Sunday morning in Britain.'

But then, as the Burton cavalcade crossed the River Seine at the Pont de Conflans and swung into the velodrome, disaster almost struck. Wadley's press car had already driven ahead to warn the organisers that Beryl would soon be arriving but found that they were in the middle of a devil-take-the-hindmost elimination track race. It was a means of entertaining the crowds before the riders arrived. When informed that Beryl was approaching, the lead official was incredulous. 'Nonsense,' he said. 'Even if she is averaging 40 kph, she won't be here just yet.' Wadley looked at his watch and simply replied: 'But she's doing 42 kph.' The official still did not believe him. 'And thus it was that I swung on to the track to find myself caught up with three riders in the final laps of an elimination race,' wrote Beryl. 'Amid much hullabaloo and scurrying, excited officials waved me round for another circuit because the timekeepers were not ready. My Grand Prix des Nations was longer, by an extra circuit of the large velodrome, than that of all the professionals behind me.' Beryl had not been caught by any of the best men's riders and, despite an additional distance of almost a quarter of a mile, her final time of 1 hr 45 min. 22 sec. was only 12 minutes slower than the winner, Felice Gimondi, who had set a new record average speed.

Gimondi is one of only six men in cycling history to have won all three Grand Tours (of France, Spain and Italy), but the media reaction in continental Europe settled on Beryl. She was already known for her world titles in track and road racing, but this was her best discipline of all – the individual time trial – and she was showing that a woman could compete with the best professional men. The magazine *International Cycle Sport* said that the Grand

Prix des Nations 'had an unexpected star', and its reporter wrote that the 'most astonished man I have seen at a cycling event' was the gendarme at the crossroads in Choisy-le-Roi who had discounted the possibility of Beryl staying in front of the men. The description of the scene also tells you plenty about how women's sport was reported: 'The gendarme's face was full of admiration for the outstanding athletic merit of the cyclist yet – belonging as it did to a Frenchman – was shaped for a whistle of appreciation that this really was a girl, with a saucy hair-do, a nice complexion and a pair of legs that would be easy on the eye at any time.'

The French were smitten, and Beryl was the subject of a lengthy report in *Le Monde* by Jean Bobet, the brother of the triple Tour de France winner Louison Bobet and himself a former cyclist, who authored the acclaimed book *Tomorrow, We Ride*. In an article entitled 'La dame à bicyclette', Bobet wrote that Beryl 'did the job with a smile and dignity that we had believed incompatible with women's cycle racing'. Another French newspaper, *Dimanche Soir*, described her as 'a feminine Jacques Anquetil'. It was an experience that Beryl savoured. Speaking almost twenty years later, in 1985, she said that 'whenever the going in life seems a little hard I close my eyes and savour again the thousands of bike-mad French fans shouting "Allez, la Britannique!"'

It also all left a question. What on earth next? Beryl was scaling new heights by the year. She had won seven world titles and, in setting historically long-lasting records, proved that women could reach a once unimaginable level of excellence in endurance sport. Aged thirty-one, she was still gripped by a desire to achieve even if the source of that motivation had seemed subtly to shift. Whereas early in her career she would often refer to the honour of representing her country, the Morley cyclists and her family alongside her experiences as a sickly child, the driving force seemed to become ever more personal. Winning and exploring the absolute limits of her athletic ability were the priority. That would increasingly also mean seeking to race directly against the very

26. Beryl became the star attraction in Paris after being invited
to race with the world's best male professionals.

best British men. 'Sometimes at the beginning of the season I get
halfway through a training run and feel so fed up I could chuck
the bike over the next hedge and forget it all,' she told that gathering of the SJA. 'But then I think of all those after my titles and I
just press on. I love racing. I am never really satisfied even when
I put up a world record. I always have an urge to do better. One
cannot go forward to new and greater things simply by harking
back.' So it was during the early winter months of 1969 that the
idea for a new challenge was formed. And it would be something
more audacious and physically demanding than anything she had
previously attempted.

Part Two

OBSESSED

9

The Mersey 24

Hidden deep among Beryl Burton's personal papers, photographs and correspondence is one striking insight into what drew her to bike racing. It is contained within some notes that Beryl herself composed on a typewriter in 1970, exactly a year after the most crushing disappointment of her career. 'One thing I can't stand is an easy ride,' she wrote. 'If I don't win, I want to feel shattered. This may sound strange, but I've got to believe that I've ridden myself into the ground. Or I'm not satisfied.' As friends, rivals and family members looked on with increasing awe and bafflement at how she continued long after repeatedly winning every major race, this need to push her body provides one core explanation. There is something cleansing, cathartic even, about riding a bike to the point of exhaustion and, in purely athletic terms, arguably the most staggering ride of Beryl's career was not a victory. It was a defeat that represented the single greatest regret of her career. It was a defeat that also invaded her body and psyche like no other.

To witness every shade of cycling's wondrous kaleidoscope you need only visit the Farndon Sports and Social Club, just off the A534 near Chester, at the end of July each year. At one level, the British 24-hour time trial championship is one of sport's most eye-watering tests of stamina, perseverance, dedication, planning and solitary fortitude. At another, it is a brilliantly eccentric annual reunion for like-minded amateurs. The range of abilities is vast and, while the prize of a national championships or perhaps even a competition record is the focus for the elite, just being there is sufficient for the majority. The scale might be hugely reduced but, with camper vans, caravans, gazebos, tents, mobile kitchens, toilets and feeding stations strategically soon appearing in the nearby garden and grass verges, it is something like the Glastonbury Festival colliding with the London Marathon. The support teams are there to provide everything from impromptu kerbside massages and new clothing to food, drink, lighting and crucially timed emotional support. It is all for one excruciating aim: to help their rider cycle as far as they possibly can in 24 hours. By the finish, the riders frequently require several people to lift them from their bikes and the surrounding roads somehow resemble a battlefield rather than the climax to a sporting event.

Even half a century on from the 1969 national championships, which was the most famous 24-hour time trial of them all, some of the key characters were still in attendance at the 2019 edition. They included Ruth Williams and Christine Minto, who, with Wyn Maddock, were also the first three women permitted to ride the event in 1967. 'I had been watching since I was a tiny girl and had wanted to ride for so long,' said Williams. 'I would write to the committee but they weren't interested. The key was getting the other women to put pressure on their husbands. When we first raced, the men were all saying, "Don't go too hard and, if you feel tired, you must stop riding".' And what did she think of that? 'I felt like making chips of them.' The anticipation that subsequently surrounded the 'Mersey 24' on the weekend of 26 and 27 July 1969 began simply with the news earlier in the year that Beryl had submitted an entry form. 'She had won everything and held every other women's record,' said Williams. 'But she had never done a 24-hour race and the 24 is different from anything else.' The women's record was held by Minto at 420.05 miles – a distance that was only 143 miles more than Beryl had achieved two years earlier in half the time. The men's record stood at 496.37 miles. But Beryl's mind was not fixed on either record. She had

1. Beryl and Charlie Burton adored the Yorkshire Dales and their daughter, Denise, would simply accompany them on the back of Beryl's bike during day-long rides well in excess of 100 miles.

2. Beryl was a special guest at the Six Day London men's professional event on the day after her historic ride of 277.25 miles in 12 hours. She had also just won her seventh world title and is pictured in her rainbow jersey, complete with the 'Jacques Anquetil' bike on which she set records lasting more than forty years.

3. Fans and fellow cyclists were fascinated by Beryl Burton. She is warming up here in 1963 at the Herne Hill Velodrome following her fourth world pursuit title in five years.

4. Beryl knew only one way to race and would routinely simply attack and ride away from the fastest women of her generation.

5. Beryl Burton was the best women's time triallist in the world from the late 1950s until the early 1980s. She is photographed here during the glorious summer of 1976, when she set both her 25- and 50-mile records and averaged 26.67 mph in winning the 18th of 25 straight Best All-Rounder titles. Note the huge single front chain ring and minimal back gearing. Beryl always rode with her right hand slightly higher than her left. Daughter Denise thinks the habit may have been formed when she nervously started racing and wanted a brake in immediate reach.

6–7. By comparing one of Beryl's original bikes – the TI-Raleigh she used during the 1980s – and a modern time trial machine inside the wind tunnel at Silverstone, experts were able to finally answer one of cycling's great debates. Just how fast would Beryl Burton be today? The amazing results are revealed in Chapter 14.

8. The stunning 60-feet-wide mural that was painted by local artists and unveiled in Morley town centre to commemorate Beryl Burton following her death in 1996.

9. The unique gold medal that was commissioned in 1967 by *Cycling* magazine both to recognise Beryl's 12-hour record that surpassed even the men and to acknowledge women's exclusion from the Olympics.

10. Beryl's 1959 3,000 m pursuit gold medal – the first world cycling championship that was won by a British woman.

11. Despite being the world's greatest female cyclist, Beryl Burton always loved competing in the most local club time trials in Yorkshire.

12. Beryl Burton, aged fifty-eight, still proudly sporting the Morley Cycling Club jersey and riding flat out in defiance of doctors' orders during her last major race: the centenary 50-mile time trial in October 1995.

13. A beaming Beryl Burton, photographed at the pinnacle of her powers in 1968 immediately after becoming the first woman to ride 100 miles in less than 4 hours. She won her campaign to race directly against men the following year. 'Beryl trounces the men!' was one typical *Cycling* magazine headline in 1972 after she beat a field of 120 male riders.

very simply set her heart that year on becoming the first person – male or female – to cycle 500 miles in a day. 'I felt sure that I had it in me to record a mileage that would make the sport buzz even more than the half-day rides I had accomplished,' she said.

There was a further added spice. The existing and previous men's record holders – respectively Nim Carline and Eric Matthews – had also entered, as had Roy Cromack. Aged twenty-nine, Cromack was a stylish time triallist who, like Beryl, was renowned for his versatility across a wide range of distances. He had represented Great Britain the previous year at the 1968 Olympics in the 100 km team time trial, and was a national championship medallist in distances ranging from the 4,000 m track pursuit through to 25- and 50-mile time trials as well as 12 hours. He had also ridden for his country the previous year in the Peace Race, which was the amateur equivalent of the Tour de France. The three star men – Carline, Matthews and Cromack – were themselves also all targeting 500 miles and *Cycling* magazine had commissioned a special gold medal as an incentive for the first rider to accomplish that feat. There was respectively £10, £5 and £3 for the first three men. The women's event had different organisers – the Merseyside Ladies Cycling Association, rather than the Mersey Roads Club – and was technically a separate event, with no prize money on offer.

It was an anomaly that did not bother Beryl and, with the cycling community now acutely aware of her capabilities, the day was again structured in a way that would permit her every opportunity to challenge the best men. Just as at the Otley 12 race two years earlier, the women began shortly after the men and Beryl, at 6.23 p.m. on what was a Saturday evening, was the third of the women to follow a field of seventy-eight men. Carline had set off 18 minutes earlier, at 6.05 p.m., Cromack at 6.10 p.m. and Matthews, the defending national champion, at 6.14 p.m. The gaps, then, were significantly larger than the 2 minutes that Mike McNamara had started before Beryl at the Otley event, but this

27. The grass verges were lined with onlookers of all ages as Beryl began her quest for 500 miles in a single day.

would last double the time. The pre-race sense of anticipation was perhaps greater than any domestic time trial before or since. 'I always knew when Beryl was near me in a time trial,' said Williams. 'Every lay-by was suddenly full of people waiting to catch sight of her. Once she caught you and had gone past, that was it. You didn't see anyone again. There was a fascination with her.'

That much is confirmed by some rare video footage of Beryl starting in the rural village of Tarvin, just a few miles east of Chester. She looks relaxed in a crisp white British national champion's jersey, complete with red and blue stripes, and is chatting with some of the club cyclists who have come to see her off. A spare tubular tyre had been attached beneath her saddle and, as well as the usual frame-fitted pump, parcels of food can be seen bulging from her back pockets. 'There were hordes of people just clapping,' said Minto, the last rider to depart. Tommy Barlow, the competition secretary, was handing out liquorice torpedoes to the riders. Charlie is also centre stage, wearing a flat cap and striped jacket while beaming proudly at the fuss being made of his wife. They both look confident, and there is a magical moment as Beryl sets off through the throng of people who, having spilled off the crowded grass verge on to the road, instinctively move back to create a narrow path that was only just sufficient for a moving bike. It was like the parting of bodies you see on a Tour de France mountain stage. Beryl, though, would soon be where she was at her most comfortable: all alone in the middle of the rolling British countryside and simply attempting to ride a bike faster than anyone else.

*

The first 24-hour races were organised in the 1880s to showcase both the reliability and the safety of the bicycle. As time trialling blossomed, the inaugural Mersey Roads event was held in 1937, and it has since only ever been interrupted twice – by the Second World War and then by the Covid-19 pandemic of 2020. The basic premise is similar to any time trial. Entrants depart at one-minute intervals and they must simply ride, without pacing, as far as they can in the allotted time. Sleep is optional and avoided completely by the most serious competitors. Back in the earlier era, there was also a rule that riders could not cover the same part of the course twice. It meant that the route travelled much further into Wales and Shropshire than today, and riders would be sent down various remote country lanes only to perform a U-turn before being sent down another random and often quite hilly road. That approach is now deemed excessively impractical, and the riders simply have a series of circuits, usually between 9 and 20 miles, that they repeatedly navigate. 'The helpers can station themselves in a few places, and it is faster, but it must be boring,' said Minto. 'I preferred touring around rather than going in circles.'

Beryl was never one to predict what she might do, but did say that she felt 'as fit as I'd ever been in my life', and her incredible start to the race confirmed that assessment. The rain was initially steady but, just as on the roads around Otley two years earlier, Beryl soon settled into a rhythm that would see her ride straight through a field of the country's best male cyclists. She was pushing a typically colossal 107-inch gear but, whereas in Otley she rode with little expectation and some caution, she attacked the Mersey course with venom. It was exactly a week after Neil Armstrong had become the first man to set foot on the moon and, as darkness descended and the stars lit up the night sky, she was obliterating the men's field. Depending on your point of view, it was the finest or the most foolish passage of cycling in her entire life. Perhaps both.

'There was no worrying about blowing up,' Beryl said. 'I went for the target as though I was riding a 10-miler.' After 32 miles Beryl's lead over Carline and Cromack was respectively already more than 2 and 4 minutes. Charlie felt alarm and excitement in equal measure. He shouted out, 'There's a long way to go,' as she passed, but there would be no backing down. Beryl felt fantastic. Aside from a brief stop to put on lights, a pale blue jumper and what *Cycling* magazine called 'a natty woollen hat', she ploughed rapidly on. With the time approaching 10 p.m., Cromack's rear light unexpectedly came into view. This was a rider who had recently been selected for the British Olympic men's team and yet was being caught for 13 minutes. Beryl clearly felt supremely confident and had the nerve to call out, 'What's keeping you, Roy?' as she passed. There was no answer. 'A brief merging of our front lights and then he was behind me in the darkness and I was alone again with my thoughts,' Beryl said.

Cromack remained unfazed. He had worked out a schedule to surpass 500 miles and was sticking to that plan, even if he also later admitted that he could not have possibly stayed with Beryl. 'I thought she could not last at that rate but, to be honest, there wasn't a lot I could do about it,' he said. The riders were now heading into North Wales, and the scene at midnight is described by Cromack's younger brother Geoffrey. 'We had parked up on a long stretch of road and were waiting for Roy,' he says. 'We saw the light up ahead and got ready with food and a bottle of water. But, as the cyclist got closer, we realised that it was Beryl. We used to see Beryl out training down our way near Doncaster. She would always be riding alone. They were both very natural pedallers – no sideways movement – but Roy tended to ride on the tops of the handlebars whereas Beryl raced always on the drops. She steamed by at a terrific speed. It was an awesome sight.'

Beryl had gone through the first 100 miles in 4 hrs 11 min. It put her 9 minutes ahead of Carline, the existing record holder, while the buffer to Cromack was now 17 minutes. It was also 7 minutes faster than her time at this stage of the shorter Otley 12. The lead continued to grow between midnight and 2 a.m., with Beryl catching Carline – her rhubarb farm boss – for 18 minutes and extending her advantage over Cromack to 23 minutes. The subsequent report in *Cycling* described her as 'pounding away, creating havoc behind, making timekeepers check and recheck their watches'. By 4.02 a.m., and nearly 10 hours after she had started, Beryl had caught all seventy-eight of the men. Many of them had set off over an hour before her. Beryl said that she was still 'feeling great, way ahead of everyone, passing the checks and knots of club folk to whistles of amazement'. Ruth Williams was in the race headquarters where the time checks were being relayed back. 'Nobody could believe what was happening,' she said.

Beryl was now at her zenith as a cyclist. She could have targeted and probably succeeded in any available aim in women's cycling that year but was so motivated by the 500-mile landmark that she had taken the unprecedented step of taking six weeks off work to dedicate herself to training. She had also decided to miss

28. Beryl would emulate and then even surpass
Nim Carline's extreme training regime.

the national road and pursuit championships and would even make herself unavailable for the world championships. Everything had been about delivering over 24 hours. In June she had won the national 25-mile championship and then cycled more than 200 miles back home to Yorkshire from Chippenham. Even more improbably, she did the same after winning the national 50-mile championship in Essex in a new championship record of 1 hr 56 min. 15 sec. only thirteen days before the Mersey 24. It had completed a fortnight in which she covered in excess of 1,200 miles.

There was, as ever, no science to these methods. More was simply better, regardless of how she felt or what else was going on in her life. It made for some punishing days. Carline's firm belief was that you should do 100 miles every day for the six weeks leading up to the national 24-hour championships. And so Beryl did the same, sometimes more, albeit with one additional caveat.

Whereas Carline would be slumped in a chair and soon fall asleep when he finished his training, Beryl refused to compromise on her usual domestic routine. 'I used to train for about 8 hours a day and then come home to all the housework,' she said. 'I always made sure I was back in time to cook Charlie's dinner, and I stood ironing for about 3 hours. The household is my responsibility.' Beryl had also just accepted the position of president of the West Ardsley Townswomen's Guild and, according to Mary Turner, the former secretary, 'did an awful lot of work for us and attended lots of meetings' during that year.

What Beryl did not tell any of her friends or clubmates was that she had begun to feel pain in her right knee in the weeks leading up to the race. Her solution? Dismiss the sensation and continue training in the same way. 'But the condition grew worse and I wondered if I should ride,' she later said. 'My instinct and outlook told me that I should. There was no point in trying for anything other than a record. In myself I was very fit, clocking up great mileages in spite of my knee, feeling that, if I was to ride, I could not miss a day's training. I was determined that nobody should know. It was perhaps foolhardy ... but I had set my heart on victory and a record which would top 500 miles.'

Cromack's methodology was very different. He had virtually grown up on his bike in Warmsworth, from where he would make the 15-mile daily commutes to the Percy Jackson Grammar School. His three A levels were in pure maths, applied maths and physics. He became a maths teacher at Tadcaster Grammar School and later joined the Royal Air Force. As they do for Beryl, his friends and family all still use the words 'single-minded' and 'disciplined' to describe him, but he was more calculated and careful in his approach. Cromack had devised his schedule on an even-paced curve that would get him to just over 500 miles, and he remained within 2 minutes of his plan during the first half of the race. He also had a theory about his gearing and would ride no more than 82 inches for the vast majority of the race. 'He had a mathematician's brain, but he could suffer,' says Geoffrey. That much was evident a year earlier when he amazed fellow riders and team officials in the gruelling 14-day Peace Race by completing the course despite suffering from bronchitis. Cromack regarded excessively long training rides as destructive and, despite also aiming to cover more than 500 miles, had never previously ridden further than 220 miles. He had also only once cycled through the night and, as dawn broke and the first half of the race was complete, he seriously considered stopping. 'He was at a low ebb,' says Geoffrey. 'He knew that he was well behind Beryl. We massaged his legs. He took off the leggings, cap, long-sleeved shirt and lights, but we really had to cajole him to go on.'

Beryl had ridden 268 miles during that first 12 hours – only 9 miles short of her record over that distance. Cromack was second with 259.5 miles, while Carline, who was now noticeably slowing, had covered 256.5 miles. Carline knew that 500 miles was slipping out of reach and stopped later that morning after 291 miles. Fuelled by bread, jam, marshmallows and a Complan liquid drink, Cromack's bad patch began to fade and he maintained his rhythm and schedule. A subtle but important change to the pattern in the time checks duly began to emerge. Beryl had amassed a 21-minute lead after 200 miles, but the rate at which she was gaining time had stabilised and, by 326 miles, had risen more slowly to 26 minutes. The expectation around the course was still that Beryl had built an unassailable advantage that would result in a record to surpass even her 12-hour ride two years earlier.

What only Beryl and Charlie knew, however, was that the discomfort in the weeks leading up to the race had been steadily building. In her autobiography, written some sixteen years later, Beryl described for the first time what she went through during the race. She had begun to feel a manageable ache at 60 miles but decided to plough on 'knowing that I was taking a calculated risk'. By the morning, and after 12 hours had elapsed, that ache had become an acute pain and was something different from anything she had ever experienced. 'It seemed to come from inside the joints,' she said. Aside from stopping briefly to take off her lights, she would make a second, much longer, morning break, during which she asked Charlie to massage her knees. He in turn reprimanded her for going so fast through the night and not stopping to take a proper feed.

Beryl was adamant that it would have made no difference. 'There had been no bad patch,' she said. 'From a riding point of view I was in good shape. My leg muscles could still answer the call.' That Cromack was not making significant inroads into Beryl's actual lead supports this analysis and, at 346 miles, her advantage had only been reduced – even including the massage – to 23 minutes. Her subsequent collapse would be abrupt and was later described by John Lewis, who was one of Cromack's helpers, as 'pitiful' to watch. 'The determination was there but the legs just would not respond,' he said. Beryl's face rarely gave much away when she was riding. Her expression was generally focused and impassive – much to the irritation of the *Cycling* photographer, Bernard Thompson – but her eyes would turn noticeably glazed and hollow as the inevitable dawned. When she then again pulled up, it was because the pain in her knees was screaming at a pitch that would be impossible to dismiss for the remaining 7 hours. And so it was, at just after 11 a.m. on the Sunday, and more than 16 hours and 355 miles after setting off, that Beryl dismounted just north of the Shropshire market town of Wem. Charlie helped her into the back of their Cortina, where, with the back seat down, she could finally stretch out. 'The veins behind her knees were bulging and felt like plastic tubes,' says Charlie. 'The muscles were like wire as well.'

Beryl eventually looked up to her husband and conceded defeat. 'My legs won't move,' she said. The backs of her knees were so tender that she could not bear to touch them for several days. She then moved to the side of the road, where the physical agony was soon compounded by the sight of Cromack pedalling by with

29. Beryl was annihilating the men's and women's records
but began to feel acute knee pain during the morning.

a reciprocal shout of 'What's keeping you, Beryl?' Cromack later
told the cycling historian Peter Whitfield that it was an 'ungen-
tlemanly' gesture. Not that Beryl cared. 'Roy was pulling out a
tremendous ride,' she said. 'I could perhaps have faced the pain
– and I could have ridden all-out in an exceedingly tough long-
distance race – but to do both was just a little too much.' Soon
after re-catching Beryl, and on being told that she had retired,
Cromack stopped at the village shop in Wolverley to buy the
biggest ice cream that he could find. 'It was not to cool me down –
just to celebrate,' he said. There was shock when the message was
relayed back to the race headquarters that the usually indestructible Beryl had stopped. 'I couldn't believe it,' said Ruth Williams.

Beryl had completed just over 70 per cent of the original 500-
mile target, and her retirement lifted much of the pressure on
Cromack. With Carline also out and Matthews poised to eventually amass 492.88 miles, he was a clear leader over the final third of

the race. The weather, which had been mild, largely windless and dry following the wet start on Saturday, also held and Cromack's schedule proved perfectly judged. He ground to a halt and collapsed on to a patch of grass shortly after 6 p.m. on the Sunday with 10 seconds of his 24 hours remaining. He had completed 507 miles and, facing him, was the aptly named Silent Woman pub.

Beryl had been on schedule for between 530 and 540 miles. The magnitude both of her early performance and of Cromack's eventual distance was underlined by the 28-year gap before his record was surpassed. Christine Minto also set a women's record that day – 427.86 miles – which stood until 1983 and has since been improved by Christina Murray to 490.28 miles. Remarkably, Beryl was on course for a distance that would have lasted as the men's or women's record until 2011 and, as of 2022, would still have been around 40 miles further than any other woman.

There is, though, only qualified respect for Beryl's record attempt among the 24-hour fraternity. Jon Williams, who was watching roadside as a boy in 1969 and now organises the Mersey 24, says that it was simply 'too early' for Beryl to have been racing so hard and that the real competition always starts in the final hours, which she never reached. 'The reality is that she failed,' he says, with a directness that Beryl would certainly have accepted. Minto also has only limited sympathy and agrees that Beryl simply misjudged the event. 'She did not ride it sensibly. She trained with Nim Carline, who was a big, powerful man and really thrashed around on his bike. Beryl was a much smoother pedaller and my personal thought is just that she used far too big a gear.' When I ask Minto whether anyone could have suggested a different approach, she just laughs. 'Beryl did her own thing – she wouldn't ask for advice and didn't care what other people thought.'

Explanations both for Beryl's failure to finish and the decision never to ride another 24-hour time trial remain mixed. Minto suggests that it 'dawned on her that she had bitten off more than she could chew'. Those closest to Beryl think that she simply over-trained. 'She was supremely fit and thrashing everyone in sight – the problem was just that she put in thousands of miles and that was too much,' says Malcolm Cowgill, the Morley secretary. Charlie concurs. 'She was on to that ride,' he says. 'It was eyeballs out from the start. She went past the whole field and then suddenly it all stiffened up. She'd over-trained.'

It was a day that still revealed just about every facet of Beryl's personality. She was brave and, like all of the greatest sportspeople, had an optimism and drive that crossed normal boundaries. She knew that her knees were injured before the race and yet refused to compromise or adapt. Instead, she was willing simply to ride herself to the point of potentially permanent injury. Peter Whitfield believes that she would have topped 500 miles and beaten Cromack were it not for the injury, but noted that, given her knee problems and the size of the challenge, 'no sensible person would even have started that particular race'. *Cycling* magazine reported that 'even the greatest female cyclist the world has ever known finally found her limit'. This analysis irritated Beryl, but she still opted not to say anything in the immediate aftermath for fear of looking like a sore loser. She would eventually describe the idea that she had 'blown up' as both 'galling and nonsensical'. Beryl adamantly believed that her only problem was her knees and the failure to ease back before the event. Not just on her cycling but all the work around the house. Lower gears, Beryl also argued, would have inflamed her knee more quickly. 'It is a wrong conclusion,' she said. 'I had been riding high gears most of my racing life.' Beryl, who was never guilty of exaggerated boasts, was also convinced, 'without a shadow of doubt', that she would have 'succeeded' and ridden more than 500 miles had it not been for her knee injury.

Beryl's definition that day of 'succeeded' helps to explain why she never again rode another 24-hour time trial. Her objective was not to become the first woman to ride 500 miles in a day – something that has still never been done and which she could surely have subsequently achieved – but simply to be the first person to achieve that feat. Having watched Cromack achieve that dream, she saw no value in missing her favourite races to focus on such a long ride. 'I couldn't just turn up and have a go,' she said the following year. An attempt to ride the national 100-mile time trial only two weeks later underlined the damage that had been inflicted on her knees. Beryl was leading but was again forced to abandon in severe pain, this time at 50 miles. Maureen Pearson was the unexpected beneficiary but took no delight in winning her one and only national title after passing Beryl in tears at the side of the road. 'It was heartbreaking – she was crying her eyes out and thought that her career was over,' she says.

The talk in cycling was of an era having ended, but the truth was that Beryl simply needed to accept an extended rest. She was then rewarded several months later, when she lowered her own competition record over 50 miles to 1 hr 55 min. 4 sec. The lasting memory of 1969, however, would be the Mersey 24 and a performance that deserves greater recognition. Not for the outcome but for the intention and the spotlight this remarkable 16-hour spectacle had shone on the sometimes irrational mindset of a champion. It was T. S. Eliot who wrote that 'only those who will risk going too far can possibly find out how far one can go'. Beryl did not achieve her goal but, by attempting something so outlandish and then almost carrying it off, she had reached a destination that few athletes ever approach.

10

An Iron Curtain Rises

It was an otherwise routine morning at Nim Carline's farm in Morley when work was unexpectedly interrupted by some unusual visitors. Two men who spoke barely a word of English had arrived at one of the barns. Through a combination of gestures and words it was eventually communicated that, no, they were not much interested in buying some rhubarb and, yes, they were actually cycling coaches. From the Soviet Union. And they had heard all about this farm and so decided to drop by to see where Beryl Burton worked. Carline shrugged. He had no issue with letting visitors have a look around. Sheila Broadbent, another cyclist from Morley, also worked with Beryl and Carline in the rhubarb sheds and was later told the story. 'At that time she was winning everything – the world championships both on the track and on the road, and they wanted to see this girl, what she did,' she says. 'They came to watch her work.' It is unclear whether this was the sole purpose of their visit to England but, having watched some digging and lifting of rhubarb, they were gone. Back, presumably to Tula, which was the base for the Soviet Union's national cycling squad, more than 2,000 miles away.

It is an extraordinary anecdote, underlining not just the Soviet Union's determination to dominate international sport but also their respect for Beryl, who had become this almost immovable obstacle in women's cycling. There were only three women's events at the world cycling championships at this time. In the sprint, riders from the Soviet Union would win 19 gold, 15 silver and

30. Beryl Burton laboured in all weather conditions on a farm
and her working patterns were studied by Soviet coaches.

7 bronze medals in the twenty-two years from the first women's
world championship in 1958 until 1980. The unpredictability of
road racing made it more difficult to dominate, but they were still
easily the most successful nation between 1958 and 1974, winning
3 gold, 7 silver and 10 bronze medals. The pursuit, though, was
different, and Beryl had spent almost a decade regularly beating
the very best specialist riders from what was a full-time, state-
funded and vastly populated system. Despite the depth of the
Soviet team, Beryl had also simply ridden away from even their
strongest riders to win both the 1960 and the 1967 road race titles.

It is a curiosity of her career, then, that world championship
success should recede during the late 1960s at a time when she was
still getting faster in domestic time trials. Beryl did win a pursuit
silver and 3 more bronze medals from 1967 until her last world
championship appearance in 1974, but this would coincide with
the start of eight consecutive victories for riders from the Soviet
Union. Six were achieved by just one woman: Tamara Garkushina,
who rode nothing internationally except for the 3,000 m pursuit

and about whom virtually nothing of any detail is publicly known. A 1967 report in *Cycling* described Garkushina's build as like that of 'a top man sprinter', while Beryl said that her muscular body made her feel like 'a drainpipe'. With a state-sponsored doping programme having later been revealed in East Germany, considerable suspicion has since developed about whether the Soviet Union's extraordinary medal haul in this period was also chemically enhanced. Bernadette Swinnerton competed in the world championships for Great Britain four times with Beryl from the late 1960s before retiring disillusioned in 1972 to focus on her teaching career. 'I went as the British sprint champion and, every year, I got through to the quarter-finals, got a Russian and was knocked out,' she says. 'It was so off-putting for everybody. You knew that you couldn't get anywhere, so there was no point doing it. Their bodies were ridiculous.'

Documenting the start and true extent of what did ultimately become an ingrained doping system inside Russia during the twenty-first century remains problematic. Unlike in East Germany, which underwent such a public reckoning with the release of the Stasi files following the fall of the Berlin Wall in 1989, in Russia the end of the Cold War has provided limited additional transparency. And, despite being one of the most striking success stories in any sport, there has only ever been the most cursory media analysis or acknowledgement of the Soviet Union women's cycling team. So is it reasonable to suspect that Beryl may have been unfairly denied further world titles? Or does that sweepingly overlook the human stories and achievements of a sporting system that was decades ahead of its time? And what became of champions like Garkushina? What did they make of Beryl Burton? And is it naive to assume that Beryl herself, who was ultimately still more successful than any Soviet rider, never succumbed to temptation? Sports history emphatically tells us that we cannot ignore these questions, even if the answers may sometimes prove nuanced, incomplete or unpalatable.

*

It took weeks of exchanging encrypted messages to set up but, with the simple click of a button on Zoom, there he was. Dr Grigory Rodchenkov. The man described as 'the mastermind' behind arguably the biggest scandal in sports history. He was seated in front of a plain white blind and wearing a check shirt, dark glasses and balaclava. Dr Rodchenkov had been under police protection somewhere so secret in the United States that the location was unknown even to his attorney, Jim Walden. 'They are desperate to silence him,' explained Walden, referring to the Russian government. And why? 'My head contains secrets of incredible calibre – a tsunami,' declared Rodchenkov, the former head of Moscow's anti-doping laboratory. The first part of that tsunami ripped through international sport between 2016 and 2020, culminating with the two-year expulsion from all major competition of an official Russia team. The Kremlin had dismissed Rodchenkov's testimony as 'slander', but key allegations of state-organised cheating were substantiated following an investigation initiated by the World Anti-Doping Agency. These centred on the years between 2012 and 2016, notably on how the urine samples of Russian athletes were systematically switched during the 2014 Sochi Olympics, but Rodchenkov is preparing further claims regarding the period before the dissolution of the Soviet empire in 1991.

Rodchenkov specifically pinpoints the period after the 1968 Mexico Olympics as when 'for sure I know steroids got introduced in a wide scale' internationally. 'It was quite equal opportunities for each country.' He says that detecting anabolic steroids remained impossible until 1976, when doping controls were first mandated and, even then, the drugs simply became 'more effective and advanced'. By the 1980s, when the record books in women's athletics and swimming were rewritten, he claims that the Americans and the East Germans, as well as the Soviet Union, had 'everything, whatever you need'.

The media reporting of that time, supplemented by later academic study, broadly echoes this timeline. The anabolic steroid Turinabol was first manufactured in East Germany in 1965 and had become a systematic part of their doping programme by 1974. Misha Dzhindzhikhashvili, a Soviet sprinter and now a sports journalist for the Associated Press, says that he was already being offered anabolic steroids in 1967 at the age of only seventeen. Rodchenkov claimed that there was an archive in the Soviet Union related to 'pharmacological schemes' that 'disappeared' after the 1980 Moscow Olympics. Bleak realities had also become evident across numerous cycling countries following the death in 1967 of the British rider Tom Simpson, whose autopsy revealed traces of amphetamines. The sport's governing body, the UCI, were clearly becoming alarmed and first constructed makeshift doping controls at the 1966 world championships, although *Cycling* magazine reported how some riders dodged the tests without any sanction by simply claiming that they were unable to produce a urine sample. 'Nobody was brave enough to tackle doping,' says Swinnerton.

The very fact that East Germany was punching as a virtual equal in Olympic sport with the United States and the Soviet Union by the 1970s, however, suggests their approach was uniquely aggressive. They were a comparatively tiny country with no history of major sporting success before the late 1960s. The British swimmers Sharron Davies and June Croft, who were themselves denied Olympic gold medals by East Germans in 1980, say that their Soviet rivals during the 1970s did not provoke such suspicion. 'It was incredibly obvious with the East Germans,' says Davies. 'With the Russian swimmers, you could always see the progression. They invested in sport. They institutionalised it. It was still a little bit brutal, a little bit inhumane, and done in an Iron Curtain way. They found talent by giving them no choice and training them like crazy. I have a Russian friend, who was picked from school and taken from her family and taken to a training facility. But she was never given any drugs. There is a massive distinction.'

This chimes with the testimony of Grigory Vorobiev, one of the most senior Soviet sports doctors between 1959 and 1996, who in an interview with the *New York Times* before his death in 2019 suggested there was ad hoc rather than systematic doping during the 1970s. He also constantly asserted the Soviet work ethic and the vast importance of winning at sport following the Second World War, when an entire state structure was created to identify the very best young athletes and maximise their talent. The USSR finished behind only the United States at the 1952 Olympics, before topping the medals table in 1956, 1960, 1972, 1976 and 1980. At a time when Beryl was amateur in the most absolute possible terms, she was directly told that the Soviets had 'combed the country (population 240 million) searching and training riders to break the Burton/Reynders stronghold'. She was up against what was, in its own focused and uncompromising way, something of a forerunner to the winning machine that Sir Dave Brailsford would create in British cycling, following the introduction in 1997 of Lottery funding.

*

Around 200 km south of Moscow is the ancient city of Tula, which, having once been the Russian epicentre for bare-knuckle fighting, was where a concrete velodrome was built in 1896 that became a focal point for the local community. It was still the only velodrome in the entire empire when the Soviet Union was formed in 1922 and, with its single wooden stand on the back straight (seats painted in the white, blue and red of Russia) and simple complex of changing rooms on the home straight, still exudes an unmistakable allure. 'It's a legendary, almost mythical place and it was where numerous champions were made,' says Marina Kotchetova, whose mother, Lubow, was the 1958 world pursuit champion, Beryl's first major Soviet rival and later Garkushina's coach and mentor.

Lubow's wider life story helps set a wider context for the Soviet Union that had emerged after the horrors of war. She was eleven when war broke out and living in Leningrad (now St Petersburg) during a torturous Nazi blockade that involved a brutal two-year plan to starve the city. Around 1.5 million residents died. Bodies were literally piled up in the streets and families were reduced to burning their belongings for warmth. An evening meal for Lubow's entire family might be a single onion or the remains of a stray cat. Ravaged by sores, gum disease and malnutrition, the family eventually fled by boat and cattle truck to the Urals. They returned to Leningrad after 1945 and, having discovered cycling racing while studying, Lubow then moved to Tula so that she could have daily access to the velodrome. She triumphed in the inaugural women's world pursuit championships and then won bronze during Beryl's victorious years in 1959 and 1963. She was also beaten by Beryl in the 1960 quarter-finals before giving birth in 1964 to Marina, who, with her mother then becoming a national coach, spent her entire childhood and teenage years living inside the Soviet cycling system. Marina became like a surrogate daughter to many of Beryl's biggest rivals and, even after moving to Canada in the late 1990s, has remained in regular contact with the great champions from her past life.

'The goal was to reconstruct the best country in the world and to work harder than ever because so many men did not come back,' stresses Marina. 'That generation of Soviet people was very special, with lots of endurance, will and both physical and emotional strength.' Sport was also used to convince people of the value of the communist system. Physical education was ingrained in state education, and leading Soviet coaches would visit schools to talent spot and to stress the benefits that came with being athletically successful. Children were told that there would be the opportunity to travel. They might represent their region or

31. With Lubow Kotchetova, the first women's world pursuit champion.

country. They would be supplied with free kit. 'Kids were curious and the parents did not have to pay anything and were happy that their children were developed physically,' says Marina.

Although the best cyclists were largely based in Tula during the summer months, they would move south during the winter for warmer training camps in Tadzhikistan, Uzbekistan, Georgia and Armenia, or southern Russian cities like Sochi or Adler. The riders received scholarships that were worth more than the salary of an average teacher or engineer, but any prize money went directly to the Ministry of Sport. The routines were strict but, in numerous ways, groundbreaking. In the equal importance that was given to women's sports, and the respect that leading female athletes were shown, they could also be considered progressive. Every morning each athlete had to be at the seven o'clock 'wake-up meeting', followed by breakfast and then a road ride of between 50 and 150 km. They would then rest, eat and have a more intense afternoon track or road session during the afternoon before swimming, massages and saunas during the evening. The riders had just one day off every three weeks. There were psychologists and doctors embedded within the team and, according to Marina Kotchetova, the doctors took responsibility for the diet – 'three good meals' – as well as daily vitamins. Smoking and alcohol were banned. In the rare event of someone being caught breaking these rules, they were sent home.

Children and partners were also kept away, and relationships between teammates were subject to clear rules. When Valentina Sahonchik and her future husband, Sergey Smirnov, for example, were once caught after 11 p.m. in the same room, they were banished from the team for a month. Even when Anna Konkina and Vladimir Semenets, respectively a world champion and an Olympic champion, were already husband and wife, they chose to live in different rooms as a mark of discipline and respect to their teammates. Any rider who overslept and missed the 7 a.m. meeting, or who went to bed later than 11 p.m., also faced disciplinary sanction. 'Go back home – no second chance,' says Marina. On trips abroad, such as at the world championships, riders could not go anywhere alone and were instructed not to socialise with rivals.

Communication, though, could not be stopped completely, and bonds would develop. Speaking in 1995, Beryl said that the Soviet riders were 'grand girls' who became 'very friendly' once an initial suspicion of strangers had subsided. Aware that certain 'luxuries' were rare in the East, Beryl would bring extra toiletries such as talcum powder to international competitions, which she would discreetly distribute. An anecdote from her autobiography, however, was revealing. Under the headline 'a disturbing experience', she recalled talking to one of the younger Soviet riders via an interpreter and expressing an interest in their shoe-plates, which were cut deeper than those in England. 'At the final get-together for riders and officials, the girl sidled up to us and produced from under her skirt a pair of these shoe-plates,' wrote Beryl. The Burtons were initially taken aback, and Charlie tried to explain that they would like to reciprocate the gift. 'The girl backed away, more frightened than embarrassed I think, and one of the minders that always accompanied the Russian teams came seemingly from nowhere, grabbed hold of her and hustled her away,' said Beryl. 'We felt terrible. I never saw that poor girl again.'

Beryl even sent a letter to the Soviet Union team in which she offered to pay for the shoe-plates and said that the incident always 'haunted' her. 'The Russian girl rode with me in spirit over many racing miles,' she later said. When I recount this story to Marina, she lets out a small shriek of recognition. She says that the incident caused a major stir inside the Soviet team and that the 'rules of moral conduct' were tightened and a 'short intensive course in manners was provided' to all the athletes. The 'culprit' was immediately struck off the national team. 'She was a victim of that system,' says Marina. 'It was brutal but, on the other hand, what a lesson for further generations of Soviet cyclists.'

Such stories of control lead to the question of doping, and whether it was perhaps an obligatory part of the programme. In East Germany numerous athletes have suffered severe health consequences after being doped from a pre-teen age by doctors who, under the direction of the Minister for Sport, told them that they were being given vitamins. Marina shakes her head and is convinced that no Soviet riders could have been inadvertently doping during this period. 'I never heard from my parents or riders of their generation about the use of doping in the USSR until the Moscow Olympics in 1980,' she says. 'I used to be among the medical staff a lot. I saw with my own eyes what they had.' And what was it? 'Multivitamins such as Undevit, Dekamevit, Anrovit … and the bottles were unpacked in front of me. They were pills, not liquids.' Marina says that the belief inside the Soviet Union during the 1960s and 1970s was that doping, especially steroid abuse, was widespread in East Germany and that it was well known that the top riders in their system were having blood transfusions. 'They did not hide it – Russians could not afford it – it was too expensive,' she says. 'So, for this reason, in Russia the emphasis was shifted to the natural strength of the riders, to say nothing about emotional pressure.' Marina is adamant that some of the perceptions of Soviet sport in the pre-1980s remain 'very unfair'.

One of the leading Soviet coaches, Nina Egorova, delivered a similar explanation shortly before her death in 2020. 'People were ready to put their heart and soul to what they were doing – we were poor but happy,' she said. They were also incredibly successful. In the road race, Anna Konkina, who had finished third when Beryl destroyed the main field by more than 5 minutes in 1967, won consecutive world titles in 1970 and 1971. There was also Galina Yermolayeva, a six-times world champion in the sprint, who became the Soviet Union's first female international cycling referee. And then there was Galina Tsareva, another six-times world sprint champion, who married Alexandr Kuznetsov, the coach to numerous great Soviet champions. They have two children – Nikolay, who was an Olympic medallist in the team pursuit, and Svetlana, a double Grand-Slam-winning tennis player. These were cyclists who have remained celebrated and visible figures in Russian sport – but the most feared and formidable champion of them all was also the most reclusive.

*

Just the photographs and record books tell a story. Short, stocky and compact, with muscular legs and tattoos across her body, Tamara Garkushina oozed a certain coiled power. 'Physically she was stronger than many men taken together,' says Marina Kotchetova. Having never known her parents, she had been brought up by distant relatives in a village in Lipetsk Oblast. There was no formal education and, according to what she later told Marina, it was marginally better than being raised an orphan. One slice of fortune was that the family moved to Soviet cycling's epicentre in Tula, where a stepbrother took her to the local club. Garkushina was fourteen and working as a building labourer but, according to Marina, it was not just physical strength that made her such

32. The Soviet Union's six-times world pursuit champion Tamara Garkushina (centre) with compatriot Raisa Obodovskaya (left) and Beryl (right).

a formidable cyclist. 'She ate it, slept it, dreamed it. No family, no profession, no friends – just cycling.' Garkushina rarely spoke and, even by those cyclists with whom she effectively lived, was considered an enigma. They could never understand why she would always insist on riding the same Soviet-built track bike from Kharkiv rather than accept the team offer of a custom-made Italian Cinelli. Garkushina so hated any fuss that she would even conceal her birthday from teammates.

The Soviet coaches, however, knew that they had an unusual talent capable of finally breaking the Burton–Reynders pursuit domination. Like the entire Soviet team, Garkushina was trained with a specific world championship event in mind and, although she also soon became fast enough to break the world 500 m record, her absolute focus was the 3,000 m track pursuit. The 1967 world championship pursuit represented her arrival as an international force and, at the age of twenty-one, she won gold with a time just under 3 seconds faster than Beryl in third. Beryl did still win the world road race that year but, spurred by her

12-hour record, became increasingly focused on longer-distance time trialling. This, coupled simply with her age, had just marginally compromised her earlier pedalling speed. 'She was less whippy, which made her more vulnerable in the pursuit and road race,' explains Denise. Beryl did still win pursuit silver in 1968, losing to another Soviet rider, Raisa Obodovskaya, in a race that was notable for Eileen Gray furiously challenging the UCI officials to ride on the dangerously wet track when they tried to stage the final immediately after a torrential downpour. 'Clowns' was Beryl's terse description of the organisers. After then missing the entire 1969 world championships to focus on the Mersey 24, Beryl returned in 1970 for what was her first direct head-to-head race against Garkushina.

The championships were being staged in Leicester, and Beryl had been angered earlier in the competition when the guest of honour, Prince Philip, had left with a group of other VIPs, including Benny Foster, the former men's team manager and Gray's old nemesis, for an early lunch. This meant largely emptying a prime area of seats in the main stand just 5 minutes before her victorious quarter-final against France's Geneviève Gambillon. 'I thought the British among them could have stayed a few minutes longer to give support by their presence,' said Beryl. The subsequent semi-final against Garkushina was close. Now aged thirty-three, Beryl actually led after the first kilometre and they were level at the bell before Garkushina's greater speed saw her draw away by just over 2 seconds in the final 300 m.

They then met at the same stage the following year in Varese, Italy, when Beryl was unsettled shortly before their race. An inexplicable late change to the schedule meant that she was paired against Garkushina even though they had been the two fastest qualifiers. Garkushina again prevailed, leaving Beryl to win a bronze medal ride-off against the Soviet Union's next best rider, Lyubov Zadorozhnaya, in 3 min. 58 sec. Beryl's time was only one second slower than Garkushina had ridden in beating her and, having been preparing mentally to ride the Russian later that day, she always felt that the scheduling change may have cost her an eighth world title. Garkushina was still improving, and it would be the same again in 1973 – gold for the Soviet Union and bronze for Great Britain – in what was Beryl's penultimate tilt at the world pursuit title and her fifteenth world championship medal. At that time it was an all-time record for any rider, male or female. The French cyclist Jeannie Longo holds the current record for the most medals, at twenty-five, but her many extra options included the time trial, an event that Beryl would undoubtedly have dominated from the late 1950s until the early 1980s. In later years Beryl would warmly describe her Soviet rival as 'unstoppable' and talk about the 'great' Garkushina. 'She wasn't a bad lass and could be pleasant at times,' she said, before adding a caveat: 'I would dearly have loved to have ridden against her at my pursuiting peak and fully trained for it.'

Garkushina was only twenty-eight when she won her sixth world pursuit gold in 1974 but, to both the relief and the surprise of her co-competitors, her disappearance from the international stage was sudden and permanent. So what happened? Marina says that there was no prospect of Garkushina ever moving into coaching and, despite still living in Tula, she simply disappeared from the cycling scene. There was no announcement. No retirement party. The cycling literature has also paid Garkushina scant attention, and even Marina became unsure of her whereabouts until her mother fell ill with cancer almost twenty years later.

Completely unannounced, and shortly after Lubow had undergone surgery, Garkushina walked through the hospital door in Tula with a huge bouquet of her mentor's favourite tulips. She was also in tears. It transpired that she had been labouring in a factory, lifting heavy boxes that contained toxic chemicals, before using her great strength to clean rugs manually by hanging them across a bar and literally beating the dust out with a stick. 'Usually it takes three middle-aged men to do the job – Tamara managed it on her own ... and she was already over sixty,' says Marina. 'It was something like exile. Usually heavy alcoholics or prisoners were given such jobs.' The reconciliation with Lubow was profound, and Garkushina continued to visit until her former coach died in 2010. She was, says Marina, inconsolable and told Marina that her mother 'had made her' and that she regarded them as her family. 'The change in Tamara was tremendous and very sincere,' says Marina. 'And since that time the miracle never finished. She has become very close – ready to help no matter what.'

So, might she now talk in more depth about her career, the races with Beryl and address the doping suspicions about Soviet cycling? Marina says that Garkushina has never given interviews and refuses all offers to appear in public. 'She makes no complaints and has no demands,' says Marina, who was at least happy to ask questions on my behalf. That was in 2020 when, at the age of seventy-four, Garkushina was living in a small apartment in Tula with several cats. When she last visited, Marina had been struck by how basic everything was. 'Tamara simply boiled a pan of water on a stove to make us tea,' she says. The request for something approaching a formal interview was duly declined with the response that she still 'hated' talking about herself but, via Marina, she did address some of my questions.

How does she look back on her cycling career?
'With pain mostly.'
Does she still keep her medals?
'She does, actually, regardless of the fact that she is not
   following cycling any more.'
What has she done since stopping cycling?
'Nothing special. For many years she worked at a factory with
   men. No memories of these dull years.'
What does she do now?
'She is just enjoying taking care of cats. She lives a life of simple
   pleasures in modesty, helping out her neighbours.'

Does she cycle any more?
'No. She does not have a bike.'
Would she cycle if she had a bike?
'Most likely no. Enough is enough.'
Does she remember Beryl?
'Very well. Beryl Burton was well known in Russia, not just
among the riders, but also among the fans. Burton was a
name on everybody's lips. Tamara did not know that Beryl
Burton had passed away. She said that she was the strongest
foreign rider and she was sort of afraid of her. She says that,
at every championship they came across each other, the
challenge was the highest.'
*And what of the question, fairly or not, that lingers over the
Eastern bloc athletes. Did Garkushina dope during her six
world title wins?*
'She totally denies using doping during her long cycling career.'

Marina says that she then 'begged' Garkushina to tell her more
about her life 'in order that it could be written about for future
generations'. The reply was blunt. 'There is nothing to say about
my bitter life. I am not a hero and never felt like one.' The conversation also ended with distressing news. Garkushina had
undergone oncological surgery for cancer, which was followed by
ten sessions of chemotherapy, and was 'ready to pass away any
time'. She was philosophical, however, about the future. 'God
gives us something to live with, and when we fulfil our mission,
it's time to go,' she said. 'I am still here – that means I have not
completed God's task yet.'

*

It should be noted that Beryl herself never raised suspicions about
the Soviet riders. Her observations always centred on their 'terrific advantages' in preparation, and her successful push for 'open'

time trials in Britain was partially inspired by the Soviet willingness to have women train with men. 'They have first-class training facilities, plenty of financial backing and the incentive of improving their lot through their sport,' said Beryl. 'When one country has four or five pursuiters who might get medals, and the same girls can race against each other for months, they must have an advantage.' Beryl was particularly friendly with Robert Guralnik, a member of the Soviet medical support staff who would buy presents for Denise. She later also discovered that invitations sent to the BCF for her to compete in the Soviet Union, as well as the Netherlands, were quietly discarded by British officials, presumably to avoid any pressure to help fund such trips. It was a source of considerable regret and, just as those Soviet coaches had come to see her daily routine on Carline's farm, so Beryl would have dearly loved to race and train in Tula.

Cycling history also tells us that it would be remiss not to consider the question of doping in the context of any phenomenally successful rider's career. So might Beryl herself have been offered amphetamines or steroids during her long career and, in so desperately wanting to win, been tempted? There is nothing in her past interviews, those of her competitors and friends or pages of private correspondence that invites suspicion. Beryl was proudly self-coached and spent almost her entire life travelling around with Charlie and immersed with Morley in the British club cycling scene. And, speaking with more than 100 people for this book, including those who were critical of other aspects of her character, there was absolute consensus on this point. 'She wasn't into any of that – it would have deeply offended her,' says Eileen Cropper. Beryl's friend Ann Sturgess was so outraged when the question was once raised on an internet forum that she telephoned Val Rushworth and Jean Dunn – two of her other British teammates – to compare their thoughts. They were all adamant that it was an impossibility. 'I raced with Beryl, went on overseas trips with her, slept in the same room as her and never ever would she have considered doping,' said Sturgess. 'Out doing more miles? Yes. But dope? No way. Never on your life.'

Beryl herself does directly address the doping issue in her autobiography, where she outlined unspecified accusations about some of her competitors. 'In my earlier years I came up against riders who had been doctored for international races,' she said. 'Some countries and riders are always one step ahead particularly, it seems, with the use of steroids.' The book was written in 1985, and in it she records particular outrage at how the American Olympic gold-medal-winning cyclists in 1984 were known to have undergone pre-competition blood transfusions. It was legal at the time and, although later banned, would become the precursor to the blood-doping generation of Lance Armstrong. 'They should hang their heads in shame,' wrote Beryl.

The emphatic way in which she dealt with the personal question of doping also feels somehow reassuringly authentic, and in keeping with a firmly binary approach to the rights and wrongs of the world. 'I always refused to seek what might decorously be called "assistance" during my career,' said Beryl. 'I have to suffer a headache for some time before even taking an aspirin, and I have the personal satisfaction of knowing that my successes have been achieved by means of training, strength of will and solid Yorkshire grub.' But how would she respond if a doctor did suggest doping? 'He would feel my toe-end up his backside,' she replied.

11

The Yorkshire Housewife

Two words most commonly accompanied the name Beryl Burton alongside her occasional forays into a national newspaper. And they were not 'world champion' or 'record holder' but 'Yorkshire housewife'. Never mind that she was the greatest female cyclist in history. Never mind that she was a rhubarb farmer. Her primary points of identity were instead that she had a husband and lived in a county of 5 million people. It is easy to imagine the outcry across social media if Dame Jessica Ennis-Hill was ever described in such terms, but it was a moniker of its time and one that seemingly caused no offence. Indeed, the supposed ordinariness of Beryl's domestic life and routine was something that she would regularly emphasise and occasionally even embellish. Denise, for example, raises her eyebrows whenever she reads accounts of how her mother would find the time and energy to cook a full family roast dinner at the end of a long Sunday spent cycling. 'It was always porridge,' she says. The wider truth was also more complicated and, while Beryl was fastidious about her household tasks, she was among the most ruthless and single-minded champions who ever lived.

It made for a family life that was far from normal and a childhood for Denise that combined extraordinary adventure with a rapid imperative to fend for herself. Denise was Beryl and Charlie's only child and, with their immersion in cycling so absolute, no serious thought was ever again given to extending the family. It was the sort of personal topic that never came up in her regular end-of-race interviews with cycling magazines but would sometimes be posed in a national newspaper feature. In 1961, when she was twenty-four and Denise was five, Beryl envisioned a future when she would soon retire to family life. 'I've missed spending a lot of time with Denise,' she told the *Daily Mail*'s weekend magazine. 'We take her everywhere racing, but there are lots of things I would like to be able to do with her that I can't because I have to train. I'd like to have more children, too, but for the moment it's not possible. That's something I shall have to catch up with when I retire.' The writer Del Cooper also emphasised Beryl's everyday qualities. 'If you saw her out shopping on a Saturday morning with her five-year-old daughter, you would dismiss her as just another attractive young housewife,' he wrote. 'But put her astride a bicycle on a floodlit race track and she'll bring 50,000 people to their feet cheering wildly. For the shapely slender legs of this 5 ft 6 in. girl produce enough pedal power to beat most men.'

The subject of more children came up again twenty years later, just before Beryl's forty-fourth birthday. 'There was never time,' she said, bluntly. 'Even Denise was an accident, but the pregnancy did not interfere with my cycling too much.' And so, wondered the *Daily Mail* interviewer Sue Mott, how would she respond to a choice between her sport and her family? 'I could never give up cycling,' replied Beryl. It was Mott's first interview as a national newspaper journalist. She would later question all the biggest names in sport, and yet there was something about that meeting with Beryl Burton that she never forgot. 'I don't think I've met a sports champion since who had the same absolute ice-sharp obsession – even sportspeople celebrated for their focus,' said Mott. 'Not Steve Redgrave, not Andy Murray, not even A. P. McCoy. She seemed tiny, sinewy, every molecule of her being converted to energy production. She was driven. Ferocious training was a goal in itself. Beryl didn't mind seeming ruthless. She was cycling to lower-wattage glory in a small pool. Fine with her. It was dangerous, demonstrated by her dices with death on the road. That was fine too.'

*

As she gazed down Harrogate's Parliament Street and the finishing straight for the 2019 world women's road race championship, a smile of wonder broke out across Denise Burton-Cole's face. 'It's very special,' she said, surveying the buzzing pre-race scene. 'I know they haven't, but I can't help feeling like they've done this for us. My mum would have loved it.' It was sixty years, almost to the day, since Beryl had won her first rainbow jersey in Liège and it felt fitting later that afternoon to see Annemiek van Vleuten win in true Burton style with a long lone break through the Yorkshire Dales. The race was 150 km – almost three times the distance during Beryl's time – and one can only imagine how many more world titles she would have won over comparably testing courses. 'The further the distance, the further ahead she would have been,' said Denise, who had spent most of the previous week out on her bike, often in lashing rain, watching the races with her husband, Clay.

After Morley, Harrogate is the town that most defined the Burton family and is now home to Beryl and Charlie's two grandchildren, Mark and Anna. It was where Beryl lived for the last twenty years of her life. It is where she died. Rudding Park is where Beryl and Denise went head to head in the 1976 national road race championships. It is also where we were seated in the autumn sun, on a bench outside Betty's Café Tea Rooms, to discuss both a mother–daughter rivalry that became utterly unique in sport and Denise's own life and cycling career. There were inevitably fewer medals, but in its own way her story is every bit as inspiring and triumphant. It also shines the most revealing light of all into the mindset of what Sue Mott called an 'absolute ice-sharp' obsessive.

Cycling naturally dominates all of Denise's childhood

memories. 'It was our entire life,' she said, recalling either being ferried on a bike via various seats, sidecars and Rann trailers or staring out of the window from the inside of a car en route to another race. 'I would sleep or look at the countryside. Reading made me feel sick. My dad would drive. My mum would be sat next to him knitting. She did that fast as well. Hats, scarves, gloves, jumpers, everything. They were beautiful – really intricate.' By the age of nine Denise was deemed ready to cycle the nearby lanes alone from the village of Woodlesford all the way to her grandmother in Morley, 8 miles away. As her independence on a bike grew, Denise would increasingly stop travelling to her mother's races and instead spend the weekend in Morley. 'I was shown the route once and that was it,' she said. 'I'd cycle to my grandma's on a Friday. Stop there and cycle back on a Sunday.'

The degree of freedom was partially a product of the time, although the extent to which Denise was a latchkey child raised definite eyebrows even during the 1960s. One club cyclist, Pam Hodson, said that Denise would be 'left with whoever Beryl could find' when she was young. That was usually her grandmother in Morley, although Denise does clearly recall being homesick when she stayed with a cycling family in York who had children her age. 'I was seven – Mum and Dad were at the world championships, and I would sob at night.' Other cyclists of the time recall being surprised by how young Denise was when she might be left home alone while Beryl was away racing. Denise had no choice but to adapt and become quickly independent, even if the passage of time only amplifies the lengths to which her mother defied any sort of parental or societal convention that might restrict her cycling.

Take school. The only function that Denise can ever remember her mother attending, including parents' evenings, was a sports day in 1969 after the Mersey 24. This was because she was being forced to rest her injured knees. Charlie and Beryl were once even reprimanded with a headteacher's letter because Denise was

33. The Burtons went everywhere by bike and
Denise was forced to grow up fast.

coming into classes with string around her neck and their house key attached. The solution was not to adjust their cycling or work schedule to meet Denise from school but instead to leave the key under the front doormat. 'I was plonked on a bike as soon as I could ride it and, if I didn't take myself to something, I didn't go,' says Denise. 'My parents never joined in with anything outside of cycling, but I loved playing out with my friends and I didn't miss an awful lot. Children are resilient. They can often do a lot more than people think.' Denise initially cycled the 2 miles to her secondary school in Woodlesford but eventually decided to walk because other children would sabotage her brakes.

So how was family life once the front door was shut? 'Quiet,' says Denise. 'Especially if there was a big race looming. My dad would be in the garage doing the bikes. You could always hear him humming or singing. My mum would be turning the race over in her mind. She could have a good laugh after – or outside of a race situation with other people – but not with me. There would be a difference between being at home and out.' And it was not a subtle shift. 'I know we have all got our social face but this was extreme,' says Denise. 'There wasn't a warmth in the home and, as I got older, I would notice the difference at my friends' houses. You would notice that there was almost a chaos with people talking and doing stuff. Our home was very orderly. You all had your jobs. If you didn't take your shoes off at the door, it would just be, "Shoes!"' Denise then giggled as she recalled how her mother would insist on ironing absolutely every item of clothing. 'Socks, knickers, the lot.'

Beryl acknowledged that the quiet at home was a consequence simply of mulling over her training schedule or next race. She would never dwell on past glories and thought constantly of the future. Denise was puzzled by how her mother could be so outgoing in the company of club cyclists but so reserved at home. She would rarely even let Denise sit on her lap as a young girl, telling her daughter that she needed to protect her legs. 'She could go hours without talking,' says Denise. 'It's hard for a child to wonder why your mum is like that. If she didn't do as well as she thought she should, or had a big race approaching, her cogs would start turning. It was as if she was rehearsing everything. She loved winning. She had to be the best. If she lost, she became more determined. She couldn't relax.' Beryl knew the value of sleep, however, and it would be lights out inside the house at around 10 p.m. She would then be up again by 6 a.m. 'My lie-in was a Saturday, but even then I had to be up by 8 a.m. – Sunday even earlier,' says Denise.

Communication was entirely based on immediate practicalities. Feelings and emotions were not discussed. Past events would never be brought up or analysed. Denise had no idea even about her mother's serious heart condition or childhood illness – and the fact that she was defying doctor's orders by racing her bike – until she herself was almost thirty. Much of what Denise learned about her mother's early life was when her autobiography was published in 1986. She was also never consulted or warned ahead of quite significant moments. When the Burtons moved house, from their council flat in Morley to Woodlesford, Denise was eight but did not know until that morning what was happening. 'I wondered what all these people were doing taking the furniture out,' she said. 'It was quite upsetting because I left all my little friends. I went to see as many as I could but I can still feel sad about that.' Visits to the doctor or dentist, even for something quite significant like having teeth removed, would also abruptly arrive without prior knowledge. A favourite Beryl reply was 'No point' if she could not see the value in doing something, and, however thoughtless it may sometimes have been, additional discussions about future or past events were evidently deemed unnecessary.

Beryl's life was also full of non-negotiable idiosyncrasies. There would be no television or telephone. She knew that a television could distract her and, whenever she visited a friend or relative, she would become utterly engrossed if they did have a television on. 'I don't dare get one,' she said. Beryl's favourite television programmes were cowboy films with John Wayne or Clint Eastwood, and *The Avengers*. A telephone would certainly have been of practical help, but she did not like the thought of being unexpectedly interrupted. The *Yorkshire Evening Post* eventually developed a system whereby they called the landline of the Burton family's next-door neighbour, who would summon Beryl if the newspaper needed a quote. Even when Beryl did give interviews, she would invariably get on with something else while she chatted, such as cooking, cleaning or picking fruit. When Bernard Thompson, a journalist and photographer for *Cycling*, once wanted material for an in-depth feature, she simply pedalled the 115 miles to his house in Lyddington, did the interview while knitting with his wife, Ethel, stayed the night and cycled home the following morning. Thompson recalled heavy crosswinds, and 'yet she arrived within a couple of minutes of the appointed time, looking as if she had merely ridden down the hill into my village'.

If an arrangement needed to be made or something needed to be said, it would simply be done in person or by post.

Other club riders have kept the letters they received from Beryl and, as well as accepting hospitality before events down south, the Burtons had an open-door policy if cycling friends were making the opposite journey for a race in Yorkshire. With Denise often at her grandparents of a weekend, Beryl would also always take it upon herself to put on a huge spread of salad, chicken and cakes for any overnight guests. The scene at the Burton home in Woodlesford was described by one writer as akin to 'an underground station during wartime, as cyclists and families bed down for the night'.

Beryl stopped swimming completely once she became serious about cycling, even though it had been one of her great passions as a girl, for fear that it would 'soften' her legs and affect her muscles. She would never take a bath for the same reason. After a race, she would simply wash herself down with a flannel or sponge from a bucket even though there were no separate changing facilities. 'We would usually all wait until the men had gone but not Beryl – she just got on with it,' says Ann Pallister. 'Some of the men would be like wooo … they'd have a right good "skeg".' Beryl, though, also had a superstition which meant never washing her legs over the duration of what could be two or three days during a world championship pursuit series. She would chastise anyone for leaving a gap between their cycling shorts or trousers and their jerseys, believing that the cold air would cause kidney problems. Clubmates who did not ride with mudguards outside of the racing season were also reprimanded and told to cycle at the back of the group.

Pallister became like a fourth Burton family member after plucking up the courage to approach Beryl for advice at the presentation evening for the Leeds St Christopher Cycling Club. Beryl spoke at length with her before suggesting a 20-mile club run the following morning from Headingley to Otley. Pallister was only eleven and duly met nine-year-old Denise, as well as Beryl and

Charlie, for what was her first ride on open roads. 'I couldn't stop looking at Denise's white bike because I couldn't believe that they made them so small,' she says. And how did she enjoy it? 'Fantastic. We had a bun and a cup of tea and then rode back. They taught me how to ride around roundabouts and in a group. Denise and I got pushed now and again up the hills but I loved it. Beryl was the coach. Charlie was the coach. Nim Carline was the coach. They were mentors. Beryl was world champion but you would never have known. She mingled with everyone. She was my hero and, within the space of 24 hours, was taking me under her wing.' Beryl's advice was uncomplicated. 'She would say, "Get the miles in," says Pallister. 'She thought you couldn't beat going out cycling with other people. She was right because you'd be sprinting for lamp posts and over the hills. We would go out regardless of the weather: wind, snow, pouring rain. My mum could never understand it but you just put on a cape. You get addicted.'

The club camaraderie can be easily sensed from old ITV footage of the Morley club setting off for a group ride in 1969. Denise would have been thirteen and it is pouring with rain, but the narrator says that they are all still heading off from the centre of Leeds on a 100-mile route. All the bikes have mudguards and saddlebags, which are packed with sandwiches and flasks. The cyclists can be seen all helping each other to put on clear rain cagoules that droop down over the handlebars, complete with knitted woolly hats. Their trousers are tucked into long socks. Charlie, with his flat cap rather than a woolly hat, provides the only slight divergence from the dress code. Denise was grinning despite the awful weather and a hat that kept creeping down over her eyes. Her enjoyment had been further sparked by Pallister's arrival and that of about twelve boys from the local area. 'We went riding all over,' she says. 'School holidays, weekends, youth hostelling. Down to London. Having a real laugh, causing chaos wherever we went, but getting some big miles in.' Denise and Ann would take a transistor radio out on club runs that they would

34. The post-race scene. From left: Family friend Dulcie Walker, Beryl, Ann Pallister, Denise, Charlie and, seated, Nim Carline.

fasten to one of their handlebars, and then listen to *Pick of the Pops* as the charts counted down of a Sunday evening.

*

Club life also soon extended into some unforgettable family holidays. The world championships were generally held in August or early September, with the domestic time trial season also finishing at the end of that month. There was no question, then, of the Burton family ever going away during the school summer break. Beryl would simply wait until it was certain that no one could catch her in the BAR – the competition decided by averaging the speeds of a rider's best times over a season – and then they would go on holiday for up to four weeks. Cycle-camping. As well as the Burtons, Carline would generally come, and later other cyclists. 'The first one was when I was ten,' says Denise. 'And we would go all over. To Sicily. Corsica. Through France. Sardinia. We did

Spain one year. The Canary Islands. Portugal. And Morocco.'
Howard Newton joined one trip in North Africa when a young
Moroccan cyclist rode with them for several hours. 'Beryl took
his name and address and sent him the full Morley kit,' he says.
They would seldom stay in a campsite, let alone any sort of bed
and breakfast, apartment or hotel. They often did not even bother
to pitch up their tent. 'We must have stunk and been filthy,' said
Denise, laughing. 'We had the sea and rivers to wash in. We would
sleep under the olive trees. Or on the beach. Anywhere.'

Beryl would take charge of the food while Charlie and Carline
would work out routes, ranging from between 40 and 60 miles each
day. Charlie says that the warm air made him think that they had
landed on a different planet whenever they stepped off the plane.
They would carry a tent, several Primus stoves and basic supplies
of food. From the back, said Beryl, they resembled a herd of pack
mules. 'My mum would calculate it all – so much corned beef, condensed milk, porridge oats and plenty of tea,' says Denise. 'We
would get grapes and tomatoes from the fields and, anywhere with
a decent shop, we would stock up on vegetables and fruit. Plenty of
fish in these coastal villages. We didn't go hungry but we really lived
quite meagre. Breakfast was porridge, bread and condensed milk.
We'd stop at lunchtime and live off sardines and grapes during
the day before stopping properly later on. It would be stew of an
evening. And every few days we would have some corned beef in the
stew. That was a treat.' Beryl especially liked the simplicity of life in
Morocco – 'it's not European, you realise how well off you are over
here, there's no sanitation, no hygiene, no nothing' – and became
frustrated by the size of Madeira and all the Canary Islands. 'It's
finding a place big enough to cycle around,' she said.

Denise joined them on seven of these holidays up until 1972,
the year before her seventeenth birthday. She loved it even if some
of the recollections of an extraordinary first trip still prompt a
grimace. 'We were following these maps over a mountain range
and ran out of road,' she says. 'We ended up going down this steep

animal track, over one mountain, and then down into a gully on to this beach area with a stone hut.' This took several extra hours and, in transporting their bikes and belongings along a narrow path, they were scratched from top to toe by thorns and branches. A shepherd who was tending his sheep and goats appeared from this solitary beachside hut and played host that evening to four unexpected guests from Yorkshire. While communicating through hand gestures and diagrams, the shepherd cracked open almond nuts with his black teeth and shared out the kernels before using heat from burned straw to cook. 'He tried to make me eat curds and whey – but I spat it out,' says Denise. After battling on for two more exhausting days through the mountains, while again sleeping at random spots among snakes and dung beetles, Denise eventually flung her bike to the floor. She refused to go on. 'What do you do with a ten-year-old who won't go any further?' she says, laughing again. The answer was that Carline and Charlie took turns carrying her bike as they steadily made their way along what was a particularly hazardous goat track.

They eventually found civilisation and a coastal road on the far east of Sicily, next to Mount Etna. One night, as they cooked on the beach, and with Etna smouldering away behind them, Carline decided that the opportunity was too great and they must cycle up this 3,300 m volcano. Charlie stayed behind with Denise, allowing Carline and Beryl to set off as the sun rose. Their day out was later described by Beryl in a talk to club cyclists. 'It was beautiful tarmac, well graded for most of the way,' she said, before recounting how the road ended abruptly and they then took a cable car as far as people were supposed to go up one of Europe's tallest active volcanoes. Undeterred, Beryl and Carline abandoned their bikes and hiked to the absolute summit. Snow was soon replaced by puffs of smoke and steam. The heat from the ground was also rising and, like walking across sand on a blazing hot day, they had to keep moving. 'It was a long way and, when we reached the edge of the actual crater, I was surprised that there were no railings,' said Beryl. 'We could see right down into a great black pit puffing up columns of smoke. Nim lay down and wriggled forward to look over while I held his feet. The flames were almost choking and I was starting to hop from one foot to the other because the soles of my shoes were hot. Not long after we were home, Etna erupted again and all that lovely road and the houses lower down disappeared.' They also almost missed the plane home from Palermo after Carline fell ill. He had paid a heavy price for accepting a roadside challenge the previous day from some locals to drink a mystery cocktail. 'We had to go like billy-o to the airport with my mum pushing me the whole way,' says Denise.

In Spain the following year they pitched their tent on a beach without realising it was a military base and were duly woken by the sight of police pointing guns at them. On another trip through Morocco, where they took in the Atlas Mountains and part of the Sahara Desert, they were joined by June Pitchford and her husband, Ken. June was an outstanding cyclist herself but was still taken aback by her rival's approach to a holiday. 'Beryl was just the same – she wanted to ride her bike,' she says. 'So it was breakfast. Ride. Lunch. Ride. Dinner. We had stones thrown at us by kids on our bikes, and Ken got really quite ill with diarrhoea and sickness about halfway through. Beryl would ration the food. It was usually a tin of sardines between the five of us and plenty of bread. She ruled the roost.' That much was apparent when Pitchford broke some spokes which needed to be urgently repaired. Charlie sourced twenty spokes from a Jeep shop and set to work rebuilding this wheel on a beach. Beryl took the chance to relax by the sea while Denise, with June and Ken Pitchford, was dispatched on her bike to the next village for more spokes. 'We had a kitty, which Beryl looked after, and we were given this money to get the spokes,' says Pitchford. 'On the way back, we stopped and used the change for an ice cream. But we never did tell Beryl. You have to laugh. We were fully grown adults and yet afraid to tell Beryl. It was like she was our schoolteacher.'

The schoolteacher analogy did not extend to their daughter's formal education. Beryl and Charlie thought nothing of Denise missing the first three or four weeks of any new school year so that she could accompany them on these holidays. 'I would go back late – brown as a berry, and covered in midge bites. The teachers would be, "Where have you been?" You would try to explain but the teachers couldn't believe it. Neither did my friends. You are talking about the late 1960s and early 1970s. Spain hadn't even been invented as far as they were concerned, let alone Morocco. My mum was in the local paper a bit, but the fact that she was world champion didn't really register outside of cycling. It were all a bit wild, a bit tough, but you just did it. Lovely. Wonderful memories.'

At Christmas, Beryl would put up the same small tree in the Burton house, but the day itself was low-key and they would then spend Boxing Day in Morley with various in-laws. Carline would also drop in for tea after working in the morning at his farm before always falling asleep in the same chair. The routine changed, however, once Denise was eleven and could ride her bike over long distances. The Burtons would then all cycle to the Lake District on Christmas Eve and stay at various youth hostels until shortly before the New Year. It soon expanded to as many as thirty adults and children from the Morley Cycling Club. The growth in numbers meant that they eventually started staying at the same youth hostel, which would put on a Christmas package. Depending on the weather or individual preferences, there would be organised walks or cycles each day from the hostel, which provided breakfast and an evening meal. Lunch would be a flask of soup, sandwiches and tea or coffee while out on their bikes. 'We were like a big family,' says Shirley Pell, who was not herself interested in racing but enjoyed the social aspect and was simply pushed up any significant incline by Carline.

Denise says that the Morley cyclists 'did everything together' and that she loved it, especially the Christmases at the hostel and local pubs in the Lake District. 'There was always a great party atmosphere,' she says. Even when Charlie was bed-bound one year after injuring his leg, there was no question of Beryl staying home with her husband over Christmas and missing out on all the cycling. It was a decision that caused plenty of raised eyebrows. 'I couldn't believe that she could be so selfish,' says Eileen Cropper, even though Charlie had long since understood and fully accepted his wife's outlook. This order of priorities is also evident from the notes of a speech that Beryl gave in 1970 when she matter-of-factly described how Charlie would drop her and Carline off at the ferry for the Isle of Man cycling week each year before returning to his day job as a wages clerk for the Central Electricity Generating Board at the Skelton Grange power station. The bottom line was that Beryl did what was best for her cycling. She would quite openly tell people that you needed to be selfish and, crucially, expended minimal time, energy or emotion worrying about what they thought.

*

Denise was also competitive. Not to the same extreme, but enough to want to race. Charlie duly measured out a 5-mile course and simply stood in the middle of the road so that his eleven-year-old daughter could practise cycling around him to perfect the sudden mid-race U-turn that was once a feature of time trialling on deserted country lanes. Denise then tried the same Morley club 10-mile course that her mother had started out on some fifteen years earlier, before entering mixed circuit races around parks in Southport and Morecambe. With Denise and Pallister increasingly riding the same time trials as Beryl, they would soon all be travelling the country together in the Burtons' Cortina. 'Bikes on the roof and wheels in the back with me and Denise,' says Pallister. The sleeping arrangements ranged from youth hostels and windmills to the hospitality of other club riders. If it was necessary to camp out, Ann and Denise would go inside what was a two-person tent and Beryl and Charlie would sleep in the back of the car. In a feature on the Burton family for the *Sunday Times* magazine in 1975, the author Gordon Burn described seeing Beryl – a rider he called 'the DiMaggio, the Muhammad Ali, of British cycling' – emerging from a borrowed van before one early morning time trial in Basildon:

> Behind her as she sat in the open doors of a greengrocer's van were her prizes that had come for winning the events of the previous two days: a Marks & Spencer cardigan worth £7 and a £6 track-suit top out of which, in accordance with her amateur status, the manufacturer's name would have to be picked. Both items were part of a pile that included damp towels spewed out of hold-alls, a spirit stove, and quilted sleeping bags whose nylon fabric glinted in the sun. Her hair, curls styled in what used to be called a bubble cut, softening her face, was greasy this morning from sleeping rough and flattened to her head where she had been lying; a scar, dimpled and drawn in the way of old soldiers' bullet wounds, was exposed high on her neck, and the fingernails of the woman who has been called Britain's greatest female athlete showed up black from accumulated dirt as they rotated in a blur against her skin.

Burn's description that day of Charlie – 'Freddie and the Dreamers hair … he resembled the proprietor of a fairground dodgem' – was also vivid. Just the sight of the Burtons' Cortina in a lay-by or car park of the race headquarters was usually sufficient to destroy the field psychologically. 'The others would all be, "Beryl's here, we've got no chance",' says Pallister. 'I never saw her enthusiasm waver. Not once. Me and Denise would moan: "Oh no, we haven't got to go out again have we?" Beryl would be, "Yes, definitely. If you want to be good, you need to train". If we got stressed or upset, she would be, "Just think yourself lucky." She was proud if we won a team prize and very complimentary if you had a good ride.' There is then a pause as Pallister confirms a difference in how Beryl might react to Denise, who was soon making rapid progress. 'I think sometimes with Denise she was OK, but it depended how she felt,' she says.

One further quirk of Denise and Beryl's relationship was that, although they lived under the same roof and were competing in many of the same races, their only shared cycling was on winter club runs and family holidays. Denise never received any advice from her mother, who, even as she passed thirty, then forty and even fifty, would remain immersed in her own world of training and racing. The singular nature of cycling was one part of the allure for Beryl and, aside from those long training rides with Carline, she almost always trained without company. She did, however, like to punctuate those rides by stopping at a café in the certain knowledge of finding fellow cyclists who instantly recognised her. Deriving strength and energy from time spent alone before still enjoying company is a classic characteristic of a more introverted personality. 'It's kind of like a battery they recharge,' says Jennifer Kahnweiler, author of *The Introverted Leader*. Beryl found that her mind would be split in two while cycling – one part on the immediate practical task and the other on wherever else it randomly wandered. 'Many things come into my mind, but I never know what they are going to be,' she said. Riding a bike was also pretty much the only time that she would actually sit down and so, for at least part of her training, there would be an opportunity to quietly unwind while still doing something completely productive.

Beryl was even reluctant to tell Charlie or Denise where or how far she was going and, if they did ask, she would often tell them to mind their own business. 'We might wave if we passed each on the opposite side of the road,' says Denise. Beryl claimed that the enforced independence of Denise's training was for the common good and they were also strict about only gradually upgrading their daughter's cycling equipment so that she truly appreciated anything new. 'She's got steel cranks and we are improving her equipment every year – but she won't have alloy cotterless [cranks] for a while,' said Beryl in 1970, when Denise was fourteen. 'I brought her up to go training on her own because I wanted her to be able to push herself. Most people can drive themselves if they've got company, if somebody's forcing them to do it but, once they're left on their own, they haven't the will.'

Denise was a great watcher of people and would still quietly absorb her mother's routines. She would sometimes even secretly follow her and was also more flexible in her thinking. 'I saw a lot but you have to work it out for yourself. You adapted. She became world champion by adapting. I don't remember receiving any help. She might sometimes say "Well done". That would be it.' Denise would also race in all types of cycling. At the age of fifteen she became the youngest rider ever to win a national senior time trial championship when, with her mother and Pallister, Morley won the team prize in the 1971 25-mile time trial championships. Beryl was 5 minutes ahead of her nearest competitor and 10 minutes clear of both Denise and Pallister, who finished within a few seconds of one another. Denise also rode with her mother in the national women's road race championships later that year. Beryl won alone by more than 6 minutes, with Denise finishing sixth among the senior women. They were exceptional performances for someone so young, and Eileen Gray, still the lone woman on any BCF committee, successfully petitioned to have her ride in the British senior team at the 1972 world road race championships in Gap.

Denise was just sixteen, and it remains the only time that a parent has lined up with their son or daughter at the start line of a cycling world championship. Denise is slightly built and looked young even for her age. When the riders from the Soviet Union, West Germany, Spain and France saw her, they did not see any

35. Beryl and Denise, with Charlie – resplendent in braces,
shirt and tie – proudly beaming in the background.

threat and simply went 'Ahh'. Already petrified, Denise began
to cry. 'Afterwards I thought, "What a wally. What a silly thing
to do", but I was so nervous. My mum would get really tense. I
needed someone to jolly me along and she was not the person to
jolly anyone along before an event, but it was fine once we got
going.' Beryl would later split the field and drive a six-woman
break, but her lack of a sprint finish meant that she ultimately
finished fifth, ahead of Denise in twenty-third. It was the first of
seven consecutive world championship appearances for Denise,
but she would only race alongside her mother twice more. They
then finished respectively eighth and twenty-third in Barcelona in
1973 before arriving in Montreal the following year and a surreal
incident on the day before the race.

The British team – Beryl and Denise, as well as Carol Barton
– had gone out to explore the course and were riding along one
especially busy section of road. Huge articulated lorries kept

whizzing past from an uncomfortably close proximity. 'My mum was on the front, I was next and Carol Barton behind me,' says Denise. 'We were hurtling along. My mum suddenly flipped around a pothole. I was too close to her wheel and went straight into the pothole. It sent me skidding along next to a high kerb. The lorries were going by inches away. I would have been killed if I fell into the road, and I still only stopped when I smashed my head on the kerb. No one wore helmets in those days. It knocked me out. Blood everywhere. I went to hospital for stitches.' It was a terrifying incident. So how did Beryl react? 'She carried on. Didn't stop cycling. Carol shouted to her. She was so upset that my mum hadn't stopped.' But did Beryl perhaps not realise until later on just how bad the crash was? Or was she just so completely concentrated on her warm-up ride that nothing, not even checking her daughter, would interfere. Denise shrugs. 'I think she was quite focused, really.'

Despite the severity of the incident, Denise still started the next day. 'I was concussed. There was a big climb on the circuit called Mount Royal. I got up it twice and then I blacked out. I was sick.' She still has a lump on her head from that crash. Beryl's only recorded feelings of regret related to how she again finished fifth after driving the winning breakaway before being beaten in the final sprint. It was Beryl's last world championship race and, while adamant that she 'could and should' have won more, it had still been a monumental sixteen years of self-funded representation for the British flag. 'I had to be left with the satisfaction of knowing that despite my seniority in years no other woman in the world could shake me off and that, given enough miles, I could beat them all … if only there was a time trial,' she said.

Denise says that her mother was clearly still the strongest rider during the three world championship road races they both rode during the early 1970s but that she had lost an ability to make sudden accelerations. 'She just went on the front and didn't know her tactics at all. The opposition knew by then that they could not let her go.' Denise did have that change of pace and a more astute tactical brain. She was also becoming faster in the 3,000 m pursuit and, after winning a national championships that did not involve her mother, was selected in the British track team for the 1975 world championships.

With Beryl now focused on the domestic time trial scene, Denise was the only Burton family member in Belgium for the world championships. Amid gale-force winds, driving rain and the same bumpy track in Liège where Beryl had won two golds, Denise produced the best performance of her career to ride to a bronze medal. The stands were again choked with crowds in excess of 40,000, even if the women still faced the usual challenge of no defined schedule within the overall programme and having to wait around in the rain for their races. Denise had been well placed to follow up her track bronze with a road race medal but was impeded by a policeman as she prepared for the final sprint and finished twelfth. It was all still enough to prompt an invite from the prestigious, and now cult, BBC multi-sport contest *Superstars*, even if Denise's main memory of that experience was falling in a canal while she tried to learn how to paddle a canoe.

Beryl was 'thrilled' by news of the bronze medal and, while it seems sad that Charlie was not at least present for his daughter's world championship success, Denise was long reconciled to how their family worked. 'She would have been racing in a time trial and my dad always put my mum first. I don't blame my dad for anything. He had a lot to put up with ...' Denise's voice trails off and she seems to be recalling a particular incident before she then simply adds: 'Oh dear. Sometimes, now that I am older, I think, "Dad, you should have stood up and said something." He should have backed me up sometimes, but I understand. It was his wife.'

It was also a unique situation. An occasionally acrimonious sibling rivalry in sport is not completely uncommon. The breakdown in a parental relationship is also relatively frequent, although this is invariably caused by an overbearing father or mother's coaching influence and the need for their child to push back and create more space. The issue for the Burtons was becoming far more complicated. At a time when Beryl's global dominance had waned amid the rise of state-sponsored Eastern European nations, the major threat to her domestic supremacy was emerging from inside her own home.

12

I Ride to Win

The full human drama would start just as a thrilling 1976 national women's road race championship had finished. Aged twenty, Denise Burton had outsprinted her mother, Beryl Burton, for a victory that would ultimately represent the pinnacle of a distinguished road cycling career.

It was a title of limited significance in the overall context of Beryl's *palmarès*. She had already won the event twelve times and, with her fortieth birthday approaching, what could be better than to see this particular baton pass into the hands of her daughter? A family one-two in a race of such domestic prestige, after all, should sit proudly on the long list of unprecedented Burton achievements.

It is a lovely narrative and one that might make perfect sense to 99.9 per cent of the population. And yet to expect Beryl to take pleasure from finishing second, especially to someone she had annihilated by 12 minutes seven days earlier in a 50-mile time trial, would be to misjudge completely the force of her competitive nature and a personal need not simply to win but always to deliver to the absolute limit of her abilities. As Beryl herself later said, 'It would be nice to record I was pleased for Denise, but this is not a story for some romantic magazine. It was a real-life narrative about ordinary people with jangled nerves and emotions.'

Eileen Cropper and Pam Hodson were among the eyewitnesses in the changing room immediately after the race. 'Beryl was banging her fists against the floor,' says Cropper, who had also ridden. 'No tears. Just pure anger. I had known Beryl for twenty years, and it never mattered to me whether she was a star or not. I spoke to her straight: "You shouldn't be like that. If a child of mine won the national championships I would be delighted." Beryl's response was that "Charlie does everything for her, it's all about her". I left her banging the floor.' Hodson, who went to secondary school with Beryl, was also dispatched to the changing room. 'It was impossible – she was like a baby,' says Hodson. 'I said to her: "You should have been leading Denise out, never mind trying to beat her."' And how did Beryl respond? 'She just said: "I ride to win."'

Cropper would then see the victorious Denise in the toilets. 'She was about to get changed for the presentation and go to the pub,' says Cropper. 'I said, "Well done, Denise." She looked at me and said, "I wish you were my mother." It was heat of the moment but dreadful. Very sad.' Beryl had still not recovered her composure sufficiently to acknowledge Denise on the podium during the prize presentation and, in full view of the cyclists, spectators and a small gaggle of media, refused the customary handshake. Beryl then did make national headlines. 'Bike ace Beryl snubs daughter,' said *The People*. 'Take that, Mother,' wrote the *News of the World*. 'How blind ambition drove Beryl's family to the brink,' said the *Daily Mail*. The event was being sponsored by the cycling entrepreneur Ron Kitching, a family friend who supplied much of Beryl's equipment. He and his wife took Beryl out to dinner that evening in a further fruitless attempt to placate her. Kitching described the stand-off as 'appalling' and, some years later, would say that 'somewhere along the line I think Beryl has been a fool to herself' and 'has some regrets'. Another confidante, Brenda Robins, says that Beryl 'loved Denise to bits' but did not know how to handle the competitive threat. 'She didn't talk about the rivalry, even to friends, for a long time,' she says. 'She knew that she was in the wrong for a lot of it, but she was the champ and she wasn't going to give it up. Bless her heart. I loved her

36. Denise Burton outsprints her mother to win the
1976 national road race championships.

dearly. Charlie was split down the middle. He felt he had to help
his daughter, but his wife did not like it at all when her daughter
went as fast as she did.'

The only time Beryl fully addressed the matter was in her
autobiography ten years later. In it Beryl highlighted a growing
tension over her feeling that Denise was not contributing sufficiently to their household tasks. As for the race itself, she also
felt that Denise had 'not done her whack' in the breakaway with
Carol Barton and had benefited from excessively shielding from
the wind in her slipstream before the final sprint. 'I had made the
race,' wrote Beryl, who also complained that she could not find
Charlie immediately after the finish. She described the absence
of her husband at the moment of rare defeat as 'the final straw'.
Beryl's account did contain some traces of contrition, albeit with
the sizeable caveat that 'it would perhaps have been better if Carol
had beaten both of us'. She did at least describe her refusal to
shake hands as 'not a sporting thing to do' and acknowledged
that her behaviour had done cycling 'a disservice'. This has since
been interpreted as an apology and there is even a scene in Maxine
Peake's play where Beryl and Denise both say 'sorry' and then

37. A distraught Beryl did not acknowledge her daughter on the podium.

hug. Denise laughs at the idea that her mother would have apologised – 'she would say that black was white' – and notes that even this qualified contrition was in an autobiography 'written with someone else'.

The broader context does not excuse Beryl's behaviour but does help to understand how circumstances collided that day in a way that she could not sensibly rationalise. Aged thirty-nine, it was a time when her athletic capabilities had irreversibly shifted. Although Beryl was still invincible in a straightforward time trial, her change of pace had eroded since the last 1960s. And what was a point of fallibility at world level during the early 1970s had become the same domestically. This then only intensified Beryl's irritation at how the competition would, quite legitimately, always attempt to beat her in a road race by staying closely behind her back wheel to shield from the wind before sprinting past at the finish. The rest of the field knew that the race was over if Beryl established clear daylight, and so would take turns to cover her attacks. The shorter distances of that era made this task even easier.

Beryl had already lost numerous world road race titles in this way, and some of the British women were now able at least to stay with the pace she set. The etiquette in Britain back then was that you 'did your turn' if you were part of any breakaway group and were not otherwise entitled to contest the sprint finish. Nobody took much notice of this unwritten code of conduct at world level, and it had never previously mattered domestically because Beryl was so far ahead of the rest. Her sensitivities, however, had previously also been exposed in the 1971 national road race championships. As usual, she had simply hit the front at the sight of a hill and quickly removed all but one of her competitors. The survivor was Bernadette Swinnerton, the twenty-year-old national track sprint champion who, in Beryl's absence in 1969, had used her finishing speed to win a marvellously unexpected silver medal at the world road race championships.

Swinnerton came from a great cycling family in Stoke, and there were other international cyclists among her six siblings, including her sister Catherine, who also raced with and against Beryl. Like many other cycling families, they would provide Beryl and Charlie somewhere to sleep if they were racing near their home. It meant that Bernadette, the eldest of the children, had known Beryl since she was a young girl. 'I absolutely idolised her,' says Swinnerton. So how would Beryl react to her joining this breakaway? 'She was quite nasty. Going up the hill really took it out of me. I was still getting my breath back. She turned around and said, "If you can't come past and do your bit, get back to where you belong."' Just as she did with Nim Carline in training, Beryl would then swing out as if to let Swinnerton through for her turn on the front but increase the speed as she did this to demonstrate her superior strength. It was pure intimidation, and Swinnerton, who says that she would not have dared contest the sprint had she been unable to aid Beryl, could not get past to help. She became so upset that she eventually dropped back to the chasing group, where she later crashed. Beryl duly crushed the entire field by 6 minutes.

Catherine, who is seven years younger than Bernadette, has comparable stories during the late 1970s and early 1980s of how Beryl would get aggrieved if anyone was tucked in behind when she tried to ride away during a road race. 'She got to know Beryl when she was on her way down and she said that Beryl would employ quite dirty tactics,' says Bernadette. 'She still expected to drop people ... but of course she couldn't do it then.' The solution could be drastic. 'She would stick her brakes on and knock them off – and she actually did that to Catherine,' says Bernadette, who thinks that Beryl's desire to repeatedly win bordered on a compulsive 'illness'. Denise does not believe her mother would ever have deliberately caused crashes or put her brakes on, but does acknowledge that she would 'sit up' in frustration and that this did once cause an accident involving Catherine.

As for the 1976 national championships, Denise remains adamant that she worked until the last lap and looks incredulous at the idea that she should then suddenly have done a great turn on the front to please her mother. 'C'mon,' she says. 'Her mind was set. My mind was set. I wanted to win. She wanted to win. I'd done the training and I knew I had a good chance.' Beryl would also claim in her book that Denise had beaten her by the 'proverbial whisker' and even suggested that there had been a long wait to discover the outcome of a photo finish. That was patent nonsense. Denise won by a clear bike length and, as the photographs confirm, there was no doubting the final outcome as parent and child crossed the line.

It would also be simplistic to dismiss Beryl's post-race behaviour as a reaction born only of defeat. Even as the family prepared to make the early morning 25-mile journey from Woodlesford to Harrogate before the start, there had been another shocking incident. Literally as they were just loading up the car before leaving, Beryl suddenly told Denise that she was not getting a lift and should instead make her own way to Harrogate. Charlie had already attached Denise's bike to the roof of the car. But there would be no backtracking from Beryl. And so off came Denise's bike and out of the car came her race wheels. With no telephone in the house, Denise had no means to contact anyone and so duly fixed her wheels to the front of her bike and began cycling. Beryl's one grudging concession was that Denise's kit bag could stay in the car.

Charlie did not argue, although what he thought is perhaps revealed by the decision to first drop Beryl off in Harrogate and then, as his wife disappeared to warm up, turn the car around and find his daughter, who had cycled about three-quarters of the route. 'He always backed my mum, although he might come up to me later and explain,' says Denise. 'Her word was law. My mum would really roast my dad at times.' The pre-race behaviour also underlines how Beryl would be quite willing to use her own brand of psychological warfare against any perceived threat, including her own child. 'There was no motherly help – she had tunnel vision and she didn't accept that she should ever come second – if she did, someone got blamed,' said Eileen Gray in the *Racing is Life* documentary, shortly before her own death at the age of ninety-five.

Denise was no longer a teenager by 1976, and Beryl also seemed to resent how she was able to combine training with part-time employment. In a joint interview with the *Guardian* in 1978 there is a quite comical moment when they even begin arguing over this point. 'I couldn't cope with working, training and racing all at the same time,' says Denise, quite openly, before stressing that she 'always had a hard part-time job'.

Beryl interrupts: 'No, you didn't, Denise.'

Denise fires back: 'Yes, I did, Mum.'

Beryl again: 'No, you didn't, Denise.'

Beryl then appeals to the interviewer to understand her point of view. 'Can you imagine what I felt when Denise said she couldn't cope? I've had to cope with training, racing, a full-time job, and cooking, washing and ironing when I get home.'

Beryl's bluntness was also apparent when she was asked how she felt if Denise won a race. 'I don't get all excited if she's done something and I've already done it,' she said. 'I'm proud. I'm pleased. But, if she'd been in a different sport and done well, I'd appreciate it more. It's the difference between being proud of someone and really looking up to them. No one at the top in sport would be any different. Denise has been closer to her dad than to me. It's natural for girls to be closer to their fathers as they grow up.'

Beryl also did not spare herself in the interview. She described herself as 'very hard to get on with' and readily admitted that, yes, she would occasionally let rip at Charlie if her cycling equipment was not perfectly assembled. Asked how she responds if people try to speak to her before a race, Beryl simply replied: 'I just don't answer them.' Her brief assessment of losing to Denise in the 1976 national championships was also rather more direct than her ghostwritten autobiography. 'We'd just had a flaming row – Denise, Charlie and me. I went berserk for three laps. Then I was smashed to smithereens. Tactically I'm hopeless. I can't honestly say I like road racing. On the road you get told to watch so-and-so. I just can't. If I'm on a bike I must just go as fast as I can.' Beryl then concludes her part of the interview by describing how she saw the domestic situation. 'It's like putting Evonne Goolagong and Virginia Wade in the same house,' she said. 'There's no friendships when we're on our bikes – it's daggers drawn. I don't think you'll find any top person in any sport that hasn't got a bitter streak. She has a softer nature. I'm very hard.' Denise did also have her say and rather pointedly noted that she'd 'be over the moon' if she had children and they won any race. She is also asked about the 'hugs and kisses' that she missed growing up. 'You just don't bother,' she says. 'You just accept that's the way a person is. We just think differently. She was pleased when I won bronze at the world championships.'

*

As we sat together for almost 3 hours that morning in Harrogate ahead of the world women's road race in September 2019, it was easy to sense that Denise has become a little weary of the most rose-tinted accounts of her mother's life. She does not want to overstate their differences, but there has been an easy caricature of domestic bliss through the week only for Beryl to ditch her apron and magically transform into a cycling goddess at the weekend. The truth was that colossal sacrifices were constantly being made and that the extent to which Beryl balanced training, racing, work, family and household tasks was frequently exaggerated.

The *Beryl* play depicts their tensions neutrally, as if Charlie was constantly split in having to choose whether to side with his wife or daughter. Beryl's brother Jeffrey remains close to Denise – and would initially only contribute to the book with her blessing – but emphasises their own strict childhood upbringing and says that Denise could be rebellious like any teenager. Peake considered delving more deeply into the tensions but, in a 90-minute play, wanted to ensure that a rightly celebratory representation of Beryl was not excessively complicated. She still does not ignore the more difficult issues and, when I attended the play with Jeffrey, there was a slightly uncomfortable moment when the audience groaned audibly following Beryl's refusal to shake Denise's hand after the 1976 national championships.

'As soon as you put forward a story, people are always saying, "Where's the conflict?"' says Peake. 'I was, "Well, there is this relationship between mother and daughter" and I was encouraged to push that, but I dug my heels and said, "I want to celebrate her life; not many people outside of the cycling fraternity know about her."' Peake, who grew up in Bolton, also has strong instincts over

the context of Beryl's character and likely wider family relationships within a northern and working-class community of that
time. 'I kept saying to people, "It's mothers and daughters. They
are difficult relationships." I thought of myself. It was me, my
mum and my sister in our house. Oh my god! We could be awful
with each other. As I saw it, you had two women competing and
Beryl had dedicated every waking hour to cycling. Then Denise
came along ... obviously younger and maybe didn't work as hard.
That would drive me nuts. Maybe there was a bit of jealousy.
But it's hard. It's your thing. You have chosen this sport. You are
supercompetitive. Of course it's going to be tricky. Why compete
if you don't want to win?'

Peake initially met Charlie and Denise at a hotel in Harrogate.
'I remember Denise coming into the room and saying, "Only an
hour on the meter – I haven't got long." I was thinking, "Yeah,
she's got a bit of Beryl in her." Although, when the hour was
up, she was, "Oh, I'll just go and put some more money on" and
carried on. But there was a protection and understandably so.'
Ann Pallister also says that Denise 'has a tough side, just like her
mother' and was not about to be put off. 'Denise was competitive,
too – she stood her ground.'

Beryl's sour reaction was also not confined to the immediate
aftermath of the 1976 national championships. There was a silent,
icy atmosphere at home, and Beryl eventually went to stay with
her mother. It was then very suddenly announced that Denise
would have a fortnight to find somewhere else to live as they were
taking up the offer of a flat in Harrogate as part of Charlie's
new job. It was a big moment in all their lives. Denise was now
twenty, and there was a feeling that she no longer needed to be
at home. The problem was that she had nowhere to go. Charlie
helped to facilitate a compromise of sorts, and Denise moved in
for the next two years with her Auntie Margaret and Uncle Sid.
'That came very hard to me,' says Denise. 'I wasn't in my home. I
was quite independent at a young age and yet needed that family

unit. My uncle and aunt were lovely people – but they were as far from sportspeople as you could possibly get.' They could not understand why Denise would lift weights in the front room or even why she cycled so much. Having been brought up only on wholemeal bread, the option in front of her was now sliced white bread. A request for rice would result in packet rice. Denise was suddenly also without the immediate mechanical backup of her dad. It was a huge emotional upheaval and her broader cycling progress would gradually stall.

The tensions were well known within the relatively small world of British cycling, and so there was considerable interest when Beryl and Denise then contested the national pursuit championships in Leicester the following summer. They had never both competed in the head-to-head environment of the track. Denise, who had won the world championship bronze two years earlier, was going for a third straight national title. Beryl, arguably the greatest pursuiter in history, had not ridden over such a short distance for three years. They met in the semi-finals and, although Beryl had beaten her daughter by 5 minutes in the 1977 national 25-mile time trial championship a few weeks earlier, Denise's now superior explosive speed ensured that she emerged victorious. There is BBC footage of the race. Beryl, decked out in the blue-and-white Morley club kit, was being held up by Charlie while Denise, who looks genuinely terrified on the start line, was being pushed off by Tom Feargrieve, the mechanic who would drive the women to the world championship races in his 'Britannia' vehicle. Knowing that he could not leave his wife's side, Charlie had personally asked Feargrieve to help Denise and push her off.

Beryl later described her mental state as 'screwed up' and told the watching reporters that she 'can't put into words how difficult it was' to be riding against Denise. Her reaction to losing against her daughter again, however, was very different. 'Trembling, I returned to the riders' enclosure and began to pull on my tracksuit,' she later wrote. 'Then somebody was standing in front of me and I looked up. Denise came into my arms and we hugged and wept, oblivious of the bikies around us and the crowd in the stand. I felt very proud when I watched her line up later for the final.' It was not quite a storybook ending, however. Denise says that the timing of their rather forced 'reconciliation' had left her unable to focus properly on a final she would lose against Maggie Thompson.

*

Having left the family home, Denise moved in 1978 to the colours of the East Bradford Club, with whom she finished second to her mother in both the national 50- and 25-mile time trials. She also moved between various flats and houses in Bradford and Harrogate, including a period at the Hotel Majestic, where she worked. She qualified as a nursery nurse and remedial massage therapist, but, at a time when she should have been entering her cycling peak, her health fell into sharp decline. Denise now knows that she was suffering from anorexia.

'It stemmed from all different reasons,' she says. 'I was travelling a lot, week in, week out, by myself. I got fed up with myself and really quite ill. It started in 1978 and just creeps on. I wasn't good by 1979. I really wasn't good in 1980 and 1981. It was not until 1982 or 1983 that I realised I had anorexia.' As well as the tensions with her parents, Denise had got married to and then separated from another cyclist, Steve Thomas. She also spent spells living and working in Essex as a nursery nurse.

It was a time when understanding of anorexia was limited, and help, not least from her parents, family and friends, was nonexistent. 'My parents didn't know what it was. I didn't know what it was. Nobody looked at you and said, "There's something wrong". They just looked at you and said, "Pull yourself together and start eating". But it's a mental thing. It is not just that you are not eating.' Denise's weight dropped from around 8 stone to below 6 stone. Beryl's incomprehension and lack of empathy were evident in her correspondence and exchanges with friends, although it is also apparent that her daughter's health was always of great concern and high on her mind. She would unhelpfully relate the personal struggles that younger people might face with her own considerable challenges in early life and say things like, 'They don't know they're born today.' With no telephone in the house, there was limited contact between mother and daughter, but Denise would speak to her father at his work and he would relay updates. In her autobiography Beryl described Denise as having 'the appearance of a starving waif' and recalled a race during which her daughter had failed to pass up a water bottle because she did not have the energy to run quickly enough alongside her as she pedalled by. Charlie had again also capsized the car in a ditch on the same day. 'I could hardly concentrate on my racing, worrying about the two most important people in my life,' she said. 'People in the sport thought I was some kind of automaton who just came out and did the rides and then retired to a castle in the sky until the next race.'

*

There are several uncomfortable certainties in the life of a racing cyclist. Stories of long winter rides through the Dales that might end with small icicles hovering down from a nostril, or being caught in a virtual monsoon sweeping across the Moors, became badges of honour among the Morley cyclists. Riding while the cold and rain had rendered the sensation of feeling in your fingers and toes a distant memory was also common. Cycling clothing was rather less sophisticated when Beryl was racing, and the sight of her sopping wet woollen jumpers, hats and socks drying out in front of a fire remain etched in the Burton family memory. Yet it is not the elements that cyclists really fear most. It is a crash.

It happens suddenly and unexpectedly, even if the bracing violence and pain of the incident can often unfold in helpless slow motion. Robert Millar put it most succinctly when he was asked in 1993 by a journalist how it feels to crash. 'Go down a hill at 30 m.p.h., jump off and find out,' said Millar. Although it happened frequently throughout her life, Beryl would say that crashing was something that she never got used to and, as she passed the age of forty, the accidents began to take a serious toll.

It was late November 1977 but, having accepted an invitation to ride an international race in Arizona during the spring, Beryl was still training unusually hard for the time of year. And, by her own account, travelling at a 'scorching' pace as she approached a snack bar on the road between Skipton and Gargrave. Beryl hesitated as she went past the roadside van, weighing up whether to stop for a drink, but was within an hour of their new ground-floor flat in Harrogate and so dismissed the idea. It had been a new start on multiple levels. Denise had now left the family home, and it was one of the rare periods in Beryl's life when she was not also working full-time. She was relishing the chance to train without distraction and contemplating how she might approach the winter months when an oncoming car misjudged her speed. The vehicle turned straight across Beryl's side of the road and, by the time she had computed what was happening, it was too late. Beryl was knocked unconscious, and her next recollection was simply the sight of a 'handsome young doctor hovering over me' in Ward 16 of the Airedale Hospital, near Keighley. She would need fifty-six stitches in her head. Her right ear, which was left hanging gruesomely from the side of her head, had to be sewn back on. Beryl's shoulder blade was also broken, but worst of all, to her mind, was the double fracture in her right leg. It would require an operation to reset the bones and a first prolonged separation from a bicycle in more than twenty years.

While previous accidents may also have caused plenty of physical pain, Beryl was always of the mentality that you ignored discomfort and got back on your bike. This was different. She was told to stay in hospital for three weeks and, although she recalled considerable jealousy on the ward at 'so many fit-looking men cyclists coming to visit', the break did prompt a rare period of reflection. Now forty, Beryl reasoned that 'it would be understandable if I retired'. She even later wrote that 'there seemed no more mountains to climb'. It was a train of thought that had little chance of persisting and, following the novelty of rest and recuperation, Beryl set herself a monumental new target. She had already won the BAR competition – for the rider with the fastest annual average speeds over 25-, 50- and 100-mile time trials – nineteen years in row, and so decided to target a round two decades of dominance. 'It seemed important to have something to make my mind transcend the physical difficulties,' she said.

It was Beryl herself who told the medics that she would be leaving hospital in Keighley shortly before Christmas in 1977. The doctors overseeing her care, led by Dr Timothy Stahl, wanted her to stay longer but they were ignored, and Charlie's first instruction from his wife was to source both a rowing machine and a stationary exercise bike. Despite still needing crutches, and being in a plaster cast below her knee, Beryl was anxious to resume training. 'Day after day I exercised until my sweat-soaked body could take no more,' she said. She also soon insisted on doing all the housework and would go out shopping on crutches with her belongings in a bag on her back. All the exercise meant that the calf muscle in her lower left leg began to grow back. The problem was that it had nowhere to go inside the plaster and she woke one night in January 1978 feeling sick and in extreme pain. Charlie telephoned Dr Stahl, who instantly worked out the problem and recommended that Beryl have the cast removed the following morning so that the infection could be treated. Not one for waiting another minute when something needed doing, Beryl dispatched Charlie to the cellar and, having retrieved a saw, he set to work in his pyjamas. 'Eventually he managed it, to reveal my calf, red raw and covered with pus,' said Beryl.

She was now back and immediately decided to take up a place in a pre-season training camp in Mallorca. Her invitation to race in Arizona also extended to simply coming over as an ambassador for what was a three-day race. The journalist Les Woodland stayed in the same accommodation and was struck by how she was treated with something approaching awe by the Americans. 'She never seemed to notice it, still less seek it,' said Woodland. 'She was instantly likeable. Instead of banging on about her greatest victories, she spoke more about always wanting the windows open and that a kitchen could never have too many power points. She got out on her bike most days, commenting on how slow Americans drove compared to Brits.'

The time in the Arizona heat, which included long rides beside the Grand Canyon, would also lay the foundation for Beryl's recovery. The first big test was the British 25-mile championship in June and, amid a new generation of challengers, and doubts over her physical condition, the chatter within the cycling fraternity was that an era might finally be coming to an end. Beryl had not read that particular script and marked her return from serious injury with a trademark demolition of the field. She was 2 min. 28 sec. ahead of her nearest challenger. To put that in perspective, the same time gap would separate the next ten finishers. The headline in *Cycling* read, 'Beryl Burton just won't be beaten' – even if the accompanying report recorded an ongoing numbness in her right leg. '[It] just didn't seem as though it belonged to me,' she said. Just how much Beryl had been through during the preceding seven months was evident from her assessment of this particular victory. 'It was a personal triumph,' she said. 'None of my time trial wins gave me greater satisfaction.'

It was a period that also reinforced her focus on time trialling and long weekends spent driving and cycling the length and breadth of the country to compete in early morning races.

Maintaining her continued dominance of the national scene was also more physically challenging than the results would often suggest. Beryl began suffering sharp chest pains in 1979 – something she blamed on pleurisy – and both her knees and her back began to cause permanent discomfort. Crashes were having an increasingly debilitating effect. Her response to any setback, though, was directly experienced by clubmate Malcolm Cowgill when she came off during a two-up 25-mile time trial they were riding together along the A1 one Saturday afternoon in April 1981.*

'We were really shifting when, all of a sudden, I heard this loud bang,' says Cowgill. 'Beryl had touched my back wheel. I stopped, looked around and she was sprawled in the road. No helmet and she had a bad head wound. If that had happened with the traffic on the roads today it would probably have been fatal.' Cowgill quickly rode back and asked Beryl if she was OK, thinking they might need an ambulance. He had not contemplated that their ride could continue. 'She just looked up at me, said, "I'm alright, let's carry on." I thought, "My God." So I started riding again, not very enthusiastically, as I was in a bit of shock. Next thing I knew, Beryl came charging past shouting at me to speed up. Blood was running off her chin, down her jersey, on her legs and all over her bike. But we still did 58 minutes. And we won.' Beryl was also back in work the following Monday but, after a full day picking raspberries, felt sufficient discomfort to seek medical advice. As well as the obvious face wound, it was found that she had two broken ribs and an infection on her bruised hip.

Beryl remained unbeatable domestically in 1981 and again dabbled with the idea of seeking financial support so that she could base herself in Leicester to prepare for a tilt at a home

---

* A 'two-up' follows the same format as an individual time trial, except that riders compete as a pair and so can take turns cycling into the wind while the other shelters close behind.

world championship the following year. She believed that daily access to a track would make her fast enough to again compete on a world level over 3,000 m but, having been turned down for a minimal SportsAid Foundation Grant, she ultimately decided to remain strictly amateur with Morley.* She also briefly considered the possibility of stepping back from racing entirely following a twenty-third straight BAR, as well as victories over the emerging Mandy Jones in both the national 25- and the 10-mile time trial championships. 'Was I crazy?' she wrote in *Personal Best*. 'I had no right to be racing and winning at my age. It would be so pleasant to contemplate some weekend rides at home, without any pressure of travelling, and perhaps a steady ride in the Dales and an hour by the Wharfe at Grassington watching the sunlight glinting on the river. Also important, it would be pleasant for Charlie to be out on his bike with me in the Yorkshire countryside, enjoying himself and recharging his batteries for the work-a-day world.' It all sounds rather tranquil and almost selfless but, without any attempt to explain why she ploughed on regardless, she then quickly added: 'In the end, the pull of the greatest and toughest sport in the world was too great.' And what would follow over the next two years, both individually and with Denise, were perhaps Beryl's greatest triumphs.

---

*The charity SportsAid was formed in 1976 and, twenty-one years before Lottery funding, provided financial assistance to elite amateur athletes. Sharron Davies and Sebastian Coe were among thousands to benefit from its support, though never Beryl Burton.

13

The Silver Jubilee

In resisting that passing thought to stop at the end of the 1981 season, there was one carrot above all else that piqued Beryl's insatiable appetite. She had just completed a twenty-third straight victory in the BAR competition and was now within sight of winning the most prestigious national time trial championship for a continuous quarter of a century. Her thoughts were recorded in her autobiography. 'Twenty-five?' she wrote. 'That was a nice sounding number. A sort of silver jubilee. Could I pull it off? I decided to try.' The BAR is a uniquely gruelling contest. There is the obvious physical test on a bike, but it is also a mental and logistical marathon. Planning each year would begin from the moment that the RTTC handbook – a thick A6 manual crammed with dates, times, addresses and records – arrived through the post. In her early racing years Beryl would simply work around the world championships, the 25-, 50- and 100-mile national time trial championships and the national track and road champion-ships. That was her order of priorities, and triumphing against the best of British in the BAR had once been simply an inevitable consequence of those objectives.

Provided that the ride was in a RTTC-approved event over 25, 50 or 100 miles between April and September, it could potentially count towards your final BAR speed. These included the national championships, but clubs from all over the country would also organise 'open' events of all distances from 10 miles to 24 hours. It meant that there was always a wide weekly selection of races and, with certain courses known for their fast conditions, and the weather greatly impacting the potential times on any particular day, choosing the best schedule could be critical. Beryl was generally so far ahead of the other women that she only needed to be sure of completing one ride over the three qualifying distances to be certain of winning the BAR. This had changed by the early 1980s and, although she always raced several times a week, it created a new pressure. A missed event previously did not matter. Now she felt an obligation to ride in case of what cyclists call 'a float day', when the meteorological atmosphere and lack of winds provide unusually fast conditions. To put the prospect of twenty-five straight wins simply in the context of this particular event, no other woman has ever won the BAR in more than three consecutive years. The longest winning streak among the men remains Ian Cammish's six during the 1980s. Beryl was out to more than quadruple such dominance.

With her mother still as competitive and motivated as ever, 1982 would also represent a pivotal juncture in Denise's life, and she cites two turning points in her recovery from anorexia. Denise had stopped racing between 1979 and 1981 but she still always rode a bike – 'just slower and fewer miles' – and was spurred by the reaction of an old cycling friend on the road near Shipley. 'I must have been very ill, because he went past and didn't recognise me at first. He then said, "Denise?" and I could see the shock and horror. He was really upset. He waited and I couldn't keep up. Something clicked. I thought, "I am not able to do the thing I love because I am so weak and thin." I had no help. No books. Nothing. That's the power of your mind. I thought, "You have to get your strength and muscle back." I needed time. It took about ten years out of my life but I did it because I wanted to get back cycling. I would not have managed it without cycling.'

Denise's initial strategy was to 'put weight on fast' and so, in her own words, she ate 'absolute junk'. That meant foods high in fat and sugar and, while that in itself would require a further rebalance over the next five years, she did gradually restore her cycling power. She eventually felt strong enough to tackle the hills of the Dales again and, during what had become weekly visits to her parents in Harrogate, it was Beryl who came up with an unexpectedly inspired idea. She suggested that Denise could get back racing with her. But not against each other. This would be the Burtons together. On a tandem. Denise tentatively agreed and, within a few weeks, Charlie had sourced a tandem for them to trial. It is an experience that Denise can now treasure:

> It was absolutely her idea – my mum wanted something to encourage me to get cycling again. She really wanted to find a way to help me and it worked. We trained on it a few times and we clicked. She had the brakes at the front and I had the gears behind. She could see the hill, roundabout or junction and would shout 'up' or 'down' for the gears or 'push' if there was a hill. I couldn't see a thing. I was just tucked down behind her back. You have to go with the flow and be relaxed but powerful on the back. I trusted her completely. And she really could pedal. She never trained on a massive gear and was so smooth in how she rode a bike. She always looked amazing on a bike but, riding with her, you could also feel it. I could take my mind off everything and just concentrate on powering it as best I could.

They decided to enter a race – a 10-mile time trial organised by the Lincoln Wheelers – and, in Beryl's words, the idea was to treat it 'as a lark'. They blasted off and, after 5 miles, an unexpected shout came from roadside. They were on course for the national women's record. 'We got quite excited – and went even faster,' says Denise. Around 10 minutes later it was all over in a new British record time of 21 min. 25 sec. Denise now wishes that they had kept chasing tandem records – 'we could have done an awful lot more but I was an independent girl' – and she would instead gradually rebuild her own individual career. After all the difficulties, the tandem record was somehow also illustrative of a wider truth. Theirs was a complicated relationship, but the bond would never break.

Despite the unlikely tandem triumph, 1982 was again characterised for Beryl by her more fragile health. She was now closer to fifty than forty and, having been dominant since 1958, was facing an increasingly desperate battle to remain the best time triallist in Great Britain. Chest pains were more frequent, and after coughing up blood over a period of weeks she attended a clinic in Leeds. They found that her lungs were dilating and diagnosed a form of asthma. She was also now using an inhaler and finding it hard to breathe out when she was pedalling quickly. Other riders would say they could hear Beryl before they saw her because of the permanent wheezing noise.

It was still a massive shock when she then lost the 1982 10-mile title to Mandy Jones in 1982. This was the first time that she had been defeated in any national time trial championships that she had completed for twenty years. Although Jones was a world-class rider, and Beryl did still win both the national 25-mile championship and her twenty-fourth BAR that year, it was now clear that the passage of time could not be endlessly delayed. The picture of the medal winners at the national 10-mile championships also told its own story. Jones was only twenty and Barbra Collins, the winner of the bronze medal, was seventeen. Beryl looked like a mother posing with her two daughters on the podium.

Beryl was not selected for either the road race or the pursuit at the 1982 world championship, even though they were being held in Great Britain, but she did travel to Leicester to watch the track events. Despite her ill health, Beryl had just beaten Jones in a 50-mile time trial but there was little evidence that she would have transferred her longer-distance qualities to the more sudden efforts required on a track or road race. Jones, by contrast, possessed an exceptional turn of pace and, having finished seventh in

38. Beryl's first national time trial defeat for two decades, but she was gracious after losing to future world champion Mandy Jones.

the pursuit, it all came together for her in the road race and she memorably rode clear to win around the motor-racing circuit in Goodwood.

Beryl had been interviewed by Barry Davies as part of the BBC's coverage and, as she outlined her ongoing ambitions, 'that bit of bitterness', as she had described it fifteen years earlier, can still be easily sensed. 'I can't really get excited spectating,' she declared. What did provoke rather more emotion, as well as a noticeable flexing of her square jaw, was the request for an assessment of her current form. 'Not too bad,' said Beryl. 'I won a 50-mile time trial the other day by 7 minutes – that really pleased me.' Davies then asked the question that would crop up in just about every interview throughout the last thirty years of her life. 'How long do you intend to go on?' Beryl looked irritated. 'Once I stop enjoying the racing or I find that I have to push myself to go training, that's it, I will call it a day,' she said. 'I think the thing in sport nowadays is to actually forget how old people are. To me, if they are producing the speed and the times, age shouldn't be taken into account.'

*

Whether Beryl liked it or not, an emerging group of domestic competitors were acutely aware of her age. One was Sue Fenwick, a tall and talented eighteen-year-old from East London who had also come from a family with little money and even less understanding of cycling. She had instantly felt liberated on a bike and duly joined the renowned Essex Roads Cycling Club. When Beryl had started out in the late 1950s, some of the other clubs in Essex did not allow women into their clubhouse, but Fenwick was among those to benefit from the transformation. 'It was very welcoming – I was a bit lost at the time and the cycling club gave me this sense of community, family and support,' she says. As they had been for Beryl, the long weekend club runs were Fenwick's introduction. She rode her first race at the end of 1982 and, quickly realising her potential, clubmates encouraged her to train seriously that winter. Bill Thorncroft, a former national champion and a major figure in the Essex time trial fraternity, lent Fenwick some race wheels and was confident that she could challenge the best riders.

There was, says Fenwick, 'a north–south divide' in terms of British time trialling, and she sensed a strong desire from her Essex friends to see Beryl finally toppled. Their early interactions were virtually non-existent. 'Beryl was very private – you would get a nod if you passed by during the warm-up, but we never exchanged more than a "hi" or "hello" during that 1983 season,' she says. Although Beryl would seldom speak shortly before a race, she was never aloof or removed from the very amateur arrangements of her competitors, and they found themselves sharing the same youth hostel room in Milton Keynes before one event. The other girls, including Fenwick, had all been standing together chatting

39. Beryl only ever sat still on her bike or while knitting.

in the dormitory when Beryl walked in at 10 p.m. 'There was this hush,' says Fenwick. 'We were all much younger and in awe. You could sense this feeling of "Here comes Beryl Burton, don't upset her."' The silence was finally broken by Beryl, who, having lifted the mattress down from her bunk bed and placed it on the floor, said simply 'Goodnight' to everyone in the room before pulling the sleeping bag over her head. Moving the mattress was actually mitigation against the now permanent pain in her spine, but Fenwick jumped to a different conclusion. 'I decided that must be the secret and, for the rest of the year, I dragged mattresses off beds wherever I was staying and slept on the floor.' And what did Fenwick make of Beryl back then? 'She was this marvellous woman, but I wanted to beat her. She was the same age as my mum and I did think, "Why is she still racing after all these years? What's the attraction? Why doesn't she retire and go knitting?"'

The irony was that Beryl was knitting even while regularly winning world titles before Fenwick had been born. Beryl wanted to leave as little to chance as possible in her bid for that twenty-fifth BAR and so, with Charlie staying at home, she took four weeks off in March and headed to Spain. Although Beryl liked to combine full-time work with her cycling – 'it stops one rusting up' – and thought nothing of fitting this in by training before daylight or after dark, she would seek work where the hours could be adapted to major races or trips abroad. Her jobs after relocating to Harrogate in 1976 included picking raspberries at a farm in nearby Knaresborough, cleaning and looking after houses, preparing sandwiches, making bread in a bakery and serving on the biscuit counter in the local Co-op. As well as Ron Kitching's bike shops, Charlie took on work at the Hotel Majestic in Harrogate, where he was in charge of ordering the restaurant's wine and food.

Beryl had firmly rejected a suggestion by the *Yorkshire Evening Post* in 1979 that her work might be 'rather undignified … for a holder of the OBE'. Indeed, her letters to friends were always crammed full of enthusiastic detail about her various jobs, such as how she persuaded the bakery to start a new line in granary and why she would lecture customers about the benefits of eating wholemeal bread. 'The other people in the shop laugh their heads off,' she wrote. Her letters are self-deprecating and humorous, starting out with sentences like 'Hi! It's that mad woman from Yorkshire' and digressing on subjects ranging from Charlie's singing while he fixed their bikes in the cellar of their flat, to her gardening, sharing the road with milk floats on early morning training rides, the pros and cons of double glazing, a love of boiled beetroot and black tea, and whether other cyclists only recognised her under a woolly winter hat because of the size of her nose. Her delight at being able to gather up cut-price dented tins or broken parcels of food that were only available to Co-op employees is also uncontained in one letter to the photographer Bernard Thompson and his wife, Ethel. 'Cycle bag full, back bag full, and usually something clutched in my hand,' wrote Beryl, who then described how the rattling noise would startle passers-by as she pedalled home through Harrogate.

The warm-weather cycling trips to Spain were something that she rarely mentioned publicly but, according to another letter she sent to the Thompsons, 1983 was actually the third consecutive year that she stayed in the same £35-a-month self-catering apartment in Benidorm. The letter, which runs to more than 2,500 words, provides some wonderful insights. The quality and vast bulk of her training are naturally evident. 'I am doing 70 miles in a morning and 30 miles steady potter in an afternoon, that is until I meet up with any English or Spanish lads then it's bit and bit,' she wrote. 'Laughed the other day. Was five miles from home – nose for the stable door – when I caught two Spanish lads. Went by, said "Hi!" Didn't know they had jumped on until I heard a couple of grunts and snorts. Thought "Oh!" Anyway, pressed on, got to the light at red. Stopped. One came alongside and said, "Always, you ride so hard!?" Oh yes! I felt great. Just those few words and I was on top of the world.'

Beryl also went into lengthy detail about her food. 'I am living like a queen,' she wrote, noting the 'kitchenette with double gas ring and fridge', and says that she is eating liver daily at midday after her morning ride ('75p our money for 2¼ lb.'), salad, tomato, onions ('all 6p lb.'). She also recounts a trip to a farm in Callosa, where you could buy 'all the fancy kinds of honey you can imagine for 50p lb.' and how, after training rides, she fills her back pockets with oranges and grapefruits fresh off the trees. 'The grapefruits I got the other day were so big every time I went over a bump I got my bum massaged,' she wrote. Beryl also recounts how she rode the 30 miles from the airport to her apartment with only a medium-size saddlebag. She reckons that she is down to 8½ stone without the home-made cakes. There is a rather comically touching interlude when she confides how, 'when I was thinking about Charlie, and how I missed him', she poured her tea into a salt pot. She also describes her husband as 'like a child with its first toy' following the recent delivery of her latest bike. She ends by ominously concluding that 'I've really got my cycling legs back' after almost four weeks' training and resting rather than being on her feet working all day.

Beryl was delighted with her winter preparation but, barely a month after returning from Spain, there was a major setback. A dangerous driver again knocked her over during a training ride. As well as wrecking her bike, she was left with three broken ribs and serious bruising to her already fragile back. Rehabilitation again began by riding indoors before borrowing Charlie's training bike. A new bike was eventually sourced, but her back pain remained acute and, as well as being unable to sleep at night, other physical problems were also now alarmingly evident. Beryl had stopped perspiring and would feel easily dehydrated, a condition that can cause rapid heat exhaustion. She was diagnosed with both spinal cord concussion and anaemia. This was on top of the asthma and dilating lungs that had caused such problems the year before. The advice from Dr Stahl was now clear. 'I was told to stop riding a bike for the time being and to forget racing for ever,' said Beryl. Yet what sounds like unequivocal advice was again interpreted as a choice, and in her autobiography she described it as 'a hell of a decision to make'. The outcome of her deliberations would have surprised nobody. 'I had set my heart on the BAR for the 25th time,' she said. 'I decided to stick it out so far as possible. If I lost, it was to be on the road, not in the doctor's surgery.'

The crash meant that Beryl was soon playing catch-up during what would become a momentous contest. She struggled throughout April, May and June, and was duly beaten in both the national 10- and 25-mile championships by Jones. Fenwick had also taken the 100-mile title and separately set a personal best over the distance to become only the second woman after Beryl to get inside 4 hrs 10 min. It was not until July 1983 – three months after the accident – that glimpses of the old Beryl Burton began to emerge. She regained the national 50-mile championships against a field that included Jones and Fenwick before riding what was the fastest 25-mile time trial of the year in 56 min. 32 sec. to pull herself right back into contention in the BAR. It meant needing a fast performance over 100 miles to take a commanding lead, but a direct consequence of Beryl's problems with temperature regulation was that longer rides, especially on a humid day, were now taking a savage toll. Beryl eventually posted 4 hrs 19 min. 57 sec. to guarantee at least one potential time but fully expected to improve on home territory in an event promoted by the Yorkshire Cycling Federation.

What followed would underline the risks that she was now taking. After 51 miles, and 'feeling hot with the strength draining from me', Beryl took the extraordinary mid-race decision to climb off her bike. She was found laid out exhausted on the roadside verge by Charlie and driven straight home. Of the thousands of races that she had started, Beryl had only previously not finished three times – when she was physically sick with a stomach virus during an event in Wales and when her knees gave way twice in 1969, during the Mersey 24-hour race and then the national '100' championship. Beryl tried to gather herself and, still combining working, training and racing with regular hospital treatment for both anaemia and her back, she targeted the Yorkshire Century in August. The outcome was no different and she again retired, dangerously sick and exhausted, after 50 miles. 'It was a disastrous day,' she later said. But still she tried again – this time in the North Midland '100' – and, having made a fast start and been on schedule for a time close to 4 hours, 'everything seemed to collapse around me and, again, I failed to finish'. In the space of just a few short traumatic weeks, the once indestructible Beryl Burton had failed to complete as many races as in her previous twenty-eight years of racing. 'I was utterly down, both physically and mentally,' she said.

Beryl would never ride another '100' but, with that one relatively slow time on the board, all was not lost. Her rapid 25 had effectively counterbalanced Fenwick's '100', meaning that the 1983 women's BAR would effectively be decided by their respective 50-mile performances. Both women knew that the season was almost certain to come down to what happened in the Otley 50-mile race. The fastest time trial courses of that era tended either to be along the A12 in Essex or those in Yorkshire, where a section of the A1 between Boroughbridge and Wetherby was known throughout cycling simply as 'The Boro'. It was a well-surfaced and reasonably flat piece of road but also sufficiently busy to create something of a 'drag' benefit for the riders. Beryl was always adamant that the Essex courses were faster and that the generally early start times for women meant that the traffic was negligible, but she did particularly appreciate the untechnical and straight nature of the A1. It helped her to concentrate and, according to Alf Engers, the most famous men's time trial-list of the 1970s, that was one of her greatest assets. 'I couldn't ride long distances like Beryl because I'd be distracted,' he says. Ian Cammish, who would win the men's BAR in 1983, believes that the reputation of 'The Boro', largely as a result of Beryl's past feats, had a psychological impact on riders. It was also home territory and, with the help of her still immaculate diaries, the weekend of the Otley 50 on 21 August 1983 is one that Fenwick can remember vividly.

Aged only eighteen, and with virtually no external backup, what Fenwick achieved herself during a first full season was remarkable. She had won a national championship and was now the main obstacle to the crowning achievement of a legend. Her logistical preparations were no more sophisticated than those of her older rival. 'I didn't have a car, so I would generally cycle to the station with my race wheels in carriers on the front and take the train,' says Fenwick. 'I would have looked for the nearest youth hostel or bed and breakfast. If there wasn't anywhere within cycling distance of the start, I would phone the event organiser and ask if there was anybody in the club who would be willing to give me a bed. It would be a tin of Ambrosia rice or a bag of chips the night before.' For the Otley race, Ann and Graham Mann, who lived in Brentwood, had offered Fenwick a lift and so she stayed with them before driving to Yorkshire on the morning of the race.

For all her mounting physical problems, Beryl's one obvious advantage was that she lived only 10 miles from the start and knew 'The Boro' better than any other cyclist. Her performances that season over 25 miles also suggested that she still had sufficient speed. The doubt was the extent to which her body could sustain her efforts into a second or third hour. Beryl's tactics were typically uncomplicated. She would set off fast and try to cling on. Her feelings that day were outlined several years later in her autobiography. 'Again it was warm, again it was breezy, again my legs no longer rammed against a high gear effectively,' she wrote. 'It was slog, slog and more slog. I poured everything into that ride, ignoring the pain, the elastic legs and the rasping body. My mind had to dominate.' She says that her rhythm went 'to pieces' in the final few miles but that 'somehow I forced myself to finish'. The result? An astonishing 1 hr 56 min. 33 sec. It was her fastest 50 for three years and quicker even than some of her BAR-winning rides in the 1960s. She had also beaten Fenwick by almost 4 minutes. According to the cycling historian Peter Whitfield, who interviewed Beryl later in her life, she privately rated it as 'perhaps the greatest ride' of her career. 'She finished more utterly drained than she could ever remember, and no one around her knew what it had cost, but it won her that 25th BAR,' said Whitfield.

It did indeed, even if absolute confirmation would not come until near the end of September, when the last two potential qualifying dates were held over a single weekend in Essex. Beryl desperately wanted to end her season immediately after the Otley race but, fearing unusually fast conditions in either the 25-mile race on the Saturday or the 50-mile event on the Sunday, she felt that she had to be there to compete against Fenwick. The severity of her health problems was known to only a few close family and friends. One of those was Margaret Allen, her former Morley teammate. Allen was never a serious contender to win the BAR in 1983 – she eventually finished tenth – but would often travel with Beryl, and they stayed together in a chalet that weekend. She saw up close just how hard Beryl pushed herself to win that 25th BAR. 'What struck me was that she was so frightened,' says Allen. 'She wanted to win so much that I think it was also making her ill.' Beryl, says Allen, had somehow also convinced herself that she would still lose on that final weekend. She would talk of 'failing dismally' and how she would retire from the sport 'utterly exhausted and beaten'. But Beryl did also keep telling herself: 'Just one more time. Then you can rest. Grit your teeth and go.'

As it was, Fenwick was also mentally and physically exhausted from all the racing and, amid wet, cold and winter weather, they both went slower than the previous month in Yorkshire. The final standings remained unchanged. Perhaps the remarkable feat of all had been achieved – and yet Beryl described almost anti-climactic feelings. 'Wearily I climbed off the bike, exhausted and my mind empty of any emotion,' she said. 'It was not until we were halfway back to Yorkshire that I realised what I had accomplished. Twenty-five years at the top! It had been a long haul for that sick little girl all those years ago in St James's Hospital.' Allen believes that Beryl's continuous domestic dominance from 1959 until 1983 surpassed even the seven world titles and the record-breaking Otley 12. 'She is the finest athlete this country has ever produced and I think it was the biggest accolade,' she said. 'It was a great release to her – and it was the hardest one she ever fought for. It was remarkable, but …' Allen then paused for about 30 seconds before finding the right words. 'The wire,' she finally said in her broad Yorkshire accent. 'Beryl took herself to the wire that year. And she had been pushing her body continuously for more than twenty-five years. You cannot do that and expect it to keep reacting the same.'

40. Beryl went to the physical brink in 1983 but twenty-five straight BAR titles will never be emulated.

There was minimal media coverage, but Beryl did receive a message of congratulations from Neil Macfarlane, the sports minister in Margaret Thatcher's newly re-elected government. The British time trial community were also determined to mark the feat at their annual awards night, which were held the following January in the Assembly Rooms in Derby. Dame Mary Peters, the former Olympic pentathlon champion, presented the prizes, but the evening almost began with a disaster. All the various trophies had been laid out on the stage, but there was a short delay after the table gave way and they all clattered down across the floor. It was otherwise a meticulously planned evening. Ian Cammish, who won the Men's Best All-Rounder for the fourth time, had been asked if he was happy for the organisers to forgo tradition and end the evening by presenting the women's rather than men's prize. Having long idolised Beryl, and once even ridden out to an event in Essex just to get her autograph (which he still has), Cammish readily agreed. On the table plan, Beryl was listed as 'Mrs C. Burton', and it was also noticeable that Charlie, as well as

Beryl, was invited up to collect the twenty-fifth BAR. The spouse of a male champion is rarely so readily celebrated. Will Townsend made the announcement. 'This magnificent Morley marvel forced herself upon the national scene in 1957, when she was second in the 100-miles championship and went on to a fifth place in the women's BAR ... how little any of us realised that we had seen the sporting birth of the greatest British woman cyclist,' he said. 'Accompanied by her husband, Charlie, I call upon you to receive and acclaim on the occasion of her Silver Jubilee of Women's Best All-Rounder triumphs, cycling's Golden Girl!'

Whenever she collected a prize, Beryl liked to slip in a joke – often at the expense of the men and warned that she might not be back next year. 'It's not me, it's the engraver – he's retired,' she said. There was also a tribute to Charlie. 'The loving care and immaculate preparation of my bikes, the constant driving at weekends, the sacrifice of his own cycling and other interests – whatever I had achieved could not have been done without him,' she said. As well as presenting her with the BAR trophy once more, the RTTC also commissioned a one-off gold necklace to commemorate the achievement. Jones, who had followed Beryl in becoming Britain's second women's world champion, also made a perfectly judged five-word speech when she took to the stage. 'Beryl, you are the greatest,' she simply said. The audience of 850 then stood for 5 minutes of continuous applause as Beryl and Charlie left the stage and were carried shoulder high around the room by their fellow cyclists.

Beryl allowed herself a rare celebration and stayed up into the early hours. Cammish, the men's champion, says that Beryl was an 'approachable enigma' off the bike. 'No airs or graces at all,' he says. Following their year-long battle, Beryl also had her first proper conversation that night with Fenwick. 'Charlie was there smiling and Beryl was very unassuming,' says Fenwick. 'I look back now and I am just gobsmacked that she was able to win it for twenty-five years. It is one of those achievements that, the more you analyse it, the more amazing it seems. I tried for one year and found it exhausting.' Fenwick would stop racing for more than twenty-five years but, when she did make a comeback in her late forties, her admiration for what Beryl had achieved at the age of forty-six only grew. 'She was in her pre-menopausal years – it was something that was never talked about – but it does have an effect,' says Fenwick. 'You can feel knackered, depressed and bloated. But she powered through all that – still training and racing with her eye on that prize. I can also look back now differently. I tried to win but it was the pinnacle. It would have been a tragedy if I had pipped her at the post after she had already got to twenty-four.'

Beryl's evening would end in the relative luxury of the Midland Hotel, opposite Derby railway station, with a small gaggle of close friends and Morley teammates. Allen and Cowgill were there. Others, like Charlie and Carline, had shared that first club ride some thirty-one years earlier. Brenda Robins made place mats with Beryl's name on them and says that the twenty-five-times champion had her friends in 'stitches of laugher' with anecdote after anecdote. They presented Beryl with a cake in the shape of a '25' that had been iced in the Morley colours of pale blue and white. She felt elated. 'They knew what it was like to push through a howling wind in pouring rain with a determination to finish; they knew the discomfort of standing and shivering in the road at a junction to point the way; they knew the tediousness of collecting entries and typing out start sheets,' Beryl later recounted. 'I sat on the floor, munched cake and mince pies, drank apple juice and realised that this, really, was what it was all about. The fellowship of like-minded folk. To be part of it gives you something nobody else has. If you are a cyclist, you understand.'

14

Just How Fast Was She?

As Beryl Burton's sparkling old handmade steel TI-Raleigh bike was released and then carefully lifted from a mount, a series of engraved letters and numbers – 'BB.1.81' – briefly became visible on the bottom bracket. The exact machine on which Beryl raced during much of the 1980s, and which is photographed on the front of her autobiography, had just completed its most vigorous workout for more than thirty years. 'People will struggle to believe this,' muttered Xavier Disley, one of the world's leading experts on aerodynamics, as he clicked through various tables, graphs and spreadsheets and began to mentally compute the information on the screens in front of him.

We were inside a wind tunnel at the Silverstone motor-racing circuit, and the objective for the day had been to finally resolve one of British cycling's classic café stop debates.

Just how fast would Beryl Burton be today? Her record times might have been broken, but would modern aerodynamic kit put her straight back on top of the pile? Or would improvements in training and sports science inevitably leave her behind? When you really stop to think about it, the idea that any athlete could overcome a handicap of more than fifty years is outlandish. Imagine plonking Sir Gareth Edwards, all 5 ft 8 in. and 13 stone of him, from the 1970s into an international rugby union match today. Or placing Billie Jean King in a time machine, letting her adjust to a modern tennis racket for a few weeks and then expecting her to hold her own on Centre Court at Wimbledon against Serena

Williams. And just consider other endurance sports like athletics and swimming. Technological advancements are minimal compared with cycling, and yet the purely human improvement through the decades is vast. The women's marathon world best in 1967, the year Beryl set her 12-hour record that lasted fifty years, was 3 hrs 7 min. 27 sec. By 2022, the Kenyan Brigid Kosgei had shaved 53 minutes from that time. Thousands of other women had also since gone faster and, although the marathon was relatively new for females in the 1960s, we can still see large improvements at more commonly run distances which are comparable to the advances in swimming records of around 10 per cent.

While mass-start road racing provides limited opportunity to pit cycling generations against each another, the simple challenge of time trialling – A to B as fast as possible – is ripe for comparison. 'You're not hiding behind anyone – it's the race of truth,' Beryl would say. By first looking back (Table 1), we can see how, over a period of eighteen years between 1958 until 1976, Beryl propelled standards far beyond even the aerodynamic revolution that was sparked in 1989 by Greg LeMond's use of body-narrowing triathlon handlebars. Indeed, throughout the fifty-nine years from 1958 until 2017, Beryl always held at least one of the RTTC's five main competition records. For a span of thirty-three years she held the entire set from 12 hours down to 10 miles, which was considered more for club riders rather than serious internationals during most of her career.

Further insight can be derived from comparing Beryl's various records with the men's standard at that time (Table 2). For around fifteen years between the late 1960s and the early 1980s she was not just the leading women's time triallist in the world but regularly up there with the very best men. Her 100-mile record ride, for example, was set in 1968 and fast enough to have won not just all but six of the fifty-three women's championships to 2021 but also most of the men's national titles during the 1970s. How unusually close Beryl was to the men's records can be illustrated by

Table 1

Distance (miles)	Record before Beryl	Beryl's record span and number of new competition records she set at distance	Beryl's personal best and % improvement over previous record holder
10	25 min. 00 sec. Jo Bowers (1960)	1960–93 8 records	21 min. 25 sec. (1973) 14.3%
25	1 hr 1 min. 49 sec. Millie Robinson (1958)	1959–96 11 records	53 min. 21 sec. (1976) 13.7%
50	2 hrs 9 min. 18 sec. Millie Robinson (1958)	1958–96 11 records	1 hr 51 min. 30 sec. (1976) 13.8%
100	4 hrs 32 min. 07 scc. Millie Robinson (1958)	1958–96 10 records	3 hrs 55 min. 05 sec (1968) 13.6%
12 hr	237.91 miles Christine Watts (1954)	1959–2017 2 records	277.25 miles (1967) 16.5%

simply calculating the difference in her personal best to the men's record at that same date. Fast-forward to 2022 and, even though all the times have improved considerably on the new technology, we can see how the comparative gap has widened enormously.

It all reinforces Beryl's status as an athletic outlier but still does not resolve that classic café stop question. What times would she have done on today's modern equipment? The anecdotal sense that aerodynamics have been a complete game-changer in modern time trialling is repeatedly confirmed by anyone with experience across the eras.

Malcolm Cowgill, the Morley club secretary, kept racing well into his seventies and, on a relatively modern time trial bike, found himself matching his lifetime personal bests after he was collecting

Table 2

Distance	Beryl's record	Gap between Beryl and men's record*	Current women's record†	Current gap to men's record†
10 miles	21 min. 25 sec. (29 April 1973)	49 sec. down 3.8% difference	18 min. 36 sec. Hayley Simmonds	2 min. 01 sec. down 10.8% difference
25 miles	53 min. 21 sec. (17 June 1976)	2 min. 21 sec. down 4.4% difference	49 min. 28 sec. Hayley Simmonds	6 min. 37 sec. down 13.4% difference
50 miles	1 hr 51 min. 30 sec. (25 July 1976)	7 min. 44 sec. down 6.9% difference	1 hr 42 min. 20 sec. Hayley Simmonds	11 min. 51 sec. down 11.6% difference
100 miles	3 hrs 55 min. 05 sec. (4 August 1968)	3 min. 24 sec. down 1.4% difference	3 hrs 42 min. 03 sec. Alice Lethbridge	26 min. 26 sec. down 11.9% difference
12 hours	277.25 miles (17 September 1967)	0.73 miles up 0.03% difference	290.07 miles Alice Lethbridge	35.48 miles down 12.2% difference

*As of date of Beryl Burton record.
†As of April 2022.

his pension. He describes the sort of steel road bikes that he and Beryl had used between the late 1950s and early 1990s as 'farm-yard implements' by comparison. Sue Fenwick, who pushed Beryl so hard for that twenty-fifth BAR title, made a comeback more than twenty-five years later, in her forties, and soon matched her own previous times – with less training – while using a modern time trial set-up.

Jamie Pringle, who worked as the head of science and technical development at the Boardman Performance Centre, immediately confirms that aerodynamic advances are anything but marginal gains. 'It's another leg,' he says. Chris Boardman himself nods and, having been tasked with identifying technological improvements as head 'secret squirrel' for British Cycling's Olympic operation between 2004 and 2012, also became an authority on aerodynamics. 'We spent one week a month in a wind tunnel for those eight years,' he says. 'We found that expenditure to go the same speed can differ enormously. It's mostly about body position. Human power hasn't changed much in the last twenty-five years. The physiology is a bit better, and we don't do so many junk miles, but efficiency has changed because of knowledge and technology.' There is, though, one enduring and related characteristic. 'Those who are good tend to get very small on the bike,' says Boardman. 'They didn't realise at the time how important it was, but people like Beryl and Alf Engers were already right down there.'

Pringle agrees and notes how Beryl 'held a terrific position', even if he is still convinced that her improvement on a modern time trial bike would be vast. Boardman could also offer his own personal experience. He was a rider who 'got small', and yet the difference between his world one-hour records on a standard track bike of the sort that Beryl would have used (49.441 km in 2000 for the athlete's hour) and the extreme 'Superman' machine with outstretched triathlon bars (56.375 km in 1996) was almost 7 km.* Both records were set in the Manchester Velodrome, although, allowing for his drop in power over those four years, Boardman estimates that the real aerodynamic upgrade was something between 5 and 5.5 kph. Subsequent wind-tunnel tests have found that the 'Superman' time trial position, first invented by Graeme Obree and later outlawed by the UCI, was very comparable to the current set-ups.

---

* The record for the distance cycled in one hour around a velodrome has existed in various forms since 1873 and has now been divided into different categories to acknowledge advances in technology.

Xavier Disley can easily empathise with Obree. He owns the AeroCoach company, which works with professional cycling teams and national Olympic squads as well as amateur riders on aerodynamics. He also invents cutting-edge equipment and clothing as part of a never-ending quest to shave seconds off a rider's time. Disley's big advantage over Obree is that he can objectively test new ideas inside a wind tunnel. He was instantly intrigued by the 'Beryl' concept and confident that he could calculate accurate projected times provided that a set of conditions was met. We would have to source an equivalent bike and clothing from Beryl's era and a rider of comparable size and aerodynamic potential. Information on the courses on which Beryl set her records would also be invaluable.

A phone call to Cowgill, and a classic pale blue Morley Cycling Club jersey, complete with wool collar, nylon body and bonus fifty-year-old mud stain, had arrived on loan from Yorkshire within 24 hours. I also discussed the idea with Chris Sidwells, a cycling historian and another of Beryl's friends, who had an idea for the bike. The frame builder Dave Marsh collects vintage machines and among those on display at his Universal Cycle Centre in the old mining town of Maltby are two of Beryl's originals. One is the red Viking track bike on which she won the 1963 world pursuit title. The other is her TI-Raleigh, which was custom-built to a size of 20.5 in. (52 cm) by the Nottingham bike manufacturer in 1981. Beryl had a Reynolds 531c steel frame during her record-breaking years and, although the Raleigh was upgraded to the slightly lighter 753c tubing, Marsh, Cowgill and Disley were all certain that the key geometry would be identical.

The next challenge was persuading Marsh to loan out the bike. 'It's priceless,' he said, grimacing at the thought of it leaving his sight. The irony was that the Burtons had literally given the bike away during the early 1990s, when Beryl began experimenting with specialist 'low-profile' machines. The lucky recipient, says Marsh, was a local joiner who hung some doors for the Burtons and had a grandchild who wanted to start racing. With its classic Campagnolo Record components and glossy red, yellow and black paintwork, Marsh had restored the TI-Raleigh to an immaculate standard. And, after a 30-minute chat about Beryl, whom he clearly revered, permission was granted for its day out down the M1 to Silverstone. 'I can tell you understand the significance of the bike and, anyway, I want to know how fast Beryl would have gone, as well,' said Marsh who, from under his shop counter, produced the added bonus of a classic pair of 'BB'-inscribed black leather cycling shoes. 'It will make it even more realistic,' he said.

That left finding a rider to be Beryl Burton for the day. Disley stressed the need for an experienced cyclist who could consistently hold her low 'tucked' position on a road bike and assume a similarly optimal position on a modern time trial bike. Jessica Rhodes-Jones, the UCI's world amateur time trial champion in 2017 and 2021, immediately agreed. In liaising with Rhodes-Jones, and subsequently also Hayley Simmonds and Alice Lethbridge, who between them held all five of the records between the distances of 10 miles and 12 hours, it was soon also clear just how aware they all were of Beryl's achievements. Both Simmonds and Lethbridge had even been regularly riding their road bikes in 10-mile time trials in 2020 and 2021 partly to see if they could go faster than Beryl's 21 min. 25 sec. personal best. 'I never dreamed of beating her 12-hour record and it still doesn't seem real,' says Lethbridge, a biology teacher from Surrey. Simmonds did eventually lower Beryl's 'road bike' 10-mile record in 2021 to 20 min. 30 sec., albeit on a carbon machine with aero wheels and tubing, while wearing specialist aero clothing. 'It shows how Beryl Burton's times are still so aspirational,' says Rhodes-Jones.

Clothing, says Disley, accounts for around a quarter of the aerodynamic improvement, and he was also keen to iron out any discrepancies that could be caused by Rhodes-Jones's long hair, which can usually be tucked beneath an aero helmet. It meant sourcing a short curly wig, which, after some additional grade-two treatment with a pair of clippers, was trimmed to the classic Burton look. In sizing up Beryl's original machine, Disley could instantly see that the Burtons were just as determined to maximise every perceived advantage as any rider today. Charlie had wrapped the handlebar tape so that it only covered the drops. There was just one front chain ring – a huge fifty-six-tooth ring – and thus only one gear lever on the side of the downtube, with a minimal 13–17 back cassette. Track tubulars had been glued on to the wheels rims, which, while light, would have a high puncture risk. Even the brake hoods and water bottle holder had been removed to save extra grams. The emphasis, however, was clearly then on weight rather than using the bike to contort the body into the most aerodynamic position. Wind tunnels have subsequently shown that minimising aerodynamic drag is actually the key to optimising performance on the predominantly flat and straight courses on which time trials take place.

Disley's methodology was fairly straightforward. By mounting a bike inside the wind tunnel and then blowing air through the area as a rider pedals, he can calculate how efficiently a bike and rider are moving, which is known as their drag coefficient (CdA). This can increase hugely just if a rider sits up from their tucked position for a drink and, when Lethbridge broke Beryl's 12-hour record, she actually carried several litres of water in a container inside her skinsuit so that she could sip through a straw without moving her body. Disley specifically needed to know Beryl's CdA once Rhodes-Jones had replicated her positions and fired up the two bikes to a speed of 45 kph (which equates to 21 min. 30 sec. for 10 miles).

With Rhodes-Jones emerging from the changing area in the Morley club jersey, wig and old-school leather cycling shoes, the TI-Raleigh was first up. She had used photographs and videos to study Beryl's pedalling style and position to the point even of raising her right hand slightly above the left. Alf Engers had also passed on his observations. 'She didn't push with her shoulders

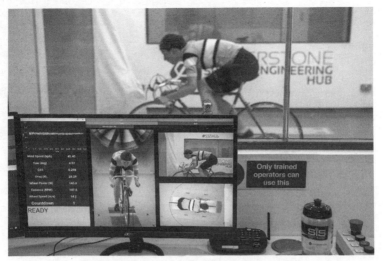

41. A day inside the wind tunnel on the very same
Raleigh bike that Beryl Burton once rode.

or rock,' he advised. 'It's not just a question of pointing your toes
and pushing but pedalling all the way around. You can roll the
bike along. That was what Beryl did. Poetry in motion.' It did
not take long for Rhodes-Jones to settle into a smooth rhythm
even if the effort to hold Beryl's position at the required speed for
around 15 minutes was clearly considerable. With Disley assessing
everything on two large screens – one showing the rider's cycling
position from three angles and another which displayed a moving
line graph and calculations for wind speed, drag, wheel power,
cadence, wheel speed and side-to-side movement – he finally signalled that he had the required information.

After a short break to rotate the bikes and for Rhodes-Jones
to change into her usual aero helmet, shoes, drag-resistant time-
trialling skinsuit and long socks, Disley then conducted the same
test on her state-of-the-art Cervelo P5 time trial bike. With its
sleek aero carbon frame and wheels, such modern machines now

retail at between £10,000 and £15,000. Rhodes-Jones's experience meant that she could immediately assume the sort of aerodynamic posture that Beryl, with her exceptionally strong core, would surely have quickly emulated. The first obvious contrast was the noise. Whereas Beryl's old bike just made the quiet whir of a perfectly oiled and maintained machine, disc wheels create an incessant hum. Rhodes-Jones also noted major differences in the respective feel. Contemporary saddles are designed to let your hips rotate as you pedal. The modern shoes and cleats are also positioned to maximise pedalling force. 'I felt very much that I was pedalling with the toes and front ball of my foot with the old leather shoes,' she said. The biggest difference, though, was in how the aero handlebars provide a stable base across the upper body. 'The Beryl bike was overwhelmingly less comfortable,' she said. 'Modern time trial bikes are designed for aerodynamics but also ergonomics and comfort. You can basically lie forward, whereas Beryl would be really tensing her triceps and core to support herself. It makes it even more impressive – how she sat in that position for 12 hours I just don't know.'

And so to the main question. What times would Beryl have set, making the same effort, on modern kit? A normal road bike usually produces a CdA (a measure of aerodynamic drag) of around 0.30m^2, but, by emulating Beryl's crouched position, Rhodes-Jones reduced this on the TI-Raleigh to a lowest sustained figure of 0.2430m^2. This dipped to 0.2258m^2 after simply changing into the modern clothing and then down to 0.1781m^2 once the same speed of 45 kph had been reached on the Cervelo P5. The wind-tunnel test also provided a power reading for the required watts to achieve the speeds and times of Beryl's various records on the TI-Raleigh. The final step was to then combine these power projections with the much lower CdA drag coefficient that was produced while riding the Cervelo P5 in the modern clothing.

It all produced the astonishing following results:

Table 3

Distance	Beryl's previous record	Beryl, new time on modern set-up*	Current record[†]	Difference to current record[†]
10 miles	21 min. 25 sec. (29 April 1973)	19 min. 29 sec.	18 min. 36 sec. Hayley Simmonds	Beryl down by 53 sec. (but third on all-time list and her record lasts until 2016)
25 miles	53 min. 21 sec. (17 June 1976)	47 min. 52 sec.	49 min. 28 sec. Hayley Simmonds	Beryl up by 1 min. 36 sec. (after 46 years)
50 miles	1 hr 51 min. 30 sec. (25 July 1976)	1 hr 41 min. 06 sec.	1 hr 42 min. 20 sec. Hayley Simmonds	Beryl up by 1 min. 14 sec. (after 46 years)
100 miles	3 hrs 55 min. 05 sec. (4 August 1968)	3 hrs 33 min. 16 sec.	3 hrs 42 min. 03 sec. Alice Lethbridge	Beryl up by 8 min. 47 sec. (after 54 years)
12 hours	277.25 miles (17 September 1967)	305.23 miles	290.07 miles Alice Lethbridge	Beryl up by 15.16 miles (after 55 years)

*Wind-tunnel test of Beryl Burton's original TI-Raleigh vs Cervelo P5, conducted on 23 June 2021.
[†]As of April 2022. Simmonds set her three records in 2016. Lethbridge set her two in 2018.

As the table shows, Beryl remains decisively faster over her three core distances – 25, 50 and 100 miles – than any rider had achieved in the decades since. At the shorter 10-mile distance, which only became a national championship for women towards the end of Beryl's championship winning years in 1978, Hayley Simmonds eventually surpassed her time in 2016. Beryl's projected 12-hour performance remains jaw-dropping – she would still even be in the top fifteen of the men's all-time list – and her ongoing dominance over 100 miles further amplifies her exceptional strength in endurance events. Most impressive of all, however, is surely the versatility over such a spread of distances. For she is effectively racing two groups of riders in these comparisons. You have an outstanding group of short- and middle-distance time-trialling champions and record holders like Simmonds, Yvonne McGregor, Dame Sarah Storey and Wendy Houvenaghel, who have won multiple world, Commonwealth, Olympic and Paralympic medals, but then also some excellent new long-distance specialists at 100 miles and above, led by Lethbridge, Joanna Patterson and Christina Murray. Few riders now challenge across so many disciplines, which is rather like the spread of 800 m to marathon in athletics, let alone with such outstanding success. And then there are still Beryl's seven world titles in the track pursuit and road race, which are quite distinct disciplines again.

Having answered our question so precisely, a follow-up call with Xavier Disley several months later was somehow even more striking. 'I just can't think of another sportsperson whose athletic feats have remained so measurably outstanding,' he said. 'I think we have made good estimates – and the fact that she broke a male competition record is, for me, the stick in the sand which cements it. Some ultra-endurance events which go on for days do increasingly favour women, but 12 hours is not the same. It's more like the Ironman in triathlon, and a female beating all the men would be completely bonkers. What Beryl did is so far out there that you would be very hard-pressed to find any other instance of that happening even going all the way back to the nineteenth century.' Disley also stressed that our wind-tunnel results can only demonstrate the difference that aerodynamic bike technology and clothing have made without factoring in aspects like tyres, which Boardman had specifically highlighted as significant, and more intangible advances in the knowledge of training, nutrition,

42. A pensive Beryl Burton prepares for action. She set an unrivalled 42 time trial records.

psychology and recovery. Beryl would have stuck largely to a 'more is more' training philosophy, but Disley is confident that there would have been further improvements to be had with the right external expertise and advice. Course conditions, notably road surfaces and traffic, throw up further possible advantages that can never be precisely measured.

The bottom line, though, is clear. Technology has progressed beyond the records that Beryl Burton set. Other athletes, even more than half a century later, have not.

15

Descent

As Beryl Burton approached her fiftieth birthday, she had scaled peaks that will surely remain out of sight. Who else has won any serious sporting competition twenty-five years in a row? Who else has even continuously won the most parochial of recreational contests for a quarter of a century? The wider question was whether she would attempt to keep climbing or could finally step back and appreciate a unique but lonely view. Perhaps the closest sporting equivalent is Sir A. P. McCoy, who finally retired in 2015 with a lifetime award from the BBC after twenty consecutive seasons as British jump racing's champion jockey. In certain key respects it is a very similar competition to cycling's BAR. You spend the season travelling the length and breadth of the country in an all-consuming search for improvement. The test is more about your stamina, hunger and relentless consistency than an ability to peak on one specific day. McCoy did not know the name 'Beryl Burton' before agreeing to our interview, but 30 minutes later he felt like he had been introduced to a kindred spirit. And, when he even began accurately predicting the endings to some of the most extreme anecdotes of Beryl's obsessive behaviour, you began to sense a rare insight into the same world.

I had begun by asking to what extent serial champions can actually enjoy winning.

'A top sportsperson is happy for those few minutes after. Then back to zero. The satisfaction is limited because you always want more and are looking for a perfection that's never going to exist. I must have had some enjoyment and fulfilment, but I didn't want to be happy. If I was happy, I was satisfied. If I was satisfied, I was finished.'

So did you fear losing?

'Terrified. Going to bed, every night, there was doubt. When I got to 100 winners in my final season faster than ever before, the voice in my head just told me that I must have been shit for the other twenty years. Only when I rode my 4,000th winner did I think, "You're OK."'

How do you live with that intensity for so long?

'You're not aware of time. Even after a brilliant day I would think, "What if it never happens again? I'd better be good tomorrow." You start off wanting to win. You end up needing to win. To keep yourself mentally sane. To stay alive.'

So can you understand Beryl not shaking her daughter's hand when she was beaten by her?

'Of course. It's about winning. She was a rival. And you have to respect that Beryl was a bit different. She did things that had not happened before. You don't get that mindset from being every other Joe Soap.'

And what about Beryl not stopping after her daughter crashed while they were training together?

'Probably looked across and thought: "She's breathing. Not going to die. Might be a bit sore but me stopping is not going to make her any better." It has to be all about you. Top sportspeople are very selfish. Keeping me happy was always the biggest problem. The family is OK. They didn't have to live with [being] me. I did.'

Does that drive come from loving your sport or just winning?

'Both. Winning is a bit of a drug, but I would have done it all for nothing. I didn't do a day's work in my life. I didn't mind the thousands of miles in the car. The injuries or the wasting and starving. The only place I felt competent was on a horse. I didn't just become a jockey to ride at Cheltenham in front of 70,000 people. I became a jockey because I love riding horses. Horses are my life.'

Did you know that Beryl died while riding her bike?
'I think, for Beryl, it is the perfect way. The hard thing is for her family. You'd have preferred her to be eighty-eight rather than fifty-eight. I've seen colleagues fatally injured. I've thought I was on the way to the ground when there were twenty-five horses behind me and I was down. It's a terrible thing to say – it's no consolation to the family – but you are dying doing what you love. It's perfect.'

Beryl also never stopped racing. Can you understand her believing that she would win even when it was impossible?
'There's never a right time to stop. You could invent flying cars but never have the egotistical thing a top sportsperson has – that feeling people are there to see you. I miss the adrenalin and the danger. Of course she thought she was going to come back and win. It's the madness inside her. That's why she was what she was. There's a fucking madness inside them all. Look at Mike Tyson, Tiger Woods, Zinedine Zidane, Maradona, George Best. Any of them. There are demons that make them go a little bit further.'

*

For Beryl, those demons were so deeply ingrained that they actually became a simplifying life force. There would be no dalliance with retirement. No conscious decision to accept the inevitability of losing. No thought process that weighed up the ongoing risk/reward of continuing to cycle with such vigour in defiance of doctors' orders. No thought process that evaluated any wider impacts on her family. After 1983, Beryl simply ploughed on, unquestioningly, in search of new objectives. It was both beautiful and harrowing. Beautiful because that basic enjoyment of riding her bike and the friendships forged through sport could never recede. Harrowing because a desire to be the best remained unwavering, regardless of the reality and the ultimately catastrophic cost to her health.

As 1984 dawned, Beryl still felt fatigued from the monumental effort she had made to win her twenty-fifth BAR the previous year. She described another early year trip to Spain as being for 'convalescence', but there were two huge potential aims. For the first time, women's cycling would be included in the Olympics. There were seven men's disciplines in Los Angeles, including a team time trial and both individual and team pursuits, but the glacial stutter towards gender equality would extend to just one single women's event. A road race. It was eighty-eight years since the first Olympic men's road race. It was also seventeen years since Beryl had won the last of her world championships and, although she did still compete in road races sporadically, a decade since the last of her twelve national titles over the discipline. Val Rushworth, the women's national coach, argued that her special status merited inclusion, but she was overruled. Beryl would never compete in the Olympics. Rushworth believes that the BCF's decision was personal and the cycling journalist Les Woodland can recall a spiky exchange between Beryl and the Olympic coach Peter Valentine. Woodland, who describes Valentine as 'bumptious', says that he criticised her training, 'to which she rightly asked how she could win so often if her training was so poor'.

An even more serious target was the inaugural women's Tour de France, which, over fifteen stages across three weeks, was the sort of endurance test that should theoretically have suited her phenomenal strength. Beryl had made a provisional British squad and, having tried again to tailor her training to road racing, was devastated not to make the final cut. The withdrawal of another rider on the eve of the race, however, did prompt national coach Jim Hendry to issue a late invitation. Charlie telephoned the farm on which Beryl now picked raspberries to relay the news and was taken aback by the firm response. Beryl had already mentally processed what she saw as rejection and, having had the working rotas adjusted, refused to unpick her plans. In reverse, it was another example of an unwillingness to bend or deviate from any course of action once her mind was set. It was also a measure of just how crestfallen she felt. The first winner, Marianne Martin, shared a total prize of just £750 with her team, and the attitude inside much of the men's peloton was summed up by the winner, Laurent Fignon. 'I like women, but I prefer to see them doing something else,' he said.

The historic administrative division in British cycling still meant that national teams were not selected by those people who organised the time trials in which Beryl so excelled. Hendry remains adamant that his only consideration was an assessment of who was most likely to challenge and in road racing the argument for Beryl was indeed less convincing. 'It was just the wrong period of time,' says Hendry. 'She would have been stupendous a few years earlier.' Hendry also wonders whether, deep down, Beryl felt uncertainty about the demands of a three-week race. Although Beryl displayed no outward signs of doubt, she had sent Rushworth a handwritten letter around this time in which she took the unheard step of seeking training advice. 'I couldn't believe it,' says Rushworth, who had known Beryl for more than twenty-five years and tried to get her to consider more rest and shorter faster sessions.

There was also one definite example in 1984 of Beryl deliberately avoiding defeat. Despite riding superbly to regain her national 25-mile title, she clearly sensed that June Pitchford was now stronger over the longer time trial distances and, having lost to her old rival over 50 miles, very noticeably did not complete a 100-mile time trial. There were sound health reasons for this choice, but that had never previously been a deterrent and it would therefore be the first time since 1956 that she did not contest the BAR. Pitchford had finished runner-up seven times during Beryl's twenty-five straight victories and was irked that her friend did not also complete a '100' and accept being beaten into second place. 'It did upset me at the time,' she says. 'She had been out to win and make it twenty-six in a row.'

Margaret Allen also sensed a rare self-acknowledgement that Beryl's powers were in decline. 'It was a 25-mile race in Yorkshire and I went under an hour for the first time. Beryl won in 56 or 57 minutes but was very down. She said, "Normally on a day like today I would do at least a 54." She had tried her hardest but the upper level had gone. That was the turning point. After that, I would never say to Beryl, "Good ride." I would always say, "Are you satisfied with your ride?" And she would normally say, "No, I am not at all happy. I can't understand it." She could not accept the natural deterioration. That is very hard for everybody, let alone someone who has been superwoman, but it became her downfall. She had been hammering herself constantly for thirty years. If someone wiser could have given her that insight, she might have been able to grasp it.'

An opportunity did arise in 1985, when Beryl put herself forward for various physical tests at Leeds Carnegie University. Her idea had been to show the British selectors that she was capable of riding the Tour de France at the age of forty-eight. After measuring her oxygen uptake and efficiency, the sports scientists concluded that she had the physiology of a twenty-year-old. They were unable to provide a fat reading because no excess flesh could be found. 'They had never seen that even in marathon runners,' says Rushworth. The evidence on the bike, however, was not sufficient to leapfrog a new group of British women's road racers, and the centrepiece of a strange year in 1985 became a trip to Arizona for an invitational 500-mile race.

Beryl had travelled to Texas with Keith Lambert, one of the ninety-nine men she had caught in the Otley 12 race eighteen years earlier, who was now a full-time professional. Lambert particularly remembered boarding their flight to America. 'She had

43. Aged forty-nine, Beryl regained the national 25- and
50-mile titles in 1986 – races she had first won in 1958.

this musette [knapsack] on her shoulder which was full of cheese,'
he says. 'We were getting $50 a day and put up in a hotel but,
typical Beryl, she took this big bag of food so she didn't have
to spend the $50 a day. But they confiscated all her cheese at the
airport. Poor old Beryl was distraught.' So much cycling did at
least provide some preparation for the following season when, in
what proved to be her last real hurrah, Beryl's still formidable
time-trialling strength allowed her to overcome an early deficit to
beat Maria Blower to the national 25-mile title and follow that by
also winning the 50-mile championship. It was respectively her

twenty-sixth and twenty-fourth win over those distances and the last of a staggering final tally of 122 individual British cycling titles. As Beryl turned fifty in May 1987, it also meant that she was still the reigning national 25- and 50-mile champion. She had been twenty-one when she first won that particular blue riband 'double' of titles.

*

There was also a familiar name back among the domestic contenders in 1986. Now aged thirty, Denise Burton was racing again with an increasing strength as she continued her recovery from anorexia. Denise had finished second to her mother in the national 50-mile championship, and wanted to give her career one final push. An international women's road racing calendar was finally developing and, after an excellent second in the 1985 Tour de l'Aude in France, which was run over ten days and included many of the best riders in the world, Denise gained selection for the 1986 women's Tour de France.

It was again staged over similar roads on the morning of the men's event and both races in 1986 would be defined by a wonderful rivalry. In the men's, it was two teammates in Greg LeMond and Bernard Hinault competing for victory. In the women's, Maria Canins and Jeannie Longo were equally far out in front. Denise had fractured her pelvis and arm in a crash earlier in the year but still finished forty-second from a starting field of more than a hundred over a course around France that took in some of the most iconic climbs of the Alps and Pyrenees, as well as the feared Puy de Dôme volcano. 'I loved it, but I really did suffer, especially in the last week,' she says. 'I could climb quite well and, although I still wasn't fully right, either mentally or in terms of my eating, it really did inspire me.'

Denise duly had an excellent winter's training. She was living back in Harrogate and, having prepared by repeatedly tackling the

2.5-mile Greenhow Hill climb out of Pateley Bridge in the Dales, had never felt fitter. 'I was pinging,' she says. Denise was favourite to win the British road race in 1987 for the first time since the 'no handshake' debacle with her mother in 1976. The race was being staged in Bedfordshire and, 24 hours before the start, she went out to ride the course and assess the uphill finish. She duly put her bike into one of its biggest gears before sprinting head-down, out of the saddle, towards where the finishing line had been freshly painted across the road. Then came a cruelly life-changing twist of fate. The spindle on the front wheel of Denise's bike snapped, catapulting her over the handlebars and straight down on to her face. 'I remember coming around,' she says. 'I was still on my bike but all skew-whiff. I undid the toe-straps, got my feet out of the pedals, sat up and found that I was spitting teeth out. Blood everywhere. A woman in a car stopped and waited with me while she got another person to call an ambulance.'

Denise was rushed to the Accident and Emergency Department of Luton and Dunstable Hospital. Her mouth was so swollen that it was impossible to speak, and her memory of that hospital was writing the word 'aspirin' on a piece of paper and giving it to a nurse as she waited 4 hours for treatment. As well as the damage inside her mouth, Denise fractured her jaw, nose and vertebrae. She now counts herself fortunate that her spinal cord was not severed. 'I could have been paralysed,' she says. 'They wouldn't let me see my face to begin with. I was black, blue and badly cut up. They put a big cage around my jaw and teeth to hold them still. I had a food processor and would whizz everything up in that and drink through a straw for weeks after.' Beryl and Charlie did drop everything that weekend to head south and visit but, once Denise was home, an ongoing distance in the mother–daughter relationship was evident. 'My mum only visited once,' says Denise. 'She said, "Can I get you anything?" I was like, "No I'm fine, I can look after myself." And she never came back up again. I was only 200 yards away.' The accident also ended her competitive cycling career. 'That said to me, "OK, that's it: finish your racing,"' she says.

*

Stopping Beryl remained rather more complicated. Although her times were respectable for a cyclist in their fifties, defeats were having to be regularly absorbed. It was a period when close friends and family members were willing Beryl to avoid those races where she would push herself to exhaustion. Charlie had the forlorn hope that she would devote more time to touring. 'She was always trying to thrash herself back into shape – trying to get back to her former glories,' he says. This meant riding even further and, perhaps most disastrously, losing weight in an attempt to rediscover her edge. And all while dealing with serious new health challenges. After Beryl finished forty-third in the national 10-mile championship of 1989, the report in *Cycling* said that she had been 'frustrated by a succession of fruitless visits to hospitals in pursuit of a reliable diagnosis to a mystery illness'. She also remained hard on herself and, considering the era, candid about the changes she was experiencing. 'I'm not on form,' she said, 'I've got to this age with females, this menopause problem, and I'm not riding anywhere near as well as I should be, but I'm riding to the best of my ability ... and I'm still beating people who are much younger.'

This virtual guarantee even of small victories and the parkrun-like opportunity to compete with yourself are two features of time trialling that Beryl could always relish. She also still had her eyes open for new objectives. Jeff Bowler, a specialist tandem rider, says that she casually suggested that they attack some mixed records while they were waiting to start a 50-mile time trial near Wetherby in the early 1990s. The simple camaraderie of time trialling also cannot be underestimated. Although Beryl remained as down to earth as ever after a race, most of the other riders knew

44. Catching up with Eileen Gray. Beryl loved the post-race
chat and club cyclists would queue for her autograph.

exactly what she had done and just mixing within an environment where she was so admired must have been wonderful for her
self-esteem. 'It was hard to believe just how normal she seemed
to be bearing in mind what she had achieved on the world stage,'
says Ian Cammish, who was the leading men's time triallist of the
time. 'I thought she would go on for ever. Although she was past
her best, she said she was still enjoying her racing and wished
people would just let her continue doing so without having her as
a target to shoot down.'

That was something that also greatly irritated Margaret Allen,
who had now succeeded her idol by winning the 1987 and 1988
BAR. 'I remember girls stood around the results board saying,
"Oh, I've beaten Beryl." And I would turn around and say, "Yes,
but you haven't done a Beryl ride."' Carole Gandy, a Kent-based

rider who would later win the 2004 BAR, recalls that some riders would be 'jumping up and down around the results board saying, "I beat Beryl today."' What struck Gandy was how Beryl always prepared with absolute focus even long after she could realistically win. 'If it was a 10, she would still ride around the course several times,' she said. 'Similar with a 25. She was a workaholic. After she had finished, I found her very approachable. No edge. I once asked for some advice and she replied by asking, "What do you want to achieve?" She then gave me some good advice.'

Another cyclist, Phil Fryer, was also struck by Beryl's kindness when he asked her about transitioning from triathlon to cycling after she had handed out prizes at a presentation evening for the Yorkshire Road Club. Beryl asked for his address and, unannounced, appeared at his front door in Morley on her bike a fortnight later. 'My heart skipped a beat and I shouted to my wife, "Karen, that Beryl was here to see me,"' he said. Having explained that he was suffering some back pain, Beryl promptly demonstrated a series of exercises on the rug in his front room. 'We were star-struck – she had a cup of boiled water, wished me luck and went on her way,' he said. Fryer went on to become Yorkshire Road Club champion, and Beryl would write him occasional letters, usually when she was winter training in Benidorm or Mallorca, in which she told him that she was 'trying to keep up with the young ones'. Beryl also never seemed precious about her records and would urge other women to set their sights higher. 'People are still thrilled if they beat me,' she said. 'To me that feels wrong. I'm going slower, so they shouldn't be aiming to beat me but the records.'

Fittingly, Beryl's last national medal would come alongside Allen in 1989 as the third finisher for the Knaresborough Cycling Club in the national 25-mile championships. 'Beryl was fighting with the realisation that she was not as good, and it was her last "best" ride,' says Allen. Beryl was fourteenth individually but only 33 seconds outside the hour to combine with Allen, who finished third, and Sally Whitfield, who finished eleventh, as national team champions. A scarcely believable span, which had started during the Eisenhower era and finished when George Bush was the US president, had culminated with 152 British individual or team titles. 'We were all on the podium and Beryl had a smile from one end of her face to the other,' says Allen. 'I was thrilled that she was so thrilled. Over the years with Morley, I had won many team medals off Beryl's rides, so it felt like I was paying her back a little. We had gone full circle. I was so proud of her that day.'

*

An extra measure of personal happiness arrived in 1989, when Beryl became a grandmother to Mark. Dennis Donovan wrote in *Cycling* that Beryl's face 'lit up' at the mention of her grandchild. Any worry that she might be excessively softened by the new arrival, however, was quickly allayed by her reaction when Charlie suffered a serious accident out on his bike just days after Denise gave birth. Charlie had been admitted to intensive care and, even after being discharged over Christmas, was still having trouble with his arms and suffering from dizzy spells. Denise paid her parents a visit and, with Charlie eventually making a full recovery, can now laugh at the scene she witnessed in their living room. 'My mum had him up on a ladder painting the ceiling – she thought it would strengthen him and get those parts moving again,' she says.

Denise and her husband, Clay, then also had a daughter, Anna, in 1993. She says that her mother 'took a while to accept that she was a grandma and people commenting on it' before then making 'a real fuss' of them. Beryl would attend all of their parties, and generally spend a Thursday afternoon looking after her grandchildren, even if she did then expect to be compensated with a meal. Denise would spend those few hours to herself out cycling for pleasure, but very consciously had no interest in following her mother's path in combining any racing with a young

45. Beryl, Charlie and their grandson, Mark.

family. 'There must have been something not quite right about my childhood because, mentally, I was "I do not want to bring my children up the way I have been brought up,"' she says. 'I did all the normal things. Taking children here, there and everywhere to various activities and parties. That was my choice.'

Beryl's more sporadic involvement in national championships over the next five years reflected the health challenges she was increasingly facing. She came respectively fifty-fifth, fifty-third and seventy-sixth in the national 25-mile championships of 1990, 1992 and 1993 but also never stopped racing in more local events. Simply riding her bike was not the problem. Most cyclists keep going for the vast health and social benefits until it is no longer physically possible. The dangerous part was her need to compete and, in having no regard for the impact on her health, never wavering from the belief that hard work and more miles were the only way back to the podium. 'I need about 3,000 miles of training before I get the speed for competition,' Beryl told the

BBC, at the age of fifty-six, in 1994. 'If it's a nice day, I go off into the Dales. I thoroughly enjoy it but I'm working hard all the time.'

Allen saw a physical change in Beryl after she had returned from a cycling trip to Mallorca with Charlie, Carline and some of the other Morley cyclists in the early 1990s. As ever, they had been camping out on local beaches while cycling hundreds of miles and, surrounded by natural fruit and vegetables, Beryl decided to stop eating meat. It was a time when there was a particular focus on low-fat diets and, in this search for an extra edge, Beryl actually made herself slower. 'Carrying weight was considered a big no-no, but she had no reserves to lose,' says Allen. 'It was just depleting her. We know more now about how protein repairs your muscles. I would tell her but, once Beryl had a bee in her bonnet, it was very difficult to convince her of something different.'

Kathleen Mitchell, another old Morley teammate, found that Beryl was a different woman in the late 1980s from the carefree young mother she had known in the 1950s and early 1960s. 'I knew two Beryls,' she said. 'We had fun before – anything for a joke. We couldn't relate back to the early days. We weren't on the same wavelength. She was very serious. She just lived and breathed her bike. It was a time when they always say that you would go faster if you were two pounds lighter. She took that seriously and lost too much weight.' Maureen Pearson, Beryl's old hairdresser, would ride the weekly Wednesday 'autumn tints' club runs, for people above the age of fifty, with Charlie and Beryl. 'It was silly what happened,' says Pearson. 'She was still going well but once she went thin that was the end of the story. She had lost her muscle weight.'

After her own experience with anorexia, Denise does now wonder if her mother 'bordered on something like that' towards the end of her life. She particularly recalls visiting her parents and how Beryl's lunch consisted of a tin of sardines, two Ryvitas and, after being gifted an entire box at a cycling event, a Power-Bar that was past its sell-by date. 'Her eating habits really weren't very good in those last years,' says Denise. 'She must have got something in her head. What that was I don't know. She never discussed it. I said to her, "Mother, why don't you eat proper food?" But she was, "I'm enjoying this." She could set her mind to anything. What made it strange was that she always loved her food. She ate lots of meat, and I think if your body gets out of balance then your head gets out of balance. It affects your blood. I think she just totally got messed up. Before she died, she was not quite the same person.' Beryl would complain to friends of feeling 'thunder and lightning' in her stomach, but doctors would struggle to offer any explanation. One theory was even that she was still being bothered by the bug that she had caught in Spain, way back in 1965, when the British team had arrived early for the world championships and stayed in such squalid accommodation.

There was then a very clearly identified health scare. A cyst was found on top of a lump on Beryl's breast and she was diagnosed with cancer. 'If I had been hit by a brick, I couldn't have been more stunned,' she said. Beryl had also undergone a hysterectomy in the early 1990s and was now told that she needed a mastectomy. It was not kept secret as such. Beryl would always answer any questions directly, but she wanted no fuss and saw no need to actively tell people. That included even Denise. 'My dad mentioned that she was in hospital having this operation, so I went to see her,' says Denise. 'And she was, "About time you came to see me." I was like, "I didn't even know." It was the same when she had a hysterectomy.' Denise then smiles. 'It's strange because I'm a right blabbermouth. I tell everybody what is going on.'

Beryl was now well into her late fifties, but her approach to recovering any lost fitness following the two operations was just the same as after any crash or illness when she was in her prime. She was back on a rowing machine and then cycling rollers just as soon as it was physically possible. During her weekly visits to see Denise, who had trained as a remedial therapist, Beryl would also still ask for a leg massage to stay supple. Maureen Pearson saw her shortly after the mastectomy. 'I didn't know she was having the operation, but it didn't seem to bother her. She was, "It's fine Maureen, I'm alright – I've got rid of them." That was her attitude.' Another old friend, Eileen Cropper, would join her on these rides and says that Beryl retained a dry sense of humour and would laugh at herself whenever the prosthetic breast that she might sometimes now wear slipped out of place while she was riding her bike.

June Pitchford was also struck by how easily Beryl dealt with such a serious situation, but now wonders if the refusal to reduce her training and racing was born of other insecurities. 'I always remember when I stopped racing and Beryl said to me, "Aren't you worried that your muscles will go funny?" I think she was frightened of what was going to happen to her body if she stopped doing all these miles. I can understand that. It took me a few years. I think that she had just done it so long that she couldn't accept that she would survive without doing all the miles. It was just ingrained. I have never met anybody so determined and one-track-minded.'

*

Beryl's last major race would come in October 1995, at a special event to celebrate the centenary anniversary of time trialling. The 100-strong field for the 50-mile event, over a version of the same F1 Bedfordshire course that Gordon Minns had covered in 2 hrs 54 min. 26 sec. back in 1895, represented a *Who's Who* of British time trialling. But there could be no doubting the biggest star. The report in *Cycling* said that 'many of the spectators had made the trip to see Beryl Burton in action' and described her 'royal progress' down the dual carriageway. The Veteran Cycle Club made a film of the event and, in the commentary, it was noted that the 'queen of time trialling' was determined to ride despite recent illness and that her participation was greeted with 'shouts and cheers' at every corner.

Beryl's rock-solid body and silky pedalling style remained instantly recognisable from the footage, and a desire still to ride as fast as possible was evident from the triathlon bars that had been fastened by Charlie to a low-profile Raleigh bike. But you could also see just from her face, and especially her open mouth, gasping for air, that she was suffering. A diminishment in physical power and her more fragile physique were also obvious. Beryl's finishing time of 2 hrs 28 min. 48 sec. was more than 37 minutes outside the 50-mile record she had set in 1976, but simply completing the course, at an average speed of just over 20 mph, had been a triumph. Three of Beryl's oldest friends and rivals – Pitchford, Allen and Joan Kershaw – also rode and, having shared literally thousands of defeats, would finish with the rare and now hollow experience of beating a woman they had come to revere. Their husbands had all happened to stop in the same lay-by along the course. 'They hadn't seen each other for years and were like, "My god, it's just like the old days,"' says Pitchford. 'It was the last time we all raced together.' And how did she find Beryl? 'She was more frail. I hardly knew Beryl in the end. We all said she shouldn't have ridden. She didn't look well enough, and I am sure it was only a few months after her operation. But there was no way you could stop her. If Beryl decided that was what she wanted, Beryl did it.'

Beryl had finished down the field but, once all the main prizes had been distributed, there was one final announcement for the presentation of a special bouquet of flowers. 'To a remarkable lady ... the one and only Beryl Burton!' said the event organiser, Graham Thompson. Beryl had been seated on the wooden school sports hall floor enthusiastically applauding all the winners and, dressed in a pink woolly jumper, blue shell-suit bottoms and brown open-toed shoes, looked thrilled to be called up towards the stage. Having received her prize, she then turned and acknowledged all the whoops of applause by holding up the bouquet, before pulling back the wrapper and pausing to carefully study the flowers. She looked gaunt, and certainly older than fifty-eight, but visibly lifted by the gesture, and her face was covered by the most beautifully natural of smiles. And there was no one in the crowd clapping with more vigour than Eileen Sheridan, that other great trailblazing champion, who had been standing directly behind where Beryl was seated.

Beryl would later ask Sheridan if they could sit down together to talk. 'She told me that she felt so tired,' says Sheridan, who was seventy-three by 1996 but still looked more robust than Beryl. 'I remember feeling very worried about her. I said, "Why don't you rest on your laurels? You have won everything. You are world champion seven times. You are twenty-five times BAR. Why don't you relax, retire and go touring?" But she still loved racing her bike and said something about how there was more she wanted to do. I felt so very sad.'

It was not just Sheridan who was now encouraging Beryl to stop racing. Charlie had taken early retirement in the hope of spending more time leisurely exploring other countries either by bike or on foot with his wife. Beryl wanted still to work and, as well as picking raspberries, was being paid to clean the home of a couple in nearby Flaxby. 'She would do all the washing and ironing and cleaning,' says Denise. 'She would say, "I have to go down to Flaxby and sort that house." It was rubbish. She didn't have to do it at all.' That same inability to do something different was evident in her approach to cycling. 'She really shouldn't have been still racing,' says Denise. 'She wasn't very well for about ten years but there would still be no half measures, no easy pedalling. My mother always wanted to win, even when there were faster, much younger, girls. My dad wanted her to stop, but how do you convince someone who loves what they do so much?' Did they try? 'Yes, by telling her that it was not good for her health any more.' And how did she respond? 'She would say, "Hard luck," and carry on. She just kept going. She wouldn't stop. She couldn't stop.'

*

Meg Jay, whose research into childhood trauma appeared so relevant to Beryl's early life, found that a tendency to become trapped in what she calls a 'superhero narrative' was another common characteristic of her 'supernormals'. This is particularly challenging, she says, for those people who have come to prioritise achievement above health and happiness. 'The brain can become addicted to the adrenalin and bodily changes associated with training and competing,' says Jay. 'It can be tough to trade that in for a "normal" life. There are bodily costs to living in fight-or-flight all the time. There is a lot of wear and tear. We become poisoned by our own stress hormones over time.'

Whether that actually happened to Beryl remains impossible to say. What we do know is that virtually all sportspeople share a certain agony when they suddenly step back from this acute competitive state. Even with a definite desire to stop racing, Denise herself found that it feels like 'you have had your life cut off' when that moment comes. 'Her whole identity would have stopped and I think that is one of the main reasons she carried on,' she says. Dame Sarah Storey, a winner of Paralympic medals in swimming and cycling over a twenty-nine-year span, believes that the extraordinary longevity she shares with Beryl can only be underpinned by 'finding joy in the journey' regardless of outside opinion. 'Never underestimate the person who loves the process because they are likely to do more than anyone,' she says. This outlook would also help to explain why Beryl remained so unusually obsessed with preparing for her next objective rather than allowing her ego to be either excessively bruised by losing or inflated by what she had previously won. As Meg Jay had earlier suggested, her entire ethos – resiliently striving to always do her absolute best – had become a permanent way of approaching life.

It all suggests a certain futility in trying to explain rationally why Beryl went on and on in defiance of both her body and medical advice. You might as well ask why a fox bites the head off a chicken. The bottom line was that she was a cyclist, and riding her bike as fast as she possibly could was what every fibre in her body longed to do. 'To ease off would be the beginning of the end,' Beryl once said. 'The rot sets in. It erodes one's self-discipline. If you are ill or have an injury, you compete the same and do the best you can in the circumstances. I couldn't not try.' Beryl's complete indifference to a question from fellow cyclists shortly before her death about her career highlights, and the incredible three-week period in 1967 when she won her seventh world championship and then broke the men's 12-hour record, was also revealing. 'It was the moment which counted,' she said. 'I savoured that. There are some who say that the 1967 season was my best. The pinnacle. Maybe so. Maybe no. For me, I enjoyed them all.'

16

Rebirth

Beryl Burton made an unusual choice on the morning of Sunday 5 May 1996. She decided to cycle across Harrogate to call in on Denise and her two grandchildren with a handwritten invitation for a picnic to celebrate her fifty-ninth birthday the following weekend. Organising even a low-key party was not something Denise can remember her mother doing but, having spent the previous day in nearby Micklefield at her nephew's wedding, it would seem that family was uppermost that weekend in Beryl's thoughts.

Beryl was 2 miles into the short ride from her home in Starbeck to Denise's house on the opposite side of Harrogate when, at the Skipton Road turning to Bilton, she made her last push of the pedals. A heart that had been severely damaged when she was a child simply gave way. Witnesses reported a slight wobble before she fell into the road and sustained a minor head injury. Two passers-by attempted to resuscitate her, and at 9.55 a.m. an ambulance was called. According to the police report, Beryl was wearing black cycling trousers, a multicoloured top and a dark peaked cap. The sketchy early media reports had assumed that Beryl was in some sort of road traffic accident but, after she had been pronounced dead on arrival at Harrogate District Hospital, Harrogate coroner Colin Moore recorded a verdict of death by natural causes. A post-mortem and histopathology test revealed heart disease and chronic anaemia.

Denise was informed by Charlie and a policeman. Beryl's

brother Jeffrey also received the same awful knock at the door. It had been his son Graham's wedding and a house full of family and friends were gathered to open presents in the very same room that Beryl had been seated the previous evening. 'I opened the front door and there were two police people in front of me,' says Jeffrey. 'They asked who I was and then one said, "I've got some bad news." We were just absolutely stunned. It made you realise how precious life is.'

Charlie, Denise and Jeffrey made the formal identification. It was, says Jeffrey, surreal to see his sister laid peacefully in hospital barely 12 hours after they had shared such a happy day. Like Denise, Jeffrey was aware that Beryl had suffered some health issues but had no inkling of how serious it all was. 'I remember her saying she was seeing some clinician and she wasn't happy about things but she never really broadcast it. She ignored it. That was her. You just console yourself that she was on her bike.' For Denise, the thought that her mother was on her way to make an unannounced visit still prompts a knot in the pit of her stomach. 'We'd never had a birthday invitation before,' she says. 'But she decided this one time that she would. It's so very strange.'

While the timing provides an enduring sadness, Denise agrees that there was something fitting – and almost inevitable – about her mother dying while riding her bike. We cannot know what Beryl was feeling that morning but, given her whole outlook on life, we can surmise that any warning signs would have been dismissed in favour of an all-consuming desire to complete whatever task and training ride she had set herself. The very characteristics that fuelled both her greatness and her demise would stand entwined. We can also suspect that, in riding her bike in the seconds before she died, she would probably have been free of any broader worries and simply immersed in a passion that had provided such purpose.

'It was the best way for my mum,' says Denise. 'She would have hated getting infirm. It would have been so against her character.

In my mind, if you really want to do something, no matter what the outcome, you are better to have done it. If not, you will get to the end of your life and think, "I wish." My mum wouldn't have thought, "I have to look after myself, or I might die." She would have just said, "I'm going to cycle. This is what I want." And what a result. It was just much too soon. Another few decades would have been nice. It's not fair.' Beryl's own response after Tom Simpson died while cycling up Mont Ventoux during the 1967 Tour de France, at the age of just twenty-nine, indicates how she might have viewed the circumstances of her demise. When told that Simpson's last reported words were 'Put me back on my bike', Beryl had simply said: 'He could have no finer epitaph.'

*

It is probable that Beryl was planning to incorporate her visit to Denise that Sunday with a longer ride in preparation for the national 10-mile time trial championships in Levens, on the edge of the Lake District, six days later. Margaret Allen had seen her old friend in the weeks before her death and, as ever, was stuck by her ambition for the forthcoming season. Beryl had been on a cycling trip to Spain and was planning to enter all the national championships again. 'She said that she was training for the nationals and had got her mind on it,' said Allen. 'In her head, she was still the best and she was going to go out there and show them what she was made of. She would get on the start line, hear those words "Five, four, three, two, one", and be thinking, "Today might be the day it comes back.' Beryl wouldn't have any recognition at all that she couldn't do it. No way.'

Beryl's death devastated the close-knit British time trial community but the letters and cards of condolence extended to literally every corner of the globe, including old adversaries from East Germany and the Soviet Union, as well as a fan club in Australia. A minute's silence was held at the national 10-mile championships the following weekend, and many of the women also wore black armbands. The added one-minute gap in the field at number three, where the now unseeded Beryl had been scheduled to start, was especially poignant. It was in keeping with Beryl and Charlie's outlook that her funeral should be low-key. Beryl's close friend Brenda Robins can now allow herself a wry smile at the memory of Charlie pulling up to the crematorium with Beryl in the back of the car that was usually used to transport all her bikes and kit to races.

A thanksgiving service the following month in Christ Church, one of Harrogate's most spectacular and historic buildings, was rather different. Around 900 people attended from across Europe. Many arrived on their bikes. People were standing in every spare corner of the church and had to spill out into the surrounding gardens. Eulogies were delivered by Eileen Sheridan, Malcolm Cowgill and John Morgan, who was the sports correspondent of the *Yorkshire Evening Post*. Sheridan reiterated the famous line that, had Beryl been French, Joan of Arc would have taken second place. Morgan recalled how he was once waiting for a bus from the Wetherby Road in Scarcroft to take him 7 miles into Leeds. 'It was a cold night and in the distance I spotted a familiar figure, bent over the handlebars with legs pumping like pistons,' he said. 'Beryl stopped for a brief chat but our conversation ended in midstream with the arrival of the bus. We pulled off in front of Beryl. But when the bus arrived in Leeds she was waiting at the terminus to finish the tale she had started telling me.'

Cowgill prompted laughter when he told the story of a disagreement with Beryl at a time trial in Nottinghamshire. It had started and finished in the exact same location but, having been irritated by a bullying headwind over the second half of the course, Beryl had complained loudly when she finished that there was more uphill on the way back. Cowgill tried to explain why this was impossible. Even after he was backed up by Charlie, Beryl simply refused to waver from her opinion. It somehow encapsulated a stubbornness that could veer into the irrational but which helped Beryl to achieve feats beyond what seemed possible. Denise then delivered a reading from the Epistle to the Philippians 3:10–14, which included a particularly appropriate passage: 'Forgetting what is behind and straining towards what is ahead, I press on toward the goal to win the prize.'

When Beryl died in 1996, the aerodynamic revolution in time trialling was already well under way, but she still held the women's competition records over 25, 50 and 100 miles, as well as 12 hours. The 10-mile record had been broken in 1993 after exactly twenty years by Yvonne McGregor, who also became the first British woman after Beryl to win the world pursuit title in 2000. McGregor, who was from nearby Bradford, was also the closest Beryl ever had to a cycling protégée, and their little-known friendship highlighted another facet of her personality.

Like Beryl, McGregor was a late starter in cycling, and a superb career, which also included Olympic and Commonwealth Games medals, was achieved from the same self-funded foundation of hard graft. McGregor wore a pair of running shorts when she raced her first national 25-mile time trial in 1990 but still finished thirteenth, and would always ride her bike to local races. For events outside of Yorkshire she would travel by a combination of train and bike with a tent on her back. McGregor says that you 'couldn't not know who Beryl was' as a Yorkshire cyclist and, intrigued, had borrowed a copy of her autobiography, *Personal Best*, from the library. She felt an instant connection. Beryl was still doing some of the same events and, in the post-race chatter around the results board, they got talking. 'Beryl was unassuming, had a dry sense of humour and I think she saw something similar in me,' says McGregor. 'From then, I would sometimes take my mum to visit them. You would never have known that it was a cyclist's house. She was easy to chat with and would write letters and cards.'

One encounter at a late autumn lunch of the Yorkshire Road

46. Congratulating Yvonne McGregor on her
world one-hour record in June 1995.

Club near Harrogate remained lodged in her mind. 'I had cycled
and it was dark when it finished,' says McGregor. 'Some of the
others were, "Stick the bike in the car and we'll drive you home."
I was, "No, this is training." Beryl was listening, and I just remember looking over at her. She gave a knowing nod. It was like, "You
go, girl."' There was an even more awkward moment shortly after
Beryl had returned from her mastectomy when McGregor was
placed one minute behind her in a time trial. 'I was catching her
and I almost fell back and thought "no". It's the only time I have
ever felt that. I did go past eventually, but I hated it. Beryl was fine.
I encouraged her, and she shouted back, "Go on, Yvonne!"'

The Manchester Velodrome opened in 1994, and McGregor
made an attempt the following year at the world one-hour record.
It was an achievement that eluded Beryl, largely due to the
absence of any comparable British track during her peak years
and the barriers to travelling abroad, but she was among the

crowd. McGregor rode 47.411 km to beat the previous marks set by Jeannie Longo and Catherine Marsal. Dave Lloyd, himself a former professional and multiple national champion, sat next to Beryl and says that she was 'shouting and screaming' encouragement at McGregor and genuinely elated. Beryl died less than a year later, and McGregor was also among those who spoke at her memorial service, reading verses 19–27 of Corinthians IX. 'To be asked, as a Yorkshire woman, was one of the biggest honours of my life – I've got tears in my eyes just thinking about it,' says McGregor, who had actually broken Beryl's 25-mile record just three days before the service. She later wrote to Charlie, telling him that she had been 'inspired' by Beryl's life and that she had been thinking constantly of her while training. She also revealed a conversation four years earlier in which Beryl had bluntly told her that it was 'about time you got some of my records'. Beryl had held that 25-mile record for the previous thirty-seven years.

Other future world and Olympic champions who made a particular point of learning about Beryl's life include Nicole Cooke, Chrissie Wellington, Lizzie Deignan and the Brownlee brothers. Having beaten the boys in Welsh national age-group events, Cooke was already deeply curious about trailblazing sportswomen when she read *Personal Best*, at the age of twelve. 'The title of the book immediately resonated – I quite like personal bests as well,' said Cooke. 'It was the days pre-internet, and I had to wait several weeks for my local library to borrow a copy from another library. It was a fascinating read. One thing that came through was that, regardless of what and how much she won, the challenges others placed in front of her never stopped. The section about 1970, at the Leicester world championships, of how the all-male management of the BCF snubbed her just as she was about to race struck a chord.'

When Deignan rode to a Burton-esque solo victory in the inaugural women's Paris–Roubaix in 2021 – staged 125 years after the first men's edition – she thought specifically of Beryl, who would have been so well suited to such gruelling one-day 'classic' races. 'I raced with the power of generations of women who were denied the opportunity,' said Deignan. Wellington, the unbeaten quadruple women's Ironman world champion, was shocked to discover that Beryl had held a men's record and that her personal best times were still fast enough to win national titles fifty years later. 'It's profoundly inspirational – and yet most top sportspeople wouldn't know her name,' she said.

Alistair and Jonny Brownlee are in the minority whose eyes also instantly light up at the words 'Beryl Burton' and, in their ultra-aggressive triathlon racing style, and simple love of punishing cake-fuelled rides through the Yorkshire Dales, perhaps come closest to embodying her spirit. They also intend to keep riding, touring and competing locally long after the quest for international titles has passed. 'I doubt if there are more than a few rural roads in our great county that we haven't both shed sweat along,' says Alistair, who, even with his own status as a double Olympic champion, asserts that Beryl 'was twice the athlete I'll ever be'. Alistair studied great sportspeople for his book *Relentless: Secrets of the Sporting Elite*, and was amazed to calculate that thirteen of Beryl's twenty-five British Best All-Rounder (BAR) titles were won with a faster average speed than the men. The women's BAR does include one shorter distance, but it was still unprecedented. 'I think it is very difficult for us to grasp that a woman in the 1960s and 1970s had the belief and tenacity to be better than the men, and how different that would be,' he says, describing Beryl as 'ludicrously ahead of her time' before concluding with four adjectives: 'Ruthless, relentless, brilliant, belligerent'.

The broader social and cultural impact was also emphasised by Sir Bradley Wiggins when we spoke while watching club cyclists whizzing around the old Herne Hill track at their annual Velofete in June 2019. With numerous women taking part in races at what was the venue for the 1948 London Olympics, it seemed extraordinary to think that half the population had no access to international competition when Beryl started out in the mid-1950s. Herne Hill was also a track that Beryl regularly graced and where Wiggins himself learned to ride. Wiggins was sixteen when Beryl died but already a student of his sport's history, and instantly recalled seeing her start a time trial in the mid-1990s. 'Her husband was there holding her up,' he said. 'There are people in sport who capture your imagination. And it is what they mean culturally, not necessarily the performance, which stays with you. Is Muhammad Ali the greatest? It doesn't matter. Ali stood for something culturally that was very important in black America. As a female cyclist at that time Beryl was also groundbreaking. The man was the household back then. She made no money out of it. Then you think where cycling is now. The women's Tour de France. Lizzie Deignan and all that. It is because of people like Beryl.'

*

The development of women's cycling has continued at an erratic and sometimes even regressive pace. The brilliant Cooke, who was able to win titles that were not available to Beryl at the Olympic and Commonwealth Games, as well as the women's Tour de France and Giro d'Italia, retired in 2012 at the age of only twenty-nine, at a moment when the international calendar for women was actually contracting. The doping scandals in men's professional cycling caused huge collateral damage to the appetite of sponsors to fund professional cycling, and it was the women who were often sacrificed. Many women's teams became financially unstable as a result. In the build-up to the London Olympics, Cooke's team had stopped paying her salary and she had to take the team to court just to ensure they honoured the basic financial terms of her contract. The contrast that year with Wiggins, on a reported annual salary in excess of £1 million at Team Sky, where he was widely branded as Britain's first Tour de France champion (Cooke had twice won the women's version), was stark. A €20,000 minimum wage was introduced in 2021 for the leading nine women's teams and, for the Beryls of the modern day, women like Marianne Vos, Anna van der Breggen and Annemiek van Vleuten, who are among around 10 per cent of professionals earning more than €60,000 a year, there is now a living to be made.

It all makes you wonder how Beryl would have fared during this era of professional women's teams, Lottery funding and brand-building via social media. Her refusal to have a phone or television, or even to learn to drive, indicates her likely reaction to being told to spend precious potential training hours marketing herself on Instagram or Twitter. Those who knew Beryl do also question how she would have dealt with formal coaching, even if one would hope for flexibility and nuance for such a precious talent. 'I can't stand a lot of instructions being shouted from the edge of a track,' she said in 1970. 'I have never had any coaching and I don't want any – Charlie is my only adviser.' Denise agrees that her mother did not need much help beyond her father's mechanical expertise early on, but does suspect she would have been fascinated by the gains that could be made in technology and aerodynamics. She also thinks that she could have benefited enormously from the psychological support, and even lifestyle advisers, who are now embedded within Olympic sport. That added expertise might have helped her find a new balance, and conceivably even saved her life, when she transitioned beyond competing for titles.

*

Sir Terry Pratchett once wrote that no one finally dies until the ripples they have left fade away, and, as the years passed following Beryl's death, the core of active riders and stalwarts from the Morley Cycling Club's extraordinary heyday in the 1960s and 1970s did inevitably diminish. Charlie Burton was faced with the sudden loss not just of his wife but of the partner around whom his life had revolved. It was an extremely difficult adjustment, but Charlie did continue to ride his bike for pleasure and enjoyed further touring holidays with the Morley cyclists. These stretched all the way from Europe to New Zealand and even the war-torn Balkans, where from their tents they could hear artillery being fired across the valley. Charlie also still travelled to Spain for group winter cycling trips, and Beryl's ashes were scattered at her favourite coastal spot just outside Benidorm, where she would train for up to a month most years. A certain trend was clearly set, and a new generation of Yorkshire cyclists, including the Brownlee brothers, still spend a part of their winters riding on the very same roads. Charlie did not like being alone in their old house and lived in a static caravan at the Knaresborough Lido holiday park, which is nestled by the River Nidd, for sixteen years after Beryl's death before transferring into sheltered, and then residential, accommodation in Ripon. 'The nurses think he's fabulous – he's still got that charisma,' said Denise, following his ninety-second birthday in 2021.

Nim Carline was also devastated by Beryl's sudden passing and died in 2007, at the age of seventy-nine. He had long been in need of knee and hip operations, probably a consequence of a lifetime lifting, digging and planting rhubarb by day and then cycling or mountaineering over such extraordinary distances. He had also seriously damaged his shoulder and neck after colliding head-on at night in thick fog with another cyclist during a 24-hour time trial. 'Nim had the money to get the operations done but was a staunch socialist and would say, "I've paid into the NHS all my life – they can do it,"' says Eileen Cropper, another Yorkshire cyclist. Carline then had a serious fall at home and, even though he was unable to get himself up off the floor, he did not raise the alarm until daylight the next morning. Laurie Morse, who worked with Beryl at Carline's farm, was among those who broke in. 'While he was waiting for his surgery, his hip broke and I

47. Denise Burton-Cole on the bench in Morley with
the blue plaque in honour of her mother's life.

think the operations really killed him,' says Cropper. 'It was tragic
because he had been as strong as an ox.'

Charlie, Denise, her husband Clay and their children and
grandchildren, as well as long-time secretary (sixty-three years
and counting) Malcolm Cowgill, are among those who continue to
pay a nominal £5 annual membership to keep the Morley Cycling
Club name going. And those ripples of which Pratchett spoke have
gathered considerable momentum since 2012 as the Beryl Burton
legend has experienced a rebirth. The most obvious physical man-
ifestation remains the mural of Beryl riding through Morley in
her heyday, but further tributes have sprung up around the town
centre, including a painted bench, a blue plaque and, on the wall
of the old Picture House in Queen Street, a large display of 'Beryl'
photographs and information which has been headlined, 'Ay lads,
you're not trying!' Two women were reading it when Denise took

48. Maxine Peake's play has been performed across Britain
since 2014. Beryl is pictured on this programme cover
during the 1970 world pursuit championships.

me on a walk through Morley in 2021, and she could not resist
interrupting them. 'That's my mum,' she said, pointing proudly.

After watching Maxine Peake's play *Beryl*, which has been
touring the country almost continuously since 2014, the acclaimed
Yorkshire folk singers Belinda O'Hooley and Heidi Tidow were
inspired to write a song. At their live shows they have found
that 'Beryl', with its catchy lyrics, is more requested even than
the BBC's *Gentleman Jack* theme tune, which they also wrote.
O'Hooley and Tidow used a bike chain, spokes and frame to replicate some of the sounds and have successfully tried to create
that sense of movement from riding a bike. 'We came out of the
play and were just, "Wow, what a woman!"' says O'Hooley. 'Heidi
tells the story of her life in the song and when we perform it I
always stop the pedalling action when she dies. We have met lots

of people at the concerts who have brought their mums along in their eighties who cycled with her. To them Beryl was a mate, and they are always blown away that someone has written a song about her.' Dame Katherine Grainger, who became Britain's most successful ever female Olympian in 2016, was similarly moved by Peake's play. 'I knew the name Beryl Burton, and that she was this huge figure in cycling, but I had never realised the longevity and scale of achievement,' she says. 'I was sitting there thinking, "I'm inspired and ashamed in equal measure." Inspired by the story. Ashamed that I didn't know more. I went with my sister and we were in silence at the end. We were stunned. In awe.'

For some of those closest to Beryl there has been a sadness that recognition remains so overdue and still largely at the margins. Kathleen Mitchell turned down an invitation to see Peake's play, not because she objected to the project but because it made her feel 'heartbroken' to think that her friend never really knew how cherished and respected she was. One accolade that was being planned before she died was the Beryl Burton Cycle Way between Harrogate and Knaresborough, which was eventually opened and named in her honour in 1997. Lord Willis, the Liberal Democrat peer who was then the leader of Harrogate Borough Council, had met Beryl shortly before her death to discuss the project. 'She came along to this meeting and her opening remark was, "And what do you want?" It was as much as to say, "Don't bother with niceties." It cut out a lot of chit-chat.'

It is Denise who now accepts any new honour on her mother's behalf, notably when Beryl posthumously joined Nelson Mandela and Winston Churchill in being awarded the freedom of Leeds in 2014. And then in November 2018, when Beryl and Eddy Merckx became the first two inductees into *Rouleur*'s international Cycling Hall of Fame. Merckx told one British cycling fan that the 'amazing, totally incredible' Beryl was 'the boss of all of us'. With Denise grinning from ear to ear and standing on the same London stage that night as Merckx, it was one of the rare occasions when the Burton name would receive its due billing. 'She would have been thrilled and quite humbled,' Denise told the audience. 'She didn't understand if people made big things out of her because she did what she loved.'

*

Beryl would have been eighty-five when the women's Tour de France was due its big relaunch in July 2022, some thirty-eight years after she was initially rejected for the first British team. In 2024, exactly forty years after women's cycling was first included at the Olympics, there will also finally be as many gold medals available at a summer Games to the women as to the men. Beryl had already lost hope by 1967 of going to an Olympics but, in a speech to sports journalists, said that 'I shall be in there, pushing the pedals around with our girls' if women's cycling was ever admitted. She would have been equally thrilled to see how Yorkshire, currently spearheaded by Deignan and Tom Pidcock, remains such a hotbed for her sport. When we drove from Leeds to Beverley to watch Peake's play together, Jeffrey Charnock said that he often thinks about what his sister would have thought of being portrayed on stage in front of literally thousands of theatregoers. And his conclusion? 'A bit confused and baffled initially but, once she had thought about it for a few days, I think she would have been quietly thrilled.' Beryl would also be stunned, he says, by how Yorkshire has staged both the Tour de France and the world road championships since 2014, as well as hosting its own Tour de Yorkshire professional men's and women's races from 2015 to 2019. 'She would have been looking down and smiling,' he says.

Had she lived, there is also no doubt that Beryl would have been out watching these races, preferably while darting around the course shortcuts on her bike in the same way as Charlie would always follow her progress. She was a force of nature and, beyond even all the records and victories, which can become almost numbing

49. Perhaps the greatest two cyclists in history. Eddy Merckx
(second left) and Beryl Burton at Tom Simpson's funeral.

to compute, the greatest legacy surely lies in how all these memories and anecdotes now live like fairy tales that are passed down
through the generations. In their inspirational simplicity they stand
as ongoing evidence that, if you work hard enough, it is possible to
shape the circumstances and limitations around you. They also serve
as a timely reminder that, for all sport's more superficial progress,
whether financial, technological, physiological or pharmaceuti-
cal, there is sometimes rather more that can be learned by looking
back. For rarely can the true essence of sport have been embodied
more powerfully than by the Burton family and the Morley Cycling
Club. One member, however, would stand apart in any era. Cycling
defined Beryl Burton. It may also have destroyed her, but, for as long
as people are still riding their bikes and sharing stories about the
greatest champions in sport, it will immortalise her.

Liquorice Allsort?

Boroughbridge, 24 May 2021

There is a point just after you join the A168 at Boroughbridge
when you might wonder how it was once the most famous and
popular time-trialling road in the country. For just over a mile
the old A1 climbs stubbornly in the direction of Wetherby at a
gradient that is sufficient to quicken the pulse, if not quite force a
change of gear. The wide, smoothly tarmacked surface and sight
of the brow of the hill mean resisting that urge in the certain
knowledge of a sweeping downhill reward. It was more exposed
during Beryl Burton's heyday in the 1960s and 1970s, but the
maturing foliage now offers protection against crosswinds and
muffles the never-ending hum of the new A1 motorway that runs
parallel. To the left is open countryside and, beyond a quarry and
fields of cows, sheep and pigs, is the dramatic outline of the North
Yorkshire Moors. Known simply to cyclists as 'The Boro', the A1
Ferrybridge and Boroughbridge Road was not just once British
time trialling's equivalent of Lord's, Twickenham and Wembley
Stadium, but a corridor between some of the most spectacular
national parks in the country. It also made up just under a third of
the 15.87-mile finishing circuit for the Otley 12 of 1967.

*

There is something instantly recognisable about the pedalling
style of an outstanding cyclist. The bike seems somehow to rest

beneath their bodies in a symbiotic relationship. With barely a flicker of movement from the waist up, their legs rotate at a brisk but smooth cadence. As the mudguards, saddlebag and old-school toe-clips clearly suggest, Denise Burton-Cole now cycles for pleasure rather than speed, but there is still something in the way she pedals that elevates her above 99 per cent of other road users. 'I just *love* cycling,' she says. 'The outdoors and the scenery. I got that from my mother. She must have loved it to do all those miles.' Denise and her husband, Clay, get out on their bikes at least twice a week, and the decision to live near Ripon in the glorious North Yorkshire countryside is no coincidence. As well as being close to Charlie, their children and grandchildren, the area amounts to a cyclist's heaven.

'We can go in any direction and virtually not see a car,' says Denise, whose expertise on the route planning extends to calculating a tailwind on the final stretch of their rides. 'We get overtaken by plenty of cyclists. They come whizzing by and I think, "Are they enjoying it?" We take our drinks and maybe stop at a café. It's 20 miles and stop; 20 miles and stop; 20 miles and home. We were in the gorgeous Hambleton Hills last week. You could look down and see the whole Vale. We also like to go to Middleham, where they have these beautiful racehorses.' Denise and Clay are never in any particular hurry, but there is one part of being a triple national champion and world championship medallist that you never lose. 'If someone passes us near the top of a hill, I usually pass them going down,' says Denise. 'You don't forget how to go fast down the hills. I still like that feeling.'

*

There are no steep descents along the 'The Boro' but plenty still to appreciate. Denise and Clay have agreed to ride the finishing circuit from the Otley 12 with me and, thanks to the Yorkshire Road Club records and two of the marshals in 1967 – John Churchman and George Baxter – we have been able to plot the course. The added bonus has been to identify exactly where Beryl finished her epic 277.25-mile ride and, better still, the precise point at which she caught Mike McNamara, the last of the ninety-nine men men she passed. 'What a day it was,' says Churchman, shaking his head and glancing over Ordnance Survey maps that are also more than fifty years old. 'Everyone on the course was "Mac's got the record!" Then it was "But Beryl's beaten Mac! What's going on!?"'

The circuit was essentially a triangle of three fairly straight roads and, as we gather speed down the last part of the old A1, Denise begins pointing out various landmarks. Ornans Hall. East Farm. The Courtyard Café and then Allerton Castle, which was once owned by the military leader who inspired the Grand Old Duke of York nursery rhyme. 'The best thing was when a military convoy came past and blew you along,' says Denise, recalling the shorter time trials which also took place on this part of 'The Boro'. She then points to what is known as the 'Red Wall', which runs for several miles between the left kerb of the road and the perimeter of Allerton Park. 'You'd be told to get in close to protect yourself from the wind,' she says. 'I'll never forget seeing Alf Engers, the king of 25-mile time trialling, flying along down this part of the course behind a pig that escaped from a farm across the road.'

Denise is still smiling as we approach the turning for the second main section of our ride, the A59 between Knaresborough and York. But a new junction is being laid and, with the steam literally rising up off the tarmac, the workmen shake their heads and point to the big 'Road Closed' sign. No matter. There are few back roads in Yorkshire that Denise does not know and, after a 1.5-mile detour that involves crossing a railway line and a gravel track, we are on the A59. We have missed less than a mile of the original course. The road is now narrower, with rather more traffic, and so I move behind Denise's back wheel until the crossroads between the villages of Cattal and Whixley. To the left is a huge lush grass verge. Up in front you can see the road climbing constantly for half a mile into the village of Green Hammerton. Baxter was marshalling along this section in 1967, and it was where scores of excited spectators had gathered. 'Mayhem,' he says. 'No cars could get through – only people or bikes.' It was also where Beryl Burton, with less than a minute of her 12 hours remaining, would climb off. Her explanation for not attempting the hill a fifth time was straightforward. 'Sod it – I can't face it,' she told onlookers. 'I don't blame her,' says Denise, sipping from her water bottle, while looking up at the hill ahead.

It was the sort of ascent that Beryl could have simply powered over in the early part of the day, but after more than 277 miles it would certainly have your body begging for respite. Onward into the village of Green Hammerton and a sharp left past the doctor's surgery, primary school and post office, as well as rows of old terraced and semi-detached houses. Residents stood out along this 400-yard section of the course in 1967, cheering and offering sponges and drinks to the riders. Denise greets a passing group of cyclists with a wave and a 'hello' before swinging right on to the B6265. The 6.5-mile return leg to Boroughbridge, on what was the A1167, is the most scenic and remote part of the course. It was also the section where Beryl would most famously pedal into cycling folklore.

*

After the ride we returned to Denise and Clay's home, where, over tea and home-made fruit flapjack, she produced several boxes worth of photographs, correspondence, scrapbooks and newspaper cuttings. It represented a tableau of an extraordinary family life that was both so groundbreakingly global and yet wonderfully parochial. Many of the items were in Beryl's own handwriting. They included a forty-six-page talk that she gave to the Cyclists' Touring Club's Birthday Rides group only seven months before her death. It is obvious from all the notes that Beryl had become an excellent raconteur, and a line from a speech in 1967, the year of her 12-hour record, feels especially telling. 'If I never raced, cycling would still be my hobby – I wouldn't swap my sport for anything,' she said. The most moving item of all is a small piece of lined card on which Beryl had made a handwritten note of her personal best times, dates and courses. Her grid has three sections: an all-time list, her fastest times over the past three seasons and also her records since 1 January 1995. The heartbreaking twist was that this piece of card, with its headings in red ink and times in blue, had been updated to include a 15-mile time trial on 27 April 1996. A ride of 40 min. 36 sec. had evidently been Beryl's quickest over the distance since at least 1993. She would die only eight days later.

In her novel *The Red Tent*, Anita Diamant wrote that 'the more a daughter knows about the details of her mother's life – without flinching or whining – the stronger she becomes', and as Denise points out cards and letters from across the cycling world while picking out some of her favourite family pictures, there is the clear sense that she has come to terms with her mother's life. She sees no point in brushing over her most difficult traits and the impact they had on their relationship, but as well as acceptance she also now feels empathy. 'I think she was an incredible person and an incredible rider who did incredible things,' she says. 'I'm not making excuses for her, because there were times when it was, "For goodness sake, mother." As a child and a teenager, some things were difficult to understand. It's still hard now but, as an adult, I can understand it better. I really think what shaped my mum was being separated from her family in that convent when she was very ill as a child. They are sparse places. Perfectly ordered. Everything minimised and in its place. Not much talking. You do things in a certain way. That was my mum to a T.

'And just imagine being a sick child and then taken away from your parents for all that time. To go into such a strict environment

50. One of Denise's favourite family pictures. She is with her world champion mother outside their Elmfield Court home in Morley in 1960.

at that age with nuns must have been absolutely horrible. Devastating. I think she became hardened to it. She had to. And she never talked about it. Never. She just pushed it to the back of her mind. She was then very young when she had me. I was born into cycling. We had some good times, but the good times were among others. Not really at home. It was clinical, and yet I wouldn't want to have been anywhere else. It was my home. That was my mum and my dad. When it is blood, there is that something there. They are yours. I love them. I love her. It was a family story. And we were this unit: The Burtons.'

*

Back along the B6265 from York to Boroughbridge, and to the right you can just make out RAF Linton-on-Ouse before the outlines of the Howardian Hills, which nestle like an amphitheatre behind the small market town of Easingwold. The road climbs very steadily upwards until a turning to Little Ouseburn and the Green Tree Inn. There are hundreds of visible yards of straight and gently undulating open road ahead. When McNamara talked about being the 'hare' for Beryl to catch, this suddenly provides a very vivid picture of what he meant. He would have been in Beryl's sights long before she finally drew level and reached for what she called 'my sweetie bag'.

McNamara and Beryl were all alone along this one-mile stretch between the villages of Great Ouseburn and Marton-Cum-Grafton. But, by triangulating the data from the results sheet and media reports, the testimony of both riders and our two octogenarian marshals (Churchman was 2 miles ahead and Baxter was stationed 5 miles further back), we can say with some certainty that Beryl caught McNamara at mile 13 of their second lap of the finishing circuit.

As we gently pull over at the assigned spot just before a turn called Gallabar Lane, Denise looks over to our right towards

51. Denise Burton-Cole at the spot her mother famously handed men's champion Mike McNamara a liquorice allsort as she passed him.

the rugged hills, before gazing back down the road we have just ridden. She agrees that her mother must have had McNamara in view for several miles before she finally went past. Denise then removes the Castelli jacket she had been wearing to proudly reveal the Morley Cycling Club jersey. 'I thought I'd put it on for her,' she says, before reaching into the back pocket and uttering two words that could only have been previously heard once on this precise stretch of road. 'Liquorice allsort?' We both smile, and I ask what her mother might say if she could see us. I had somehow expected to hear one of Beryl's more brusque remarks. Maybe something along the lines of, 'You're only riding one lap? I did nearly 280 miles that day. C'mon, you're not trying hard enough!' But Denise shakes her head. 'No. She would be impressed. My mother liked to see people riding their bikes. She were passionate … and blinkin' good.'

Appendix

The Championship-Winning Years

"HE'S WASTING HIS TIME — HE'LL NEVER CATCH BERYL BURTON."

Year	58	59	60	61	62	63	64	65	66	67	68	69	70	71	72	73	74	75	76	77	78	79	80	81	82	83	84	85	86	Titles
RTTC national championships																														
10 miles (event introduced in 1978)																					1	1	1	1						4
25 miles	1		1	1	2	1	1	1	1	1	1	1	1	1	1	1	1	1	1	1	1	1	1	1	1	3	2	7	6	26
50 miles	1		1	2	1	1	1	1	1	1	1	1	1	1	1	1	1	1	1	1	1	1	1	1	2	2		3	1	24
100 miles	1		1	1			1	1	1	1	DNF	1	1	1	1	1	1	1	1	1	1	1	1	1						18
Best All-Rounder	2	1	1	1	1	1	1	1	1	1	1	1	1	1	1	1	1	1	1	1	1	1	1	1	1	1				25
3,000m Track pursuit																														
National championships			1	1	2	1	1	1	1	1	1	1	1	1	1	1	1			3										13
World championships		1	1	2	1	1	2	Q	1	3	2	1	3	3	4	3	Q/F													5
Road race																														
National championships	1		1	2		1	4	1	1	1	1		1	1	1	1	1		2											12
World championships		5	1	2	8	DNF	10	23	5	1	13			9	5	8	5													2
																														Total titles
																														129
Competition and world records																														
10 miles			24m 35s	24m 27s			24m 23s	23m 17s	23m 05s / 22m 45s	23m 05s					22m 06s / 21m 25s							Record lasts until 1993								

312

Year	58	59	60	61	62	63	64	65	66	67	68	69	70	71	72	73	74	75	76	77	78	79	80	81	82	83	84	85	86	Titles
25 miles	1h 1m 27s				1h 1m 10s	59m 25s	59m 02s						54m 55s		54m 44s				53m 21s					Record lasts until 1996						
					1h 0m 34s		58m 39s																							
							58m 02s																							
50 miles	2h 9m 17s	2h 6m 38s	2h 5m 45s			2h 5m 16s	2h 4m 29s			1h 56m 0s		1h 55m 4s				1h 54m 7s			1h 51m 30s					Record lasts until 1996						
							2h 1m 12s																							
100 miles	4h 33m 26s	4h 20m 4s	4h 18m 19s		4h 14m 29s			4h 13m 4s	4h 8m 22s	4h 4m 50s	4h 1m 41s													Record lasts until 1996						
	4h 29m 21s										3h 55m 5s																			
12 hours		250. 37m								277. 25m														Record lasts until 2017						
3,000 m pursuit		4m 12.9s		3m 59.4s																										
			4m 10.4s																											
		4m 6.1s																												

DNF - Did not finish   Q/F = Quarter-final   Q = Qualifying heats

313

Acknowledgements

It must be odd to have a stranger contact you out of the blue to say that they would like to write a book about a close family member. The Burton and Charnock families may have quietly sympathised with *The Times*'s verdict in 1971 that Beryl Burton was 'the least publicised, least rewarded great woman athlete ever to be disregarded by her own country', but their deep pride is modestly displayed and they were never seeking additional recognition.

I am immensely grateful, therefore, for their candour and trust in agreeing that only a complete portrait of Beryl's achievements and multilayered personality made sense. To get to know them over these past four years was truly the most rewarding part of the project.

The book could not have been written without the kindness and help of Beryl's daughter and son-in-law, Denise Burton-Cole and Clayton Cole, Beryl's husband, Charlie Burton, her siblings, Jeffrey Charnock and Maureen Bell, and her sister-in-law, Elaine Charnock.

Another hugely uplifting aspect of the research was meeting so many of Beryl's old friends, teammates and rivals, who are still regularly riding their bikes well into their seventies, eighties and even nineties. They were invariably generous in providing interviews and information.

Particular thanks are due to members past and present of the magical Morley Cycling Club: Malcolm Cowgill, June Cowgill, Ann Pallister, the three Larkin sisters (Kathleen Mitchell, Maureen Pearson and Margaret Allen), Laurie Morse, Sheila Broadbent, Shirley Pell, Howard Newton, Pat Clayton and Trevor 'Tad' Noble.

Beryl Burton was revered throughout the British cycling community during what was the golden age of time trialling. The input from numerous people who competed, volunteered, reported on or worked with Beryl during her forty-three years in the saddle between 1953 and 1996 collectively painted a wonderfully vivid picture. She may have been virtually invincible, but she was also utterly accessible and I never tired of hearing about their everyday

Acknowledgements

encounters with this most compelling of sportspeople. Thanks to: June Pitchford, Joan Kershaw, Mike McNamara, Val Rushworth, Bernadette Swinnerton, Ann Sturgess, Brenda Robins, Val Baxendine, Eileen Cropper, Christine Minto, Graham Barker, Keith Lambert, Kay Scales, Pam Hodson, Sue Fenwick, Jim Hendry, Ruth Williams, John Churchman, Dave Trapps, Phil Hurt, Chris Sidwells, Marjorie Dunn, Rod Goodfellow, Les Woodland, Jeff Bowler, Brian Keighley, John McNamara, Bob Howden, Barbara Penrice, Mike Williams, Maggie Thompson, Mary Horsnell, Jean Baylis, Jim Love, Barbara Cromack, Geoffrey Cromack, Sally Whitfield, Phil Fryer, Sue Dashey, Sue Mott, Carole Gandy, Baz Breedon, Dave Lloyd, Margaret Smith, Sue Sill, Alan Sturgess, Keith Bingham, Jon Williams, Stephen Gath, John Taylor, Harry Jackson, Brendan McKeown, Darryl Webster, Betty Phillipson and John Fenwick.

Various greats of British cycling also provided interviews, and their willingness to contribute was a constant reminder of the esteem in which Beryl is held. Sincere thanks to: Sir Bradley Wiggins, Nicole Cooke, Eileen Sheridan, Dame Sarah Storey, Lizzie Deignan, Chris Boardman, Yvonne McGregor, Mandy Jones, Brian Robinson, Philippa York, Barry Hoban, Sean Yates, Alf Engers, Ian Cammish, Hugh Porter, Alice Lethbridge and Phil Liggett.

It was critical also to hear the perspectives of Beryl's main international rivals, and the author Isabel Best was extremely generous in opening doors. Jos and Chritt Vekemans provided welcome company and translation during a wonderful afternoon in Antwerp with the seven-times world champion Yvonne Reynders. Marina Kotchetova was also incredibly kind and helpful in taking me behind the 'Iron Curtain' and contributing such insight into the extraordinary Soviet Union cyclists of the 1960s and 1970s. Her conversations on my behalf with Nina Egorova and the reclusive six-times world pursuit champion Tamara Garkushina were invaluable. The swimmer Sharron Davies and the whistleblower Dr Grigory Rodchenkov further deepened my understanding of sport in the Soviet Union during this period. Thank you also to the German journalist Matthias Hufmann for his expertise in trying to track down Stasi records related to the 1960 world championships and Beryl's cycling trips to East Germany.

Beryl Burton's story has touched people far beyond her immediate sporting community. Maxine Peake's play helped reach a new audience, and it was fascinating to speak with her about portraying Beryl, as well as to the actors Jessica Duffield and Annie Kirkman, who played the characters of Beryl and Denise so superbly at theatres in Beverley and London. The folk singers Belinda O'Hooley and Heidi Tidow also provided fresh perspectives, as did sporting greats across other disciplines and eras. Thanks to: Dame Mary Peters, Sir

Geoffrey Boycott, Sir A. P. McCoy, Alistair Brownlee, Jonny Brownlee, Anita Lonsborough, Dame Katherine Grainger, Chrissie Wellington and Dorothy Hyman.

For their expertise in relevant areas of psychology, physiology, cycling aerodynamics and Yorkshire's social history, I am also grateful to Dr Meg Jay, Dr Xavier Disley, Professor Dave Russell, Chelsea Warr, Dr Jamie Pringle, Lord Willis, Professor Dave Collins and Tim Kerrison.

There were moments during the Covid-19 pandemic when I doubted whether the wind-tunnel idea would come off, but Dave Marsh kindly loaned out Beryl's original bike and the cyclist Jessica Rhodes-Jones then agreed to become BB for the day, even happily sporting a tightly curled wig to complete our comparison. The results spoke just as eloquently as Beryl's incalculable tally of victories in demonstrating her rightful place among the greatest athletes who ever lived.

Many other people provided practical help in connecting me with various interviewees and research material, or simply a timely word of inspiration. I am grateful to D'arcy Darilmaz at Morley's West Yorkshire Archive Service, the ITV and former *Yorkshire Evening Post* journalist Jonathan Brown, *Cycling Weekly* editor Simon Richardson, *Rouleur* editor Andy McGrath, the cycling historians Peter Whitfield and Ray Pascoe, the former Cycling Time Trials chair Sheila Hardy and British Cycling's Scott Dougal, as well as David Barry, Justine Potter, Duncan Craig, Chris Hodge, Louise Sheridan, Rob Arnott, Emma Wade, Keith Harrod, Kate Long, Alyson Rudd, Dave Joynson, Ant McNamara, Paul Cooper, Paul Grover, Paul Jones, Michael Hutchinson, Colin Sturgess, Colin O'Brien, Robert Dineen, Ken Cooke, Tom Morgan, Adam Sills, Donald McRae, Anna Kessel, Oliver Holt, Richard Williams, Marcus Armytage, John Cross, Rob Wilks, Rachel Welch, Alastair Johnstone and Tom Cary.

I am thankful also to the literary agent Max Edwards, who showed such instant enthusiasm for the idea when I told him about Beryl Burton in January 2018. The team at Profile Books were then hugely supportive. Thanks to my editor James Spackman, Andrew Franklin, Penny Daniel, Peter Dyer, Matthew Taylor, Flora Willis, Hannah Ross and Alison Alexanian for their expertise and encouragement.

Family members also provided crucial feedback – thanks to Di, Martyn and Ben, and above all to an unbeatable home team of Clare, Casper and Owen for their limitless patience and support.

Bibliography

Books and Periodicals

Bacon, E., *Great British Cycling* (Bantam Books, 2014)

Best, I., *Queens of Pain: Legends and Rebels of Cycling* (Rapha Editions/Blue Train, 2018)

Brown, J., *Cycle Yorkshire* (Great Northern, 2015)

Brownlee, A., *Relentless: Secrets of the Sporting Elite* (HarperCollins, 2021)

Burton, B., *Personal Best* (Springfield Books, 1986; repr. Mercian Manuals, 2009)

Clemitson, S., *Ride the Revolution* (Bloomsbury Sport, 2015)

Collins, D., and Macnamara, A., 'The Rocky Road to the Top: Why Talent Needs Trauma', *Sports Medicine*, vol. 42, issue 11, pp. 907–914 (2012)

Cooke, N., *The Breakaway* (Simon and Schuster, 2015)

Dineen, R., *Kings of the Road* (Aurum Press, 2015)

Dyer, K., *Catching up the Men: Women in Sport* (Junction Books, 1982)

Foster, B., *The Benny Foster Story* (Kennedy Brothers, 1971)

Fotheringham, W., *The Greatest* (YouCaxton, 2019)

Goertzel, V. and M., *Cradles of Eminence* (Little, Brown, 1962)

Hermans, M., *Yvonne Reynders: Zeven Maal in de Zevende Hemel* (BMP, 2002)

Hodge, E., and Gray, E., *Rebel with a Cause* (Hodge Printers, 1999)

Jay, M., *Supernormal: Childhood Adversity and the Untold Story of Resilience* (Canongate Books, 2017)

Kitching, R., and Breckon, B., *A Wheel in Two Worlds* (Ron Kitching, 1993)

Kynaston, D., *Austerity Britain, 1945–1951* (Bloomsbury, 2008)

Laing, S., Hardy, L., and Warr, C., 'The Great British Medalists Project', *Sports Medicine*, vol. 46, pp. 1041–1058 (2016)

Rodchenkov, G., *The Rodchenkov Affair* (W. E. Allen, 2020)

Ross, H., *Revolutions* (Weidenfeld & Nicolson, 2021)

Russell, D., 'Mum's the Word: The Cycling Career of Beryl Burton', *Women's History Review*, vol. 17, issue 5, pp. 787–806 (2008)

Sheridan, E., *Wonder Wheels* (Nicolas Kaye, 1956; repr. Mercian Manuals, 2009)

Sidwells, C., *The Call of the Road* (André Deutsch, 2016)

Slot, O., Timson, S., and Warr., C., *The Talent Lab* (Ebury Press, 2017)

Taylor, J., *The 24 Hour Story* (Btown Bikes, 2005)

Thompson, B., *Alpaca to Skinsuit* (Geerings of Ashford, 1988)

Thompson, M., *Memoir on Two Wheels* (Maggie Thompson, 2020)

Wagg, S., and Russell, D., *Sporting Heroes of the North* (Northumbria Press, 2010)

Ward, N., *Yorkshire's Mine* (Littlehampton Book Services, 1969)

Whitfield, P., *12 Champions* (Wychwood Publishing, 2007)

Woodland, L., *Cycling Heroes* (McGann Publishing, 2011)

Editions of the following publications between 1957 and 2014 all contained useful material:

Cycling, International Cycle Sport, Sporting Cyclist, Yorkshire Evening Post, Morley Observer, Guardian, Daily Mail, Le Monde, Dimanche Soir, Sunday Times, The Times, Daily Telegraph, The Independent, Rouleur, New York Times, People, Daily Mirror and *News of the World*.

Television, Film and Radio

Calendar Summer Sports Special, *Beryl Burton* feature, Yorkshire Television, 1986

Pascoe, R., *Racing is Life: The Beryl Burton Story*, Bromley Video, 2012, and *Racing the Clock: Time Trialling Filmed in the UK (1979–1983)*, Cycling History and Education Trust, 2019

Peake, M., *Beryl: A Love Story on Two Wheels*, BBC Radio 4, 2012

Sporting Witness, *Beryl Burton: The Yorkshire Dynamo*, BBC World Service, 2015

A variety of other ITV Yorkshire and BBC archive material between 1960 and 2019 was also useful.

Additional Material

Denise Burton-Cole shared family scrapbooks, photographs, speeches and personal correspondence. The Ron Kitching Library in Otley also contained a treasure trove of information.

Cycling Time Trials and Peter Whitfield shared material from Bernard Thompson's archive and British Cycling provided access to their Beryl Burton display cabinet at the Manchester Velodrome.

The websites ttlegends.org, timetriallingforum.co.uk and the 'Legends of the RTTC' Facebook page were also a wonderful resource.

List of illustrations

Frontispiece: Portrait of Beryl Burton. Photo: Len Thorpe/Burton family collection, p. ii

1. Cycling near the Yorkshire Moors. Photo: PA/Alamy, p. 9
2. Time trialling in the rain. Photo: Bernard Thompson/Cycling Time Trials, p. 12
3. Starting the Otley 12. Photo: *Cycling Weekly*, p. 17
4. The Otley result sheet. Courtesy of Ruth Williams, p. 27
5. Portrait of Mike McNamara. Photo: Bernard Thompson/Cycling Time Trials, p. 27
6. Childhood portrait. Photo: Burton family collection, p. 33
7. Home again after recovering from rheumatic fever. Photo: Burton family collection, p. 37
8. Starting her first time trial. Photo: Burton family collection, p. 51
9. Wedding day, April 1955. Photo: Burton family collection, p. 58
10. Members of the Morley Cycling Club. Photo: Arthur Wright/Burton family collection, p. 60
11. Mother, daughter and bike seat. Photo: Burton family collection, p. 61
12. Eileen Sheridan en route to another record. Photo: Courtesy of Peter Whitfield/Eileen Sheridan, p. 69
13. Eileen Gray and the women's team transport. Photo: Hodge Printers/ *Cycling Weekly*, p. 77
14. Britain's first world cycling champion. Photo: Etienne Auwera/Burton family collection, p. 81
15. Between pursuit races in East Germany. Photo: Burton family collection, p. 87
16. Riding to the 1960 world road title. Photo: The Horton Collection, p. 92
17. A kiss from Tom Simpson, *Cycling* magazine front cover, 17 August, 1960, p. 93

List of illustrations

Beryl

Plates

While every effort has been made to contact copyright-holders of illustrations, the author and the publishers would be grateful for information about any illustrations where they have been unable to trace them, and would be glad to make amendments in further editions.

Index

Page references for photographs are in *italics*

Index

Index

Index